"How much easier this book would have made my life when I was a teenager. I wish every parent of a teenage daughter would buy this book for her."

PAULINA PORIZKOVA
Supermodel

"A must read. If you want questions answered on how to be in control of your own life, this in-depth guide is for you."

TRACIE SPENCER
Singer

YOU'RE IN CHARGE

*A Teenage Girl's
Guide to Sex
and Her Body*

**Niels H. Lauersen, M.D., Ph.D.,
and Eileen Stukane**

FAWCETT COLUMBINE • NEW YORK

This book is not intended to treat, diagnose, or prescribe.
If you or anyone else has a serious health problem,
we suggest that you consult a professional health worker.

A Fawcett Columbine Book
Published by Ballantine Books

Library of Congress Catalog Card Number: 92-90375
ISBN: 0-449-90464-4

Text design by Holly Johnson
Cover design by Georgia Morrissey
Cover photography by Michele LeGrou

Manufactured in the United States of America

First Edition: March 1993

10 9 8 7 6 5 4 3 2 1

To strengthen the bodies and minds
of girls becoming women

Contents

Acknowledgments

We thank all of those who believe, as we do, in the intelligence of today's youth. They have helped us make *You're In Charge* a relevant guide for teenage girls.

The young women who confided in us directly, and those who answered our questionnaires, honestly told us how they felt and what they wanted to know about—everything from hair care to sexually transmitted diseases. They grounded us in real-life issues.

Many professionals who are devoting themselves to the education and betterment of young women took time to give us invaluable assistance. Our gratitude goes to all of them, especially Robyn Stein and Gloria Roberts of Planned Parenthood Federation of America; Lillian Drvostep of Hunter High School in New York; Eileen Hayes and Susan McCarty of the YWCA Teen Parents Program in New York; Laurel Stavis and Lt. Kim Delaney of Wellesley College; Dr. Alexandra Kaplan; Giselle

Harrington of Barnard College Student Health Services; Diane Pollack of the National Abortion Federation, who helped us on some very sensitive issues; Dr. Leonard Levitz, Judi Goldstein, Hap Rogers, Dr. Merrily Karpell and Ginny Panish of The Renfrew Center; Jonathan Schenker of Ketchum Public Relations; Liz Milwe; Dr. Reed Mangels of The Vegetarian Resource Group; Dr. Hillard H. Pearlstein; Jeanne Kassler, M.D.; and Philip Kingsley.

Original artwork for this book was created by Enid Hatton, and single illustrations were executed by Rick Meyerowitz and Tony Kramer.

Our appreciation also goes to our agent, Ellen Levine, for her irreplaceable know-how, and to Diana Finch, for keeping watch.

Finally, we are fortunate to have worked with Joëlle Delbourgo, Sherri Rifkin, and the staff at Ballantine Books. With their clarity and dedication they have molded this book into an essential companion for every teenage girl.

Niels H. Lauersen, M.D., Ph.D.

Eileen Stukane

Authors' Note

In an effort to clarify the writing, we use the male pro-
nouns—*he*, *his*, *him*—when referring to a doctor. We have
given the book's hypothetical gynecologist a masculine
identity to distinguish the doctor from the patient. This
doctor/patient gender identification must not be viewed
as political or chauvinistic labeling; the distinction is made
only to avoid confusion. While in the past, the majority
of ob-gyn specialists have been men, today many more
women are entering the practice of obstetrics and gyne-
cology. A young woman now has a greater field of choice
for selecting a female or a male doctor.

YOU'RE IN CHARGE

CHAPTER ONE

Friends Together

"You just don't trust me," Amanda told her mother.

"It's not that we don't trust you," her mother explained, "but your father and I cannot let you have a party here without us. After all, Amanda, what if something happens? We're the ones who are ultimately responsible."

"What's going to happen?" asked Amanda. "Do you think I'm going to have a party with drugs or something? You know I don't do those things."

"Of course, we know." Amanda could tell that her mother was using her controlled voice. "But nonetheless we are not leaving the house. You can have a party; we want you to have your friends over. Look, we don't want to be at the party with you, but we do want to be in the house. We'll stay in the bedroom."

Amanda couldn't believe her parents. They said she

could have a sixteenth birthday party. They told her how grown-up she was getting, and then they treated her like a child. It would be embarrassing to have the party with her parents there. She didn't think they would stay in the bedroom, her father would find some excuse. Yet she knew her home was a great place for a party. She lived in a loft in New York City. Unlike an apartment, the loft had high ceilings and wide, spacious areas for living and dining rooms, with good floors for dancing.

Amanda was frustrated.

"I think you should do it," said Jennifer, Amanda's best friend, on the phone that night.

"It's so uncool, Jen," Amanda argued back, "a party with my parents here. No one will want to come."

"Look, they're all right," Jennifer told her. "How many times have a bunch of us slept over and not even seen them till morning? I think they'll be cool and stay out of it."

Amanda didn't say anything.

"Do you really think it could work?" Amanda asked.

"Absolutely," said Jennifer reassuringly, "and I'm in the mood for a party. How often do you turn sixteen, anyway? You've got the space, why not use it?"

"I guess you're right. I just didn't like the idea of having them there."

"Well, they really won't be there," said Jennifer. "My advice is to give them a few things to do for the party and they'll be satisfied. Then you do the rest. They'll be so glad you decided to have a party at home, they'll leave you alone."

Jennifer's confident, quick decision-making left Amanda awestruck. She wondered if she would ever be so sure of herself.

Amanda told her mother that she wanted to organize the party herself. Her mother went along with everything so easily that Amanda thought she might have been too quick to judge the situation. Most of the people she asked to come weren't making a big deal over the fact that her parents would be in the house.

On her birthday, Jennifer and Nicole arrived early to help set up the food and drinks. Nicole made guacamole to go with the corn chips. Amanda opened apple cider for the people who didn't want to drink soda, and Jennifer put popcorn, potato chips, and nuts in bowls. Amanda's mother made chili, which was warming on the stove.

"What do you think, Jen, will Eric show up tonight?" asked Amanda. "I think he's cute. He did say he'd see me tonight when we were leaving school yesterday, but between Friday and Saturday who knows what can happen."

"Of course he'll show," Jennifer said. "The word is that this is the place to be tonight."

"Isn't it amazing?" said Amanda. "I didn't want to have this party here, and now it's turning out that *here* is where everyone wants to come. A few seniors I hardly know asked if they could stop by. I felt like a celebrity or something."

Just as the girls finished setting up, the buzzer sounded. Melissa, a girl Amanda had met in Spanish class, was the first to arrive.

The party was going pretty well, thanks to the guacamole and Jennifer's party mix tapes. Amanda was completely surprised by the brownies that two friends had baked, but when Nicole covered them with candles, Amanda made a wish, and blew.

Amanda's wish, of course, was that Eric would pay

more attention to her. She spent half of her time in orchestra practice thinking of him instead of her flute pieces. She liked the way he moved his hands along the saxophone when he was playing. He had more blond hairs on his arms and hands than she had ever seen. The only good thing the flute had done for her, she thought, was to get her in the school orchestra where she met kids who were juniors and seniors.

Suddenly, Eric was walking toward her. He was actually here in her house.

"Happy birthday," he said as he touched her arm.

"Thanks," said Amanda. She thought he had a great face; it had lots of angles.

"I brought a few friends," said Eric, leaning his head in the direction of two boys whom Amanda recognized as seniors. They were holding large bags.

"We brought a few refreshments," Eric said, as he reached over into one of the bags and pulled out a six-pack of beer.

"Oh, I don't know," said Amanda, looking at the sweating bottles. She didn't want to appear uncool, especially in front of Eric, but she also didn't want to get into trouble. "I'm a little nervous about that. You know, my parents are in the house."

"Don't worry, we'll be cool," Eric assured her. "If we see them, we'll just stash the bottles somewhere."

Amanda was really torn between what was the right thing to do and what she wanted to do. She knew that she wasn't allowed to have any drinking at the party, so the right thing would be to tell Eric and his friends to take the beer out of the house, but she wanted to be hip and throw a party everyone would talk about.

She weighed her options. If she told the boys to forget about the beer, she'd probably be considered totally out of it. The other thing was that she wanted to go along with Eric. She had been trying to get him to notice her all year. Yet what if her parents wandered into the party and saw beer around?

"I like your hair," Eric said, as he gently pulled on her braid. "Where's the bottle opener? This is making my hand cold." He held up a bottle as if it were the torch on the Statue of Liberty.

"The opener is in the kitchen," Amanda answered. Suddenly, her decision had been made for her. She couldn't tell him no.

Amanda led Eric into the kitchen, and the other two boys followed. She handed the opener to Eric and watched as the others unpacked two of the four six-packs, and put the other two, still in a bag, into the refrigerator. Amanda imagined her father suddenly having a craving for something to eat, opening the refrigerator, and seeing that bulging paper bag in there. She didn't want to think about what would happen next.

Eric and his friends took the beers into the party and began passing them out. No one seemed the least bit surprised by the beer. Maybe everything will work out all right, thought Amanda, but she was still scared. It would be different if she were at someone else's party; then she wouldn't be the one who was dangerously close to being in big trouble right now.

Even though Eric seemed to be telling everyone to cool it and keep the beer out of sight, Amanda realized that her good time had ended. She would be a nervous wreck until the party was over. She began to think that maybe she shouldn't try so hard with Eric, but he was so cute.

In the midst of her concern, Amanda felt a tug on her arm. "Can you come into the bedroom for a minute," asked Jennifer. "We need you in there."

"What's wrong?" asked Amanda.

"It's Lisa," answered Jennifer. "She's falling apart. I think she and Andrew are breaking up."

"Oh, my God," said Amanda. This isn't fair, she thought. This is my birthday.

Lisa was sitting cross-legged on Amanda's bed. She was hugging Amanda's stuffed tiger with one hand, and blowing her nose with the other. Amanda saw that Lisa's tears had smudged her mascara, and she looked as if she had two black eyes. Nicole was trying to comfort her.

"Lisa, what happened?" asked Amanda, as she sat down next to her friend. Actually, Amanda was glad to be thinking about something other than the beer.

"Guys can be so insensitive," Lisa said between sniffs. Now her nose was running.

"I know what you mean," said Amanda, thinking of Eric.

"I mean, Andrew's the one who got me in trouble and he acts as if I did it to myself."

"What kind of trouble?" questioned Amanda. "Start from the beginning. Did something happen just now? You two were sitting on the couch together just a little while ago."

"That's when I told him," Lisa said.

"Told him what?"

"That I think I'm pregnant."

"You're kidding!" Like most of her friends, Amanda was a virgin. Everyone was sort of private about what they did. The idea was that when it was right for you, when you were ready, you would do it. Amanda felt that she wasn't ready yet. She didn't really know what some of the girls who had relationships were doing, but if it was right for them to have sex, then that was their decision. "How do you know you're pregnant?"

"My period is late, and it's never late, never," said Lisa rather loudly.

"Well, did you and Andrew, you know, do it?" interrupted Nicole, who appeared stunned by the news.

"Not really," answered Lisa, "because I haven't wanted to, but there was this one time when we were in his room. Oh God, I hate talking about it." She blew her nose again. "Well, we were in his room and we started kissing and he was getting crazy. Usually we stop at a certain point but he was going nuts. I'd never seen him like that before. He said he wanted to do it, and I didn't say yes or no. I figured we could, you know, go a little further, but stop when we wanted to, but it didn't happen that way. He pulled down my jeans and his, took off our underpants, and we were on his bed, and I thought, Oh God, this is it, we're going to do it, and I freaked. I just freaked, but it was too late." She paused.

"What do you mean 'too late'?" demanded Jennifer. Amanda realized that the three of them, Jennifer, Nicole, and herself, were spellbound by the story, and a little afraid for Lisa.

"Well, by the time my brain reached my mouth and I said, 'No, let's wait until I'm on the Pill,' he had come all over me," sobbed Lisa, "and now I think I got pregnant."

No one said a word, but the three girls hugged Lisa, who was crying so hard she was gasping for breath. When they separated, Jennifer took charge.

"Look, Lisa, maybe you're not pregnant," said Jennifer. "Did you have a test? Did a doctor say you were pregnant?"

"No," she answered, "but my period has never been late."

"Also," Jennifer added, "I don't think you can get

pregnant if he's only in the neighborhood, if you know what I mean. You didn't actually have sex."

"I think Lisa is right, Jen. Unless the sperm is inside, I don't think you can get pregnant," said Nicole.

Amanda realized that they didn't know what they were talking about. Lisa hadn't had a pregnancy test, and none of them knew whether she had done anything to become pregnant in the first place. Maybe she was so upset with Andrew that her emotions had affected her period.

"I think you ought to buy a home pregnancy test before you get any more hysterical," Amanda told Lisa.

"Exactly what I was going to say," said Jennifer.

"Those test kits they advertise on TV with the husband and wife? I'm too embarrassed to buy one of them. What if somebody saw me?" asked Lisa.

"Don't worry," said Amanda. "Look, tomorrow is Sunday. We'll pick a drugstore to meet at tomorrow and we'll buy the thing together. Then we'll read the directions and figure out what to do next. Don't worry. I bet you're not pregnant, but you do look like a mess. Better wash off your eye makeup. Are you and Andrew still talking?"

"He's been so awful. When I told him I was scared that I was pregnant, he said 'No problem, that can be taken care of,' as if it was about as hard to handle as a hangnail," said Lisa. "I'm so mad at him right now. But don't worry, Amanda, I won't ruin the party."

Amanda had almost forgotten there was a party going on on the other side of the bedroom door. "Right, the party," said Amanda. She gave Lisa a hug and told her not to worry. They would all stick together and help her. Amanda then opened the door and noticed that someone had dimmed the lights since she had gone to see what was wrong with Lisa.

I hope I live through this night, thought Amanda,

what with the beer, and Lisa, and now the lights. She considered how feelings got you into trouble. Her feelings for Eric had led to the beer at the party, and Lisa's feelings for Andrew had her in a state of terror right now. How do you handle the pressure from boys and the things they make you do? Well, as long as she and her girlfriends had each other to work things out, they'd probably be all right. But did they really know what they were doing? She wondered.

WE CAN THINK WE KNOW MORE THAN WE DO

You might feel that you know how to handle yourself, and are clear about what you'd do in certain situations, but real life puts everyone to the test. Every time you have an experience that requires you to use your judgment, your knowledge and self-assurance are being tested. Have you ever started explaining something and suddenly realized that you didn't know what you were talking about? Or become nervous when you thought you were completely confident? You are not alone. Everyone gets rattled from time to time.

Amanda, for instance, thought she could handle a party with no problem, but did she know that Eric and his friends would bring beer? Maybe she had an inkling that someone would show up with alcohol, but the fact that Eric was that person complicated her feelings. She lost her perspective about whether she did or didn't want alcohol at the party.

Then there was Lisa. Amanda, Jennifer, and Nicole really cared about Lisa. They wanted to help their friend deal with this situation. Lisa knew what a home pregnancy test was, but she didn't think of buying one, or was too embarrassed to buy one, until the other girls

1. What's On Your Mind? Do you daydream about who you are and who you will become? With determination you can make any idea a reality, because you're in charge.
ILLUSTRATION BY RICK MEYEROWITZ

pushed her into it. Of course, they were going to support her all the way and help her take the test, but none of them had even read the directions yet. How do you do a home pregnancy test? No one really knew.

At the same time, no one knew whether Lisa had anything to worry about. Could she have become pregnant even though she was still a virgin? They needed a book like this to give them immediate answers. Lisa had reason to be concerned.

What none of her friends asked her, however, should have been an immediate question: Why wasn't Andrew using a condom? I'm sure they all had heard about the need to use condoms, not just for pregnancy prevention but safety. All young women and men who are sexually active before marriage ought to be protecting themselves against the possibility of catching a sexually transmitted disease.

One of the values of friendship is that what you may

forget, your friend may remember. When faced with the "Eric" in your life, facts can disappear as your emotions override your mind. That's when a friend can offer you direction, and that's when *You're In Charge* is there. This book can stay beside your bed, and give you answers before your questions arise. If she had browsed through this book, Lisa would have known her chances of becoming pregnant *before* she was in Andrew's arms.

THE TIMES ARE CHANGING

With the growth of the women's movement in the 1960s and '70s, women started to demand more information from their doctors. Both male and female physicians began listening to their female patients with greater respect. Books about women's bodies became more prevalent, and bookstores even set aside shelf space for a section marked "Women's Health." It seemed that a woman would forever be able to control the decisions that were to be made about her body.

Lately, however, courts have begun deciding whether a woman has a right to end her pregnancy, and state legislatures have been passing new, more restrictive abortion regulations. Naturally, I am in favor of preventing an unwanted pregnancy rather than trying to deal with a conception. A human life ought to be created only when two people are able to offer love and care to a new, fragile being. Yet I continue to believe that a woman's body is her own property.

I want to educate a girl about her body, so that she can wisely discuss her health with her parents, friends, and doctor, and make smart, capable decisions. It's disturbing to me that organizations that provide information about birth control and abortion may be prevented from counseling teenage girls who do not have their parents' consent to seek help. I want you to learn as much as you can about your health, because ultimately it's your body, and no one else can take care of it the way you can.

BEING A TEEN: YOU'RE ON TOP OF THE WORLD, BUT IT'S TOUGH UP THERE

These are the years when, while listening to music and talking on the phone with your friends, you're figuring life out for yourself. Yet sometimes it's hard to have the proper perspective. You may think that you're over-weight when you're not, or that your breasts are small when they're fine. You may want to ask a doctor about physical changes that have been happening since you got your period, but you feel too old to see a pediatrician and too shy to visit a gynecologist.

How do you find out the answers to questions about yourself, your friends, and even boys? You can turn to *You're In Charge*. My hope is that you'll think of this book as a smart, close friend who can give you advice on things that are really happening to you. Do you want to know how to handle stress? Why sex can make you feel vulnerable? Where a depressed mood comes from? What actually happens to a woman's body during pregnancy? Sometimes the questions you'd most like to have an-swered seem embarrassing when you say them out loud. *You're In Charge* gives you a chance to get answers by yourself.

I know you are looking for answers, because many girls have asked me to help them. They are searching for knowledge. Hoping that your questions may be among them, I have devoted space in every chapter to answer actual questions from teenage girls. (If you have a personal question that I have not answered in this book, and you need help, please write to me: Dr. Niels H. Lauersen, 784 Park Avenue, New York, NY 10021. I will do my best to give you an answer.)

Yet although a book like this can be an invaluable guide, ultimately you are in charge of yourself. When it comes to handling situations involving alcohol or drugs, or knowing what to do when a boy makes advances, you are the one deciding how to behave. Armed with as much real-life information as can fit into these pages, you can feel smart and, above all, confident about your decisions.

Smart, confident women, however, must also be prepared for the unexpected. Think of it this way: a top-notch driver on a well-traveled highway can get into an accident if a maniac is behind the wheel of another car. As much as you may be determined to take charge of yourself, you can never know what others will do. When you have this book to turn to, you'll have a few tips for steering clear of trouble, and staying on course.

CHAPTER TWO

How Your Body and Looks Are Changing: What They Didn't Tell You in Health Class

THE POWER OF HORMONES

Hormones are awesome forces. Brace yourself for a few facts you've never before heard or, perhaps, understood. Did you know that hormones—in amounts so small that the first laboratory equipment for measuring them didn't even exist until the 1970s—give you sex drive, brain power, looks, strength, and more? The special effects of hormones are more fantastic than anything you've ever seen in the movies.

Here are the hormones, chemical messengers moving within the bloodstream, programmed by the brain to hit different target organs. They're keeping you healthy and at the same time shaping your personality. And they're most potent now, during your teens.

Even researchers who have been studying hormones

for years discover new facts about them regularly. Trying to understand hormones is like attempting to solve a mystery: Follow the path of the hormones, and see what kind of person appears at the end of the trail.

Along with your genes, hormones are making you a person, and since this book is about helping you understand yourself, hormones seem a good place to start. They give you harmony. Without hormones, you could be a body of separate parts. Just think, right now your hormones are carrying messages from Mission Control—the brain—to the rest of you. They're the go-betweens in the relationship that your mind has with your body. Hormones influence how you feel about your figure, while they're giving it shape. Here's how far-reaching hormones are.

HORMONES CONTROL YOUR BODY

Want to know why you can crave pizza every day for a week? Why your period isn't always the same? Why simply *everything* bothers you sometimes? Why your breasts either aren't growing enough, or don't seem to stop growing? Hormones are a big reason. They affect your moods and direct your growth. Hormones control whether you'll be short or tall, fat or thin.

While you're reading this page, hormones are pacing your heartbeat and governing your liver and kidneys. When you eat, they control metabolism, the way your body turns food into energy. Hormones direct the processes by which food fortifies blood, bone, muscle, and tissue. There are hormones to balance blood sugar levels, and hormones to monitor the amount of salt in your body.

You entered puberty when your hormones decided the timing was right. They orchestrate the menstrual cycle and have much to do with having a baby. Hormones are involved in getting pregnant and in every stage of pregnancy, from the first ripening of an egg cell to those final contractions of labor that push a newborn into the world. Hormones also bring on the breast milk that feeds a baby.

When you're scared or in danger, hormones help you to protect yourself. The hormone adrenaline flows into your body and gives you the strength to fight and to get out of a dangerous situation fast. Hormones also help you by defending against invading germs and working with white blood cells to fend off illness. They keep the body's machinery operating at peak performance and affect your mental and emotional well-being.

When a hormone is released, or secreted, from a gland, the type and amount can trigger a change of attitude. With hormonal flows in balance, you feel well and happy. Should hormonal motion be upset, you can feel down or physically ill. Much depends on the delicate give-and-take of hormones.

THE BODY'S GLANDS: HOME OF THE HORMONES

Glands are any internal organs or structures that release secretions, the way sweat glands put out perspiration. Hormones are secretions from the powerful endocrine glands located at strategic points in the body. (See illustration, page 20.) Some of these glands are tiny, just a few cells, but others, like the thyroid and pituitary glands, can be clearly seen. For all their power, the glands that house the hormones don't take up much space. The total weight of all the endocrine glands—the pituitary, pineal gland, thyroid, parathyroids, adrenals, thymus, pancreas, the ovaries in a girl, and the testes in a boy—is no more than seven ounces.

With the pituitary, the brain's master gland, as director, the other glands send hormones through the bloodstream to different organs. For example, when levels of hormones from the thyroid gland drop off, the pituitary gets the signal and sends back a thyroid-stimulating hormone, or TSH. After receiving TSH, the thyroid gland increases its production of hormones. This new supply goes into the bloodstream, aimed for target organs. The heart, for instance, uses thyroid hormones to maintain a regular beat.

It's a constant internal conversation. The endocrine glands "listen to" the hormonal messages they receive from the brain's pituitary, and respond by releasing more or less of their own hormones to the body. The glands also report messages back to the brain. In response to the feedback from the glands, the pituitary sends out a round of hormones again. This give-and-take is going on in your body right now. You can't hear it, but you do feel it.

THE PITUITARY

Everyone's body chemistry is controlled by the **pituitary**, or master gland, in the center of the brain. Protectively surrounded by bone, the pituitary is located behind the nasal cavities, just below an area called the **hypothalamus**.

The hypothalamus links the thinking part of the brain, the cerebral cortex, to the pituitary, which has power over the other endocrine glands. The mind/body connection goes something like this: Say you're stressed out about finals and, at the same time, your period is late. Your stress probably affected the hypothalamus, which

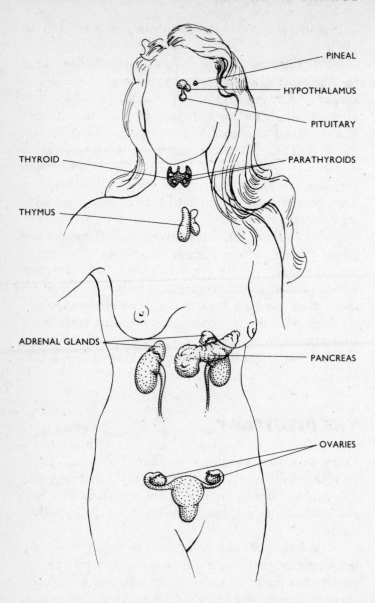

PINEAL

HYPOTHALAMUS

PITUITARY

THYROID

PARATHYROIDS

THYMUS

ADRENAL GLANDS

PANCREAS

OVARIES

2. Where the Body's Endocrine Glands Are Located.

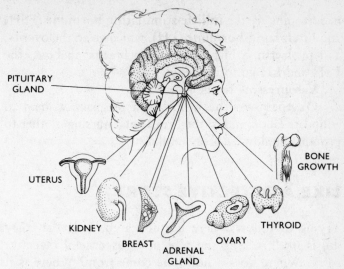

3. The Pituitary Gland, the master gland, directs sex hormone production, helps maintain pregnancy, governs the kidneys, stimulates the flow of breast milk, affects hormone production in the adrenal glands, ovaries, and thyroid, and controls growth.

sent its "stressed out" message to the pituitary. The pituitary then relayed its "stressed out" signal to other endocrine glands, causing a change in the hormones that regulate the ovaries and menstrual cycle. The result? A delayed menstrual period.

As you can see from the drawing, each hormone that the pituitary sends out has a particular function and is directed to a specific area of the body:

Growth hormone—mostly to the bones.

Thyroid-stimulating hormone (TSH)—to the thyroid gland.

Adrenocorticotropic hormone (ACTH)—to the adrenal glands.

Gonadotropins—to the sex organs. In girls, the gonadotropins are the **follicle-stimulating hormone (FSH)** and **luteinizing hormone (LH)**, which go to the ovaries, and **prolactin**, which goes to the breasts; in boys, the **FSH** and **LH** go to the testes.

Vasopressin—to the kidneys.

Oxytocin—to the womb of a pregnant woman to stimulate labor, and to the breasts of a nursing mother to prompt the flow of breast milk.

LIKE A DETECTIVE STORY

Trying to follow where hormones go, and what they do, is like tracking the plot of a suspenseful detective story. Where does a hormone come from? Where is it going? What is its aim? What are the clues? Even researchers never know exactly where the path of a hormone will lead, and when they think they've made a discovery, sometimes they've only uncovered the beginning of a whole series of interconnections that keep the body together. Here, though, is what they do know about the way hormones from the master gland are changing your looks, while keeping your body together.

GETTING TALLER: GROWTH HORMONE

How tall you get has a lot to do with **human growth hormone (HGH)** from the pituitary. This hormone to the bones is so powerful that if the pituitary misfires and lets out too much of it, you can be too tall, maybe even a giant. With too little growth hormone, you could be a dwarf. Other hormones contribute to overall develop-

ment, but growth hormone has by far the most important influence on height.

The greatest amounts of growth hormone are released
when you're asleep. A baby, who is growing at a rapid
rate, sleeps all the time. You may take naps more than
your parents or your ten-year-old sister, because you're
growing. Usually a girl has her biggest growth spurt when
she's between nine and twelve years old; boys normally
shoot up later, between twelve and fourteen. Those are
the years when growth hormone is surging through your
body.

Your growth may have slowed down a bit by now,
and you may have started to gain weight if you're in
the mid-teens. Don't panic and try to drop a few
pounds just yet, though. It's important to eat properly
and not diet until your weight has leveled off. When
your body is changing it needs proper nutrition, and
your growing bones require calcium. Milk and other
dairy products, fish, beans, leafy green vegetables, all
have calcium. (For more on the metabolism of food,
see the next section, The Energizers: Hormones from
the thyroid.)

The median height for girls, by age eighteen, is five
feet four and one-half inches; for boys, it's five feet ten
inches. Whether you're shorter or taller may depend on
the genes your parents gave you, but food is no small
influence. If you are not eating properly and are mal-
nourished, you may not grow to your full potential. (Improved nutrition, by the way, is one reason why teenagers
today are generally much taller than teenagers in the
1700s. Stand in a preserved colonial house in one of the
historic regions of this country and see how low the ceilings are!)

A hormonal imbalance, as well as certain diseases, can
bring on growth disorders. By eating wholesome food

and staying healthy, you give your body the best advantage.

THE ENERGIZERS:
HORMONES FROM THE THYROID

Every cell in your body is affected by hormones from the thyroid, the butterfly-shaped gland in your throat. The thyroid is positioned in front of the windpipe, or trachea, just below the voicebox, or larynx.

After the pituitary directs **TSH** to it, the thyroid then sends out its hormones, which affect the development of the brain, muscles, bones, organs, and other glands. Two thyroid hormones, **triiodothyronine (T3)** and **thyroxine (T4)**, are quite important since they affect metabolism, the way your body converts food into energy.

You might watch a friend eat enormous lunches, snack on chips and chocolate, and never gain an ounce, and you might think that she's the luckiest person in the world. Don't be too envious. Your friend could be growing so fast that she's using up all the calories she's consuming, but she also might have an overactive thyroid gland. An **over-** or **hyperactive thyroid** can make you nervous and jittery, pale and weak. Your menstrual cycle can become irregular, and you may not be able to get pregnant when you're ready to start a family.

When it's sending out the proper amounts of T3 and T4, the thyroid gives you a reliable source of energy. You feel good. Too much thyroid hormone, and you're edgy; too little, and you're sluggish. If you never indulge in fattening foods, yet still gain weight, and if you generally feel sleepy and tired, you may have an **under-** or **hypoactive** thyroid. You don't have to live with this or an overactive thyroid, however, since medications are available to correct both conditions.

Your monthly cycle is so hormonally sensitive that if the thyroid gland is over- or underproducing, the menstrual pattern will change. In fact, if you ever experience menstrual problems and also seem to have too much, or not enough, energy, your condition might be connected to an imbalance in thyroid hormones.

ADRENALINE AND OTHER HORMONES

The adrenals are triangular glands atop the kidneys. In both girls and boys, the adrenals release **estrogen**, the female sex steroid, and **androgen**, the male sex steroid. While these steroids supplement the sex hormones coming from the ovaries in girls, and the testes in boys, they also are giving some male sex hormone to a girl, and some female sex hormone to a boy. The male sex hormone may affect the amount of pubic and other body hair on a girl, as well as her sex drive. Too much male hormone may give her a deeper voice, a larger clitoris, and a heightened interest in sex. These are only a few of the forces of the adrenals, however.

The inner part of the adrenals releases the **catecholamines**, the fight/flight chemicals that are also produced in the brain and nervous system. The best-known catecholamine is **adrenaline**, also called epinephrine. Adrenaline is the major fight/flight hormone. Should you ever feel threatened, your adrenal glands would get a "danger" signal from the pituitary in the form of **ACTH** and quickly send out adrenaline. The adrenaline puts your body on red alert. It makes your heart beat faster, rushes blood to the muscles, and breaks down fats and sugars for an energy boost. With a surge of adrenaline, you can fight harder or run faster than you ever thought you could.

SEX HORMONES

Your breasts, hips, menstrual flow, the sound of your voice, the feel of your skin, the wetness of your vagina, are all products of the female sex hormones, estrogen and progesterone. They're more essential to your sexuality than your genes.

Early in pregnancy a fetus, whether it has XY (male) or XX (female) chromosomes, is unisex; it possesses neither penis nor vagina to identify it as male or female. During the eighth to twelfth weeks the fetus with the male chromosomes begins to manufacture testosterone and other androgens (male sex hormones). As testosterone levels climb, masculine sex organs take shape. The fetus with the female chromosomes, since it barely produces male sex hormones, doesn't change. It continues life as a female. You, the female, are the basic human being! In spite of what the Bible says about Adam being fashioned first, male hormones are added to the basic female for a male body and brain to be created.

ESTROGEN

With computerlike precision, during puberty the pituitary gland began sending an increased amount of **follicle-stimulating hormone (FSH)** and **luteinizing hormone (LH)** to your ovaries. Like two pearls at the end of the Fallopian tubes (see illustration, page 28), the pinkish-gray ovaries began manufacturing more and more estrogen. A girl on an estrogen surge might notice her skin glistening a little more and her breasts becoming more shapely. Her hips may widen, pubic hair grow, and genital area enlarge. Both girls and boys have some estrogen, but when the FSH and LH from the pituitary targets the ovaries, the amount of estrogen a girl has soars tremendously. (A boy receiving a wallop of FSH and LH to his testes during puberty begins producing the male sex hormone testosterone. With testosterone, a boy's muscles become more pronounced, his voice deepens, his beard starts to grow, and his penis gets bigger. See Chapter 4, *What Boys Are Going Through.*)

Estrogen has the starring role in your body. It is the force behind puberty, menstruation, and pregnancy. It's curious, though, that you attain most of your height before your first menstrual period. When estrogen rises and menstruation begins, your bone growth virtually stops. From then on, you do not grow much taller, but sexually you flourish.

With menarche, the onset of your first menstrual period, your body enters its first stage of womanhood. The pituitary and the ovaries begin a close working relationship for the production of the sex hormones. The monthly cycle is a finely tuned interaction between the pituitary hormones in the brain and the sex hormones from the ovaries. (See The Synchronized Menstrual Cycle.) First, the pituitary sends out FSH and LH to the ovaries and estrogen rises. An egg is then released. (This is ovulation.) **Progesterone**, the costarring female sex hormone, makes its appearance in the cycle's second half.

Don't forget that there is a mind/body connection, though. If you have a shift in emotions, you can feel as if you are in someone else's body. If the master pituitary receives a distress signal, then the hormonal chain reaction may well be out of sync. When the interplay of hor-

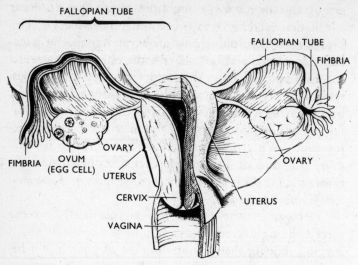

FALLOPIAN TUBE

FALLOPIAN TUBE

FIMBRIA

OVARY

FIMBRIA

OVUM
(EGG CELL)

OVARY

UTERUS

CERVIX

UTERUS

VAGINA

4. Internal Female Sex Organs. Notice how the vagina leads to the cervix and passage into the uterus. At the upper portion of the uterus, the Fallopian tubes extend outward to meet the ovaries. It is here, in the ovaries, that the female sex hormones estrogen and progesterone are produced.
ILLUSTRATION BY LAUREL PURINTON RAND

mones is off, you may not ovulate, or have a period. One thing sets off another that sets off another, and so on and so on.

THE MILK-CONTROLLING HORMONE

Should you become pregnant, the pituitary will direct a hormone called **prolactin** to stimulate the production of milk in your breasts. Sometimes, though, the prolactin level may rise without pregnancy.

If you are under a lot of stress or have premenstrual

syndrome (see discussion on page 149), your hormone levels may become imbalanced and may cause an over-abundance of prolactin. In some cases, too much prolactin may signal a pituitary tumor, but more often the rise is from something else. Suction on the breast, pain, frustration, anxiety over an upcoming operation, and sexual intercourse may cause a jump in this hormone.

When prolactin is high, you may leak milk from your nipples. You may also become infertile, unable to conceive a baby. If this happens, you can be treated with a medication called Parlodel (bromocriptine mesylate), which normalizes the hormone.

THE KIDNEYS

The kidneys are not glands, but organs. Nevertheless, the pituitary sends the hormone **vasopressin** to the kidneys, as if they were glands. The kidneys, in turn, are stimulated to produce two important hormones: **renin**, a regulator of blood pressure, and **renal erythropoietic factor (REF)**, which influences the amount of red blood cells that are manufactured in bone marrow. Body fluid is also affected by hormonal output from the kidneys, since renin influences thirst.

THE BIRTHING HORMONE

Once doctors believed that when the pituitary sent the hormone **oxytocin** to the uterus of a pregnant woman, she would go into labor. Today physicians know that although labor contractions are helped along by oxytocin, they probably start when the unborn baby releases its own set of hormones. It may be that each person decides when to be born. Yet oxytocin plays a big part in labor. It works in combination with **prostaglandins**, hormone-like substances in the lining of the uterus and other body tissues. In fact, mother and baby are both releasing oxytocin and prostaglandins at the start of labor.

After labor, oxytocin is the hormone that helps breast-feeding. As a baby sucks on a nipple, nerve impulses to the brain signal the pituitary to release oxytocin. The oxytocin triggers contractions within breast tissue that help send milk to the hungry infant.

Studies at the National Institute of Mental Health have also linked oxytocin to mothering. In animals, oxytocin prompts licking and cuddling between mother and offspring; in humans, oxytocin may explain why a mother instinctively responds to her child's cry in the night.

MENSTRUATION IS NOT AN UNSOLVED MYSTERY

Of all the hormone changes, the one we call the menstrual cycle belongs only to girls, and sometimes boys make fun of it. If you're in a bad mood, a boyfriend might say, "What's the matter? Is it that time of month?" While such comments acknowledge the power that hormones have to create mood swings, they also dismiss your feelings as some minor side effect of menstruation, at moments when you may not be menstruating at all! These remarks are often made by people who do not understand how the menstrual cycle works.

The menstrual cycle has been considered mysterious for centuries. The word *menstruation* comes from the Latin *mens*, meaning "month," but *month* is a derivation of *moon*, and in Greek, *moon* is *mene*. Clearly, the ancients linked the female monthly cycle to the phases of the moon. The moon takes twenty-nine days to pass through its cycle of phases from new moon to new moon—the same timing as a woman's menstrual cycle. And like the moon, which peaks midway through its cycle, a woman's body experiences ovulation, an egg moving out of an ovary, midway through the menstrual cycle. Finally, both cycles end, one with an invisible new moon, the other with menstruation.

Legend gave the menstrual cycle this mysterious link to the cosmos. Ancient peoples blamed or credited women with everything from blight to harvests of plenty, from deaths to miracle cures. Yet the feminine cycle is no mystery. It is a hormonal ritual that your body goes through about every twenty-eight to thirty-five days.

The ritual began with your first period, which you may or may not have experienced yet. The first sign of a period, a spot of blood on your underpants, may show up during any normal day, from the time you're ten until you're about fifteen. If you haven't started menstruating by your sixteenth birthday, however, it's a good idea to consult a doctor. (You should find out whether there is a hormonal imbalance or a problem with the sex organs that is preventing menstruation.)

When all is in perfect order, here's how your hormones make your period happen.

THE SYNCHRONIZED MENSTRUAL CYCLE

The First Half of the Monthly Cycle (Days 1–14)

Day 1 of a brand-new cycle is the day you first notice your menstrual flow, which is a shedding of bloody tissue that has been building up on the wall of the uterus. The tissue was to be nourishment for a fetus during pregnancy, but since you are not pregnant, the tissue leaves your body as blood, or menstrual flow.

A few days into your period, as the flow lightens, the hypothalamus sends its hormonal message—the releasing factor—to the pituitary gland. The pituitary then moves the follicle-stimulating hormone (FSH) into the bloodstream, where it follows a course to the ovaries. When FSH arrives at the ovaries, the action begins.

All the little follicles, the potential egg cells in the ovaries, begin to grow and increase the production of the female hormone estrogen. Hormone-producing ovarian tissue also adds estrogen to the buildup. As estrogen climbs, your skin is at its best. Blemishes disappear and your complexion glows. Your natural odor also becomes more appealing, and your breasts may take on a new fullness. (Estrogen, in fact, is credited with a number of "female" characteristics and personality features. See the sections following Holding Hormones Responsible, in this chapter.) The rise in estrogen also changes the amount of mucus that the cervix, the mouth of the uterus, secretes into the vagina.

Right after your period begins, the mucus is barely there, but toward the middle of the cycle, when estrogen peaks, cervical mucus is abundant. You may sense some wetness in your vagina. The mucus at this time is clear and thin, like raw egg white. You can see it, if you want to, by inserting your thumb and index finger into your vagina, withdrawing the two fingers, and stretching them apart. The stretchy, clear mucus threads between your fingers signal that you are at your most fertile. (The mucus's ability to stretch like this is called spinnbarkeit.)

While all this is happening, one of the follicles that started the estrogen buildup, for some unknown reason, grows faster than the rest. That one egg cell, called the Graafian follicle or the egg-of-the-month, swells out, making a bubble on the outside of an ovary. Inside the bubble, the egg continues to develop. Eventually it will break out and travel to the uterus.

The level of estrogen continues to rise, and halfway through the cycle (about fourteen days) the pituitary responds to the abundance of estrogen by slowing down its release of FSH. As estrogen reaches a certain level, it stimulates the pituitary to send out luteinizing hormone (LH), which is designed to promote the escape of the monthly egg.

The presence of LH makes the Graafian follicle burst its bubble and send out a mature egg cell. This release of an egg is called **ovulation**. When the cycle is in sync, ovulation corresponds to spinnbarkeit. This is the time of the month when you would be most likely to get pregnant. *You are most fertile midway through your cycle.*

Some girls report that they feel sexy at this halfway mark. In the animal world, females are said to be in estrus (or "in heat") when their estrogen is high and they're ovulating. Male animals sense the change. The same is true for the human male: he has sensors, too. Actually, both sexes may sometimes experience urges they do not understand.

The Second Half of the Monthly Cycle (Days 14–28)

Now, back to the egg. To release an egg, the ovary turns its ovulation side toward the fringed end of the Fallopian tube. The fringes on the end of a Fallopian tube are called fimbria. In a sense, the fimbria are like tentacles, or fingers, that reach down and catch the freed egg. Once it leaves the Graafian follicle, the egg is moved along on a five- to seven-day journey inside the Fallopian tube to the uterus.

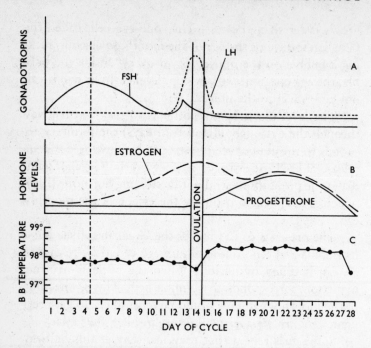

Chart 1. How Hormones and Body Temperature Change
During the Menstrual Cycle.
   • Curve A shows the fluctuations in the hormones FSH
and LH during the menstrual cycle.
   • Curve B indicates the fluctuations of the female
hormones estrogen and progesterone.
   • Curve C indicates changes in body temperature.
   • How the Changes Are Related: Day 1 marks the first
day of menstrual bleeding. The FSH stimulates the ovaries to
produce estrogen. When estrogen reaches a peak, it triggers
the release of LH. The heightened LH then stimulates
ovulation, the release of an egg from an ovary. Estrogen and
progesterone increase after ovulation and cause a rise in
body temperature. This temperature jump is a sign that
ovulation has taken place.

The second half of the menstrual cycle is now in progress. The scar tissue that the traveling egg has left behind becomes the **corpus luteum**, the producer of progesterone.

Progesterone is called the pregnancy hormone because it causes the lining of the uterus to change into a soft, spongy nest rich in blood vessels, making it the perfect bed for the egg coming down the tube. In other words, progesterone readies the uterus for pregnancy and helps the conception survive. If the egg unites with sperm while in the Fallopian tube, the uterus, thanks to progesterone, will be prepared to nourish the fertilized egg. Progesterone also relaxes the uterus to give the egg a better chance to implant itself in the **endometrium**, the transformed lining of the uterus. If progesterone is low, a miscarriage may occur.

The two female sex hormones, estrogen and progesterone, now increase together. Ovulation is in the past. The LH level drops off. In this second half of the cycle, the relationship of estrogen and progesterone may bring on menstrual problems, however. These are explored in Chapter 5. Meanwhile, the cycle is nearing an end.

If the egg-of-the-month is fertilized and pregnancy occurs, estrogen and progesterone stay at high levels. When there is no fertilization, which is more often the case among teenage girls, the pituitary does not get a message to keep the corpus luteum, the producer of progesterone, going. Without the signal from the brain, the corpus luteum disintegrates, estrogen and progesterone levels drop, and menstruation is triggered. When the sex hormones drop, the level of prostaglandins, hormonelike substances in the lining of the uterus, rises. They cause the uterus to contract and shed the endometrium. Sometimes, if levels are exceptionally high, prostaglandins may trigger menstrual cramps.

As the cycle winds down, the surface of the endometrium, which is useless without pregnancy, leaves the body as menstrual blood. One menstrual cycle ends and another begins. The first day of menstruation marks the first day of a brand-new cycle.

A GIRL AND HER EGGS

A girl is born with about two million follicles, or eggs, in her ovaries. By the time she begins menstruating, however, more than half of these follicles have disintegrated and about 300,000 are left. With each menstrual cycle, one or two of these 300,000 follicles will ripen into the egg-of-the-month. A girl uses about 400 eggs in her lifetime, so she has plenty to spare. If one ovary becomes damaged or is surgically removed, she still has at least 150,000 eggs in her other working ovary. After childbearing years, the unused eggs simply disappear.

WHAT IT ALL MEANS

To explain the activities of hormones, *Newsweek* magazine once compared the human body to "a hotel switchboard, lit up by a constant stream of room-service orders and complaint calls: 'Can you lower the temperature in this room?' 'Would you send up a couple of cheeseburgers, please?' "[1] In this human "hotel," the messengers rushing from room to room to satisfy each need are hormones.

The word *hormone* comes from the Greek *hormon*, which means "to set in motion." Almost all aspects of the human experience are touched by hormones, and sci-

[1] Matt Clark, David Gelman, et al. "A User's Guide to Hormones," *Newsweek*, 12 January 1987, 50.

entists are frequently discovering new ones. About twenty human hormones were known in 1970, but researchers today believe that there may be as many as two hundred. They have identified at least forty-five separate hormones in the brain alone. The natural high you can get from bicycling for miles, swimming laps, or skiing down a mountain comes from the release of the brain's opiates, or "feel good" hormones.

The most interesting questions, and touchiest issues, however, are about the sex hormones: estrogen in girls, testosterone in boys. Studies have focused on how these hormones affect sexual development, intelligence, and behavior. Does estrogen make girls smarter? Is testosterone a violence-promoting hormone? Hormones always seem to cause controversy.

HOLDING HORMONES RESPONSIBLE

The latest findings on sex hormones can help you understand your personal passage to adulthood. The rise and fall of estrogen in your monthly cycle and the amount of testosterone in your body are important to who you are. Since hormones are helping you become a woman, you ought to know what all the fuss is about.

ARE GIRLS SMARTER THAN BOYS?

On the average, boys are better than girls at solving mathematical equations and problems with lines and patterns, while girls excel at expressing themselves verbally and using their hands with dexterity. Scientists argue about whether these differences are due to hormones or upbringing. Yet male and female rats, who certainly have no cultural upbringing, have male and female ways of getting through a maze. Researchers at Barnard College found that male rats relied on geometric tips alone, while female rats used geometry and landmarks.

Male and female brains are structurally different, and some researchers feel that they're probably chemically different, too. It's difficult to pinpoint what forces are at work in the mind. Some experts feel that girls could be just as good in areas of "male thinking" as boys if they were encouraged in those directions. It has been said that we are living in a sexist society that discourages girls from involving themselves in mathematics or being interested in, say, architecture. Other experts, however, believe that society is not all-important, that a boy's prenatal exposure to testosterone actually alters his brain, making it more sensitive to such things as math.

The controversy over whether biology or environment is a greater influence on the way girls and boys think will go on long after you and your friends have grown into adulthood. What's for sure right now, though, is that girls have their mental strengths and boys, theirs.

WHEN ESTROGEN IS HIGHEST, YOU MAY BE AT YOUR SMARTEST

You may be sharper at different times of the month. Canadian researcher Doreen Kimura, Ph.D., a psychology professor at the University of Western Ontario, along with Elizabeth Hampson, a graduate student, decided to find out whether changes in hormone levels within a monthly cycle affect a girl's thinking. Estrogen, the main female sex hormone, is low at the beginning of the menstrual cycle, but at the midway mark, just before ovulation, it rises. Estrogen drops shortly before a girl begins menstruating.

Dr. Kimura and her colleagues tested over 150 young

women. The women could handle tongue twisters, such as "A box of mixed biscuits in a biscuit mixer," much better on high-estrogen, than on low-estrogen, days. They also had greater hand-and-finger coordination during times of high estrogen. (Could it be, then, that halfway through the menstrual cycle a girl is at the peak of her powers?)

Toward the end of the monthly cycle, when estrogen fell, the women studied were better at solving problems related to space, such as mentally rotating designs drawn on paper. Even though men usually surpass women at solving these types of problems, during low-estrogen days women come closer to thinking like men in this regard.

The left side of the brain, which controls logic, communication (speaking, reading, writing), and manual dexterity, may be more sensitive to estrogen than the right side. It's curious, because the business of the right side of the brain, the understanding of patterns and complex relationships that may not be logical, more traditionally has been linked to "male" thinking.

Generally, a woman who is lost while driving will stop to ask directions, while a man will keep driving in patterns that he believes will help him find his way. Yet a woman would be better able to communicate the problem on high-estrogen days, according to Dr. Kimura. In spite of the differences that sex may bring to the brain, however, researchers emphasize that in many ways, men and women still think alike. Let's hope so.

EXCESS BODY HAIR: WHEN A GIRL HAS TOO MUCH TESTOSTERONE

As mentioned before, teenage girls have lower levels of the male sex hormone testosterone. Testosterone influences the growth of pubic and underarm hair. The rise of testosterone levels during a boy's puberty is responsible for the growth of hair on the face, chest, armpits, and genitals. Since a boy has more testosterone than estrogen, he has more areas of coarse, sex-linked hair than a girl does.

During the monthly cycle, a girl will experience a slight rise in testosterone. If she normally shaves the hair on her legs, she may notice that she has to shave more frequently. Sometimes, though, hairiness can seem excessive. A girl may have hairs on her face, around her nipples, or on her stomach. A hormonal imbalance in the adrenal glands can cause an overabundance of hair-growing testosterone, but often excessive body hair springs from an ovarian problem.

Sometimes a girl may inherit a special form of polycystic ovaries, the **Stein-Leventhal syndrome**, a condition in which the ovaries are slightly enlarged and produce too much estrogen and testosterone, which can lead to a general hormonal imbalance. Brain hormones do not function properly and ovulation is off. If you look in the mirror and see hair growing up from your pubic area toward your navel in a triangular fashion, and you notice hair around your nipples, you may have the condition.

Before you decide that you have a hormonal imbalance, however, you should look at your mother. Often dark-haired Mediterranean women have more body hair than fair-haired northern European types. Asian women have the fewest hair follicles and the least amount of body hair. Your body hair may simply be a matter of heredity.

If a doctor does diagnose a hormonal imbalance, the condition can be treated with synthetic hormones. The Stein-Leventhal syndrome, for example, can often be corrected with birth control pills. A drug called Spironolactone may counterbalance the increase of testosterone from the adrenals and has been known to reduce the amount of body hair.

Unfortunately, however, the hair doesn't usually go away after treatments. The ways to eliminate excess body hair are still electrolysis, waxing, depilatories, and shaving. (See Chapter 3, *How to Be Happy with Your Body*.)

The idea of having too much testosterone can be disturbing to a girl. She may wonder whether the male hormone can affect her personality. She needn't worry. The imbalance of testosterone, which may promote hairiness, usually involves such low levels of the hormone that a girl remains unaffected in other ways. Her voice doesn't deepen and her biceps do not start to bulge. As for what's considered the masculine trait of aggressiveness, doctors disagree on whether testosterone is a strong influence. Researchers studying hormone levels in girls and boys from nine to fourteen years old found that sometimes boys with *lower* testosterone levels had greater problems with aggression than did boys with higher levels of the hormone. (See Chapter 4, *What Boys Are Going Through*.)

HOOKED ON STEROIDS: FAKE TESTOSTERONE

Although the thought of too much testosterone is scary to a girl, a boy may want extra male hormone. Synthetic testosterone is illegally sold in the form of anabolic steroids, which can be injected or taken in tablets. Recent research from Penn State University has shown that one out of fifteen male high school seniors in the United States are taking bodybuilding anabolic steroids.

In a survey of high school seniors, almost half the boys who were steroid users said they took the drugs to improve their athletic ability, but 26.7 percent of them just wanted to look better. The drugs can make a boy bulk up like Arnold Schwarzenegger. Some think that the more they look and act like "The Terminator," the more girls will like them.

With steroid use come side effects, which include a slowdown of natural testosterone production. Testicles shrivel up and breasts grow. The drugs can kill, since they cause kidney and liver damage, liver cancer, and heart disease. There are also psychological effects—moodiness, depression, irritability. Users are keenly aware of what's called " 'roid rages," when the smallest thing can drive them to irrational tantrums that can lead to death. One seventeen-year-old boy in Michigan put a .22 caliber rifle to his head and pulled the trigger when, his family believes, he became annoyed because the door was stuck on a car he wanted to drive. He had been buying steroids from suppliers at local gyms.

A girl who thinks that a lean, average-looking boy is cute may want to let him know. It might be a good idea to shatter the stereotype of the girl who gets a thrill from rippling muscles. Girls know they're not so easily swayed, but apparently boys are still in the dark. (See Chapter 4, *What Boys Are Going Through*, for more on steroids and how boys feel about their looks.) A girl must be aware of the dangers of steroids for herself as well. If she is drawn to competitive bodybuilding, she might be tempted to "juice up" on anabolic steroids, and she'll be risking her health just the way a boy does. Whenever the delicate balance of hormones is interfered with, chaos can reign within the body.

SOME PEOPLE ARE LIVING WITHOUT SEX HORMONES

Sometimes a baby might be born without that important pituitary gland, or with damaged reproductive organs, and will not have sex hormones. Fortunately, synthetic sex hormones offer replacements. They can be given to a person by injection or orally throughout his or her lifetime.

The ovaries are the source of the sex hormone estrogen. A woman may have her ovaries surgically removed, thereby losing the chief supplier of this hormone. Estrogen replacement can enhance her physical female characteristics, although the woman will not be able to become pregnant.

Historically, the removal of sex organs and hormones, or **castration**, has been most frequently linked to males. In some ancient civilizations a man could be castrated because he committed a crime, but sometimes poor families made money by selling young sons for castration, since there was a market. Castrated males, called eunuchs, were sought after for royal households. In the Far and Middle East, a eunuch might be a harem guard or a personal servant of a ruler's mother. Without a beard or body hair—but fatty tissue on his chest that gave him breasts, wide hips, and a high voice—a eunuch was smooth, pudgy, and sweetly tempered. Today's synthetic sex hormones, though, would change all that. If a man must have his testicles, which supply the hormone testosterone, surgically removed, he can take synthetic testosterone.

THE BODY ELECTRIC

The action within your body is electrifying. As hormones travel from the brain to different organs and hormonal "messages" are sent back again, the body's systems are kept in operation and you continue to be a thinking, feeling person. If you ever sense that "something is wrong," if you feel that your body is not developing the way your friends' bodies are and you suspect a hormonal problem, you can have it checked out. Today, with a blood test, a number of hormones can be measured and analyzed.

Research is advancing so rapidly that even your health teacher may have difficulty staying up-to-date on what science is able to tell from hormones. Just recently twenty-one healthy men from ages sixty-one to eighty-one were injected with genetically engineered growth hormone for six months. The result was that their bodies seemed to become twenty years younger. The surge of growth hormone, which normally begins declining at age thirty, added bulk, strength, and youthfulness to their aging muscles, organs, and backbones. By the time you become a senior citizen, there may well be a hormonal way to keep the body young while growing old.

Scientists are learning more and more about the body from hormonal discoveries. Your goal should be to keep yourself as healthy as possible, so that your hormones will move where they're needed in your body, keeping you in great shape.

CHAPTER THREE

How to Be Happy with Your Body

Hair just doesn't do what you want it to sometimes. How often have you thought that if your hair were straighter or curlier, longer or shorter, thinner or thicker, or a different color, you'd be deliriously happy? How many times have you wished that you could change your skin, breasts, hips, or legs? Is there a girl who cannot list a few improvements she'd like to make on herself?

With hormones keeping you together, shaping your silhouette, gauging your height, and mapping out your body hair, you own a basic package. Within that package, however, are options. Take a moment to stand naked in front of a mirror and think about how you want to treat the body you see before you.

Chapter 2 described the hormonal, inner workings of your body—the invisible you. This chapter offers an understanding of your visible parts, a head-to-toe survey of what you may see in the mirror. You have the power to improve your image. By being smart about your looks and keeping your best features healthy, you can set your personal standard of beauty.

HOW YOUR FIGURE IS CHANGING

Except for their sex organs, girls and boys in grade school have fairly similar bodies. Girls may have a little more fat and boys, longer forearms, but basically they're the same. As a girl's sex hormones, estrogen and progesterone, get going during puberty, the contours of her body change. Her face even changes; the lower half gets longer and fuller.

Depending on your age, here's what you might see in the mirror at:

• *Nine to ten years old:* Your pelvic bones are beginning to grow and give you a female form, and more fat is settling on your breasts, hips, and thighs.

• *Ten to eleven years old:* You're getting taller, and your nipples are starting to bud. If you look down, you can see pubic hair appearing on the mons pubis, also called the mountain of Venus, triangle between your legs.

• *Eleven to fifteen years old:* You're nearing your full height, and you probably have been gaining weight. Your breasts are filling out and your pubic hair looks coarse and dark. You might also have armpit hair. Sometimes you may notice a vaginal discharge, but you've already begun menstruating. You're a bit heavier than you used to be because your body added extra fat in preparation for your period.

• *Fifteen to eighteen years old:* You're probably as tall as you're going to get. For the most part, bone growth is over, but it's still possible to grow an inch or so before

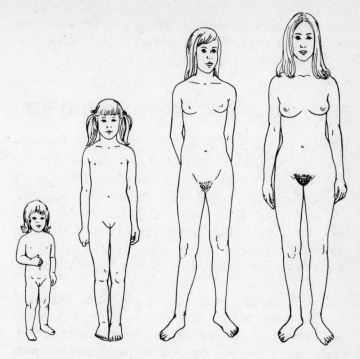

5. *How Your Body Changes to a Woman's. The female body at ages 4, 8, 12, and 16.*

you're twenty-one. (For eighteen-year-old girls, the median height is five feet four and a half inches.) Your body is more a woman's than a girl's by now. You have full, soft curves. Your breasts have taken on their own shape (see sections on breasts in this chapter) with the areolae, the circles of darker skin surrounding the nipples, forming their own mounds of distinction. Your periods are more regular, and you can see a defined triangular nest of pubic hair.

The woman's body you have acquired may be angular or curvy, sturdy or delicate, slim or endowed, tall, petite, or somewhere in between. Every body type has its assets, and you can make the most of yours. Take a good look in the mirror, and rejoice in being you.

THE FASHION OF WOMEN'S FIGURES

Women periodically reshape themselves. The movies from the 1950s, when Marilyn Monroe was a star, show that the fleshy, big-breasted woman was in vogue. A woman back then wanted to have full cheeks, pouty lips, and big breasts. In the 1960s and '70s she traded in that look for a slim, long-legged, small-breasted figure to match the braless, mini-skirted image of that period. Although thin has remained in, current body fashions allow more variety.

Fashion models continue to be pencil-thin, but movie stars like actress Melanie Griffith, who has a soft, rounded face and a certain amount of flesh on her bones, are setting a more "normal" standard. Yet no "standard" need exist. The key to having a good-looking figure is to feel good about your body. Girls have different body types, but instead of being pleased with their differences, so many want to meet that "perfect body" standard. A voluptuous girl starves to make herself skinny, and a slim girl eats to have more curves. Meanwhile, the girl who is most truly attractive is the one who likes herself and her body, and wants to be fit.

While you can cut back on calories (see Chapter 11, *How You Eat Reveals How You Feel About Yourself*) and exercise to alter your figure, you ought to ask yourself if changes are really needed. Some girls judge themselves by an impossible standard. How unfair they're being to themselves! As you judge the body that your hormones, nutrition and genes have given you, remember that a great shape comes from good health and a sense of satisfaction about yourself. Both of these traits can be yours with a head-to-toe understanding of your body. Let's start at the top.

HOW HAIR GROWS

Your head has about 100,000 hairs on it. Each hair sprouts out of a follicle, a minute pocket in the scalp. Until recently, scientists believed that hair grew straight out of a papilla, a knob of hair-making tissue at the base of the follicle. In 1990 researchers discovered that a hair bulge slightly above the papilla sent down special cells that got the papilla's own hair cells going. The discovery of the hair bulge means that, in effect, hair grows down before it grows up.

As hair cells pile up, a single hair grows longer and harder and eventually pops out of the follicle as a hair shaft. Your hair grows about a half inch each month.

Not every hair on your head is growing at the same time, however. While about 90 percent of your hairs are always growing, another 10 percent are "resting." Those at rest stay that way for about three months, then fall out. You lose between fifty and a hundred hairs every day, so don't worry when you shampoo and see all those strands swirling down the drain. It's perfectly normal.

When a hair falls out, the papilla in the follicle starts to generate another hair. The new hair grows for about three years before it "rests" and falls out, then the cycle begins again. It's estimated that in a person's lifetime, twenty-four growth cycles take place in each of the 100,000 hair follicles.

So, if hairs continuously fall out and are reborn, it would be difficult to have hair that was, say, longer than you are tall. Yet the country singer Crystal Gayle has grown her locks well below her waist, and it's not unusual to hear about a woman who has "hair she can sit on." It might be that these women don't have a resting phase in their hair cycles.

What's more common, though, are too many resting hairs. When someone, usually a man, goes bald, it's because the resting hair that falls out doesn't grow back again. The papilla stays dormant forever. Women rarely go bald.

WHERE HAIR COLOR COMES FROM

The color of your hair normally matches the color of your skin. Melanin is a brown-black pigment that colors and protects the skin, hair, and eyes. Dark-skinned, black-haired people who live in hot, tropical climates usually have the highest amount of melanin in their skin and hair cells. The melanin acts as a shield against the burning rays of the sun.

In temperate areas, like the United States, people tend to have less melanin, lighter skin, and brownish hair. In the cooler parts of the world, like Scandinavia, people have little melanin. Their skin is fair and their hair is generally blond. Sometimes you might run across someone who is an albino, a person with no melanin at all, with snow-white skin and hair.

Some people may have chemically different melanin granules that give off a reddish hue. By themselves, these melanin granules create strawberry-blond hair. If a moderate amount of them are combined with ordinary granules, a true redhead appears; however, if only a small percentage join with ordinary granules, hair has red highlights. Shades spontaneously invented by nature, sometimes lightened by the sun, become the color of a girl's crowning glory, her hair.

HOW TO HAVE HEALTHY, SHINY HAIR

You may think that girls with shiny hair have simply chosen a good conditioner. In truth, shiny hair is a reflection of how healthy you are. Just as a cat's shiny coat dulls when the animal is sick, so your hair can appear faded when you aren't eating properly or feeling well. Sometimes certain drugs can affect the luster of hair (and occasionally lead to hair loss, but this is a more severe problem).

A low-fat, balanced diet is important to good looks. Within that diet, foods containing the B vitamins, which boost energy, fight depression, and help maintain balanced hormone levels, also contribute to good-looking hair. For example, B_6 promotes hormonal balance, and hormonal signals keep healthy hair growing; B_{12} increases the supply of red blood cells, and an enriched blood supply to the scalp nourishes the hair. The B vitamins are found in whole-grain breads and cereals, nuts, beef, liver, chicken, fish, peas, beans, milk, eggs, and dark green vegetables.

But just as important as what you eat is when. Philip Kingsley, a British-trained trichologist (a specialist in scalp and hair science), reports that the hair-growing energy levels in a hair follicle begin to diminish four hours after you eat. To keep those follicles active, you should not allow more than a four-hour break without nourishment. If you have lunch at noon and dinner will be at six, then a midafternoon snack of fresh fruit, or even half a sandwich of tuna, lettuce, and tomato on whole-grain bread, can keep hair in good health—just as long as you don't automatically reach for greasy potato chips or other junk food.

High-fat, high-sugar foods affect your scalp, just as they influence your skin. If you notice that after eating french fries or chocolate your skin becomes oilier and breaks out, remember that your scalp is reacting too. This chapter's sections on how to have beautiful skin can also be considered good sources of advice for hair care.

By watching what you eat and drink, you can strengthen your hair from within. Those eight glasses of water a day that are recommended for good skin are also needed for healthy hair. When hair is lacking in moisture, it takes on a dull, dry look. Yet while good food and lots of water and juices are essential, diet isn't the whole story.

At the end of the day, a good night's sleep renews your skin and hair. Sometimes when you don't sleep well, your hair is droopy and lifeless. Of course, it could be that stress is keeping you awake, and stress is known to cause negative hormonal changes and to deplete B vitamins.

Although hair can be damaged by too much blow-drying, perming, or coloring, its dullness can also be a signal that something is wrong—that you're sick, stressed, not eating well, not getting enough sleep, smoking, or on drugs of some sort. Stress, smoking, and drugs, both legal and illegal, can cause changes in your body chemistry. Before you buy a more expensive shampoo or conditioner, consider ways to beautify your hair from the inside out. A smoke-free, drug-free body that gets a balanced diet and sound sleep brings forth shiny hair. A scalp massage can also stimulate the blood vessels that keep hair healthy.

WHAT TO EXPECT FROM SHAMPOOS AND CONDITIONERS

If you examine a hair under a microscope, you can see that it's made up of many overlapping cuticle cells, with their tips pointing upward. A healthy hair has smooth cuticle cells; its shine comes from light reflecting off the surface. A split end is a sign that layers of cuticle cells are being worn away. Blow-drying, vigorous brushing, perming, and coloring can cause the cells to swell, separate, and weather. The surface of the hair shaft changes and hair looks dull and dry. Light no longer reflects because the cells are not smooth. For the shaft to stay moisturized and shiny, hair needs regular shampooing and conditioning.

When selecting a shampoo, remember that hair itself does not absorb nutrients such as honey, protein, and vitamins. The best shampoo for healthy hair is the one you think is best for you.

A conditioner contributes to healthy hair by returning the cuticle cells to their original places and sealing in the moisture that's in the hair shaft. Since hair grows a half inch every month, if your hair is twelve inches long, it's two years older at the ends. Those older ends are going to be more weathered and drier, and they'll need conditioning more than the hair at your scalp.

MOMENTS IN THE HISTORY OF HAIR[1]

For your amusement, I have briefly departed from health matters to reprint here some information about hair history from writer Alice Love.

8000 B.C. (New Stone Age)—
First Hair-Doings

First known use of hairpins and hair ornaments, as discovered by archaeologists. No signs of mousse.

1700s—First Hairdressers

By popular demand of English women competing to produce the highest and most lavishly ridiculous hair designs in semi-civilized history, hairdressing as a full-time occupation came into being. Towering hairdos up to three feet in height were supported by wire frames, stuffed with wool, rope, and straw, then decorated with flowers, feathers, jewels, ribbons, and assorted household appliances.

1870s—Heated Tongs

Invented by French hairdresser Marcel Grateau to create what became known as marcel waves. Forerunner of curling irons.

1890s—Hair Dryer

The first hair dryer, courtesy of French hairdresser Alexandre F. Godefroy, had a bonnetlike covering attached to the chimney pipe of a gas stove.

1905—The Perm

German-born hairdresser Charles L. Nessler came up with the first permanent-wave process, which took twelve hours.

1922—The Bob

Inspired by idolized ballroom dancer Irene Castle, the short boy-cut bob became a post–World War I symbol of political and social emancipation for women of the time. Men raged, preachers ranted, and barbers sniffed, but women held their ground and danced on.

1941—The Peek-a-Boo

Veronica Lake's long, blond hair, covering one eye and dubbed the peek-a-boo, was a national craze. It was so popular, in fact, that government officials asked her to pull her hair back for the duration of World War II because women in war plants were catching their clone 'dos in machines. Deprived of her signature hairdo, Lake's stardom quickly faded, and she herself labored under no delusions: "You could put all the talent I had into your left eye and still not suffer from impaired vision."

1949—The Record

Swami Pandarasannadhi, head of a monastery in Madras, India, was reported to have grown his hair to twenty-six feet in length, the longest in recorded history, according to *The Guinness Book of World Records*.

1953—The Blonde

Marilyn Monroe had gone from her natural Norma Jean–brown to platinum seven years earlier, but in her twentieth movie, she convinced the nation that *Gentlemen Prefer Blondes*.

December 12, 1965—Mia My-Oh

This date marked Frank Sinatra's fiftieth birthday and the day girlfriend Mia Farrow "set fans and Hollywood gasping by cutting her own hair to less than an inch long all over her head." Sinatra's response on first seeing it: "Now you can go out for Little League like the rest of the boys."

1966—Hot Rollers

Clairol introduced "the instant hairdo" with Kindness and Carmen hot rollers. In combination with blow dryers, this innovation put an end to the long-popular alibi: "Not tonight; I have to wash my hair."

February 1966—Twiggy

A scrawny seventeen-year-old from London by the name of Lesley Hornby also shed her long tresses and emerged as Twiggy, the ninety-pound cockney sensation who made buzzed napes, bony knees, and painted-on lashes fashionable.

November 1966—The Fall

Women who took the Twiggy look too seriously could become instantly feminine again with the rise of the fall, a mane of store-bought hair that was pinned to the top of the head to produce a not particularly realistic long-tressed look. "It's the finest investment in the world," Washington, D.C., socialite Margot Hahn told *Time* magazine that year. "You can't do anything in Washington without one."

1967—*Hair*, the Musical

Hair, the musical, opened, causing a furor over its nudity and simulated sex acts.

September 22, 1976—Big Hair

With the debut of the hit television series *Charlie's Angels*, Farrah Fawcett became an instant industry. And big, winged Farrah hair—the look created by Hollywood hairdresser Jose "Shake Your Head, Darling" Eber—became a national, even international, craze for far too long.

1979—Bo Braids

Bo Derek's slo-mo ocean romp with braids and bosom bouncing sent women flocking to hairdressers for the cornrow treatment. Most appealing was that the hair could be left in braids for three to four months.

1981—To Di For

Prince Charles of Great Britain married twenty-year-old Diana Spencer, and princess wannabes around the world demurely sidled up for the big-banged Shy Di 'do.

1981 + —MTV Hair

With the advent of round-the-clock rock videos, musical performers became household faces, and women looked to cable TV for hair inspiration. Leading the way: the Madonna goddess bob, the Tina Turner thatch, and the Stevie Nicks curl 'n' swirl.

HOW YOUR SKIN REFLECTS WHAT YOU EAT

Like hair, skin reflects your diet. You can eat for healthy, glowing skin by making sure that your diet is high in vitamin A, which directly affects skin tissue. You can find vitamin A in animal products, yellow-orange fruits and vegetables, and dark green leafy vegetables.

The low-fat, fruit-and-vegetable sources of vitamin A are the first choice of nutritionists, because these foods help to keep your heart healthy while they're creating a glow. Squash, pumpkin, sweet potato, carrots, cantaloupe, papaya, spinach, watermelon, kale, collard, and mustard and turnip greens contain a compound called beta carotene that converts into vitamin A in the body. Among the higher-fat foods, liver, cheese, eggs, butter, chicken, and whole and fortified milk have vitamin A.

There is some evidence that the mineral zinc might work with and help the release of vitamin A in the body. Laboratory mice that were given diets low in zinc were found to also have low levels of vitamin A. Doctors, though, think that zinc may be an anti-inflammatory agent which has a special role in keeping skin healthy. However zinc works, it's obviously a good idea to have it in your diet. Foods high in zinc are oysters, liver, lean ground beef, lamb, pumpkin seeds, tuna, and the dark meat of turkey and chicken.

Chocolate and Other Foods Linked to Skin Problems

Some girls think that all they have to do is look at a piece of chocolate and they'll break out. They're sure that chocolate gives them pimples. Doctors disagree about whether sweet, salty, and fatty junk foods like candy bars, soft drinks, potato chips, greasy french fries, and burgers actually contribute to acne. (See Acne, page 63.) One study in which acne sufferers who ate large amounts of chocolate didn't have any worsening of their conditions is cited as proof that chocolate doesn't cause blemishes.

You know how your skin reacts, however. If you break out after eating a particular junk food, then stay away from it. A diet high in sweet, salty, and fatty foods won't improve the health of the rest of your body anyway, so you might as well cut back when you can.

. . . AND DRINK

The best health and beauty aid for your skin is H_2O—water. If you live in a temperate climate, you lose two and a half to three quarts of water a day. You lose water in urine, of course, but less obvious are the losses from water vapor that escapes when you exhale and from light sweating that goes on no matter what the temperature. If you exercise forty-five minutes a day, you can easily lose four quarts of water, and if you don't replenish the water supply, eventually your skin will show it. You will become pale and the texture of your skin will be less supple.

Although eight 8-ounce glasses of water a day is the general rule, you're taking in water from foods (even bread and potatoes contain water) and beverages. Water, though, is nature's own moisturizer for the skin and cleansing agent for the body.

Beer, wine coolers, and other drinks that contain alcohol can dry out the skin. This "skin wrinkling" feature is one more reason to keep away from alcohol.

SMOKING AND OTHER INFLUENCES

Smoking can cause a lot of wrinkles, making your face look old while you are still young. Researchers do not know the scientific reason why skin wrinkles faster for smokers, but one theory is that smoking lowers estrogen levels. Normally, estrogen gives skin a healthy glow. About halfway through the menstrual cycle, when the estrogen level is at its highest, your skin shines. A falling estrogen level can have a drying effect on the face. A smoker may have a dusty, gray cast to her face from smoking, whether the cigarettes are tobacco or marijuana. Besides affecting estrogen, smoking also causes blood vessels to constrict, or narrow, and makes rosy cheeks pale.

Drugs like cocaine and crack can also make the skin dry, thin, pale, and unhealthy. Besides the many other assaults on the body, these drugs can make users look ill fairly quickly.

Stress caused by worry over such things as an important test, or how you'll look on picture-taking day, or whether a certain first date will go well can bring on hormonal fluctuations that make your skin break out. A hormonal imbalance can affect blood flow and the skin's ability to fight infection.

It hasn't been possible for scientists to prove through laboratory tests that stress causes pimples, since not everyone is susceptible to skin problems. Girls who are vulnerable, though, aren't surprised when a pimple appears the day before yearbook pictures are to be taken. If your complexion is a sure target for stress, then try to find a healthy release for your anxiety. You might discover that swimming, painting, or just listening to music helps you relax, and the more stress-free you are, the less likely a blemish will break out.

THE GOOD SUN

While lots of unprotected time in the sun can be damaging to the skin, the sun still is important for good health. Sunlight causes a chemical in the skin to make a substance that your body metabolizes into vitamin D. That's why vitamin D, which helps calcium and phosphorus strengthen bones and teeth, is called the "sunshine vitamin."

Sunlight also influences hormones. A study conducted in the late sixties showed that light entering the eyes may cause a surge of luteinizing hormone (see Chapter 2), which triggers the release of the egg-of-the-month from an ovary. Adding support to that finding are egg farmers, who strongly believe that leaving lights on in henhouses during darker, shorter winter days keeps egg production up.

So get out into the sunshine, but don't stay too long. While a little sun is beneficial, a lot can lead to trouble.

THE BAD SUN

In spite of its benefits, the sun can truly fry you. You may spend hours and hours in pursuit of the perfect tan and see sun-damaged skin when your bronzed body fades. One blistering sunburn in your teens or twenties and you'll develop fine lines, brown spots, and skin that's lost its elasticity. If you're a devout sun worshiper, the ultraviolet rays may also lead to cell changes that cause skin cancer.

Skin cancer is the Number One cancer in the United

States. The rate of skin cancer has nearly doubled since 1980 and today strikes one in every six people. Basal cell carcinoma is the more frequently occurring, less serious type of skin cancer that usually appears on the face and hands and, in almost all cases, does not spread to other parts of the body. At the other end of the spectrum, however, is malignant melanoma, a most deadly type of skin cancer. Researchers are working on a vaccine against melanoma, which spreads beyond the skin to other organs. This is one of the toughest cancers to treat, and it's a cancer that can kill.

Girls who have a family history of skin cancer, fair complexions, blond or red hair, or freckles are more susceptible to skin cancer, but every girl has to be careful. Even though the melanin in the skin of black and Asian girls gives them more protection against the sun's rays, they can still get skin cancer. If you spend a lot of time in the sun without protection, you're placing your skin in jeopardy.

Sunscreens, which block out both the ultraviolet A and the more intense ultraviolet B rays, offer the best protection. It's important to check labels for active sun-blocking ingredients, especially if your skin has become irritated by sunscreens. The favored sun-blocking ingredient is one of the B complex vitamins called para-aminobenzoic acid, or PABA. Chemical derivatives, or esters, of PABA may also appear on labels. These esters are even more effective than the original 5 percent PABA solution in sunscreens, but dermatologists have found that both PABA and its esters can cause allergic reactions. If a rash or irritation appears on your skin after using a PABA-containing sunscreen, try one of the new, PABA-free products on the market. Choose a sunscreen with ingredients that are compatible with your skin and that offer a substantial level of protection.

The higher the sun protection factor (SPF) of a sunscreen, the longer you can stay outdoors without burning. While SPFs range from 2 to 45, the Skin Cancer Foundation recommends using sunscreens with at least a 15 SPF all the time. Dr. Hillard H. Pearlstein, who is assistant clinical professor of dermatology at the Mount Sinai School of Medicine in New York, tells me that number 15 sunscreen is a biological necessity and that you should keep reapplying it for as long as you're in the sun, because most of it gets washed off with sweat and water.

Sunscreens slow, but don't completely prevent, tanning, since some ultraviolet and visible light passes through. Zinc oxide, the old-fashioned white coating sometimes seen on the noses of lifeguards, is still the only impenetrable shield against the sun's rays.

BATTLING BLEMISHES

Blackheads are not dirt, but plugs of sebum, natural oil that your body produces, and dead skin cells that are clogging your pores. When exposed to oxygen in the air, the sebum and pigment in the skin cells blacken. You didn't have blackheads when you were younger because your oil glands weren't manufacturing as much sebum as they are now. The hormonal changes, particularly the rise of male hormones (see Chapter 2), during your teens are causing oil glands to make more pore-clogging sebum. (The link between male hormones and the rise in sebum is the reason why boys seem to get acne more often than girls.)

A certain amount of sebum is good—this oil is supposed to move through the pores and soften the skin—but too much leads to a blockage. Then, not only sebum, but dead skin cells and bacteria that are normally in hair follicles crowd the pore, creating a blackhead.

The medical term for a blackhead is a comedone, and a comedo extractor is a tool, which you can buy at a surgical supply store and occasionally at a pharmacy, to remove blackheads. Dermatologists, doctors who specialize in treating skin conditions, use comedo extractors all the time. The device puts an even pressure on a blackhead and pops it out without scarring the skin. If you squeeze or pick a blackhead, you may make matters worse by inflaming the area.

Whiteheads are also sebum-clogged pores. With whiteheads, the pore openings are covered by the skin's surface, whereas blackheads have pushed their way out. To get the better of either type of blemish, wash your face with a gentle soap twice a day and buff the skin with a mildly abrasive pad. Buffing helps to remove outer layers of skin cells. Products with benzoyl peroxide in 5 or 10 percent strengths, such as Clearasil creams, Oxy lotions, and Fostex gels, when applied to the skin also help to remove skin cells. It's best to start with a 5 percent strength, which will be less irritating.

Note: The Food and Drug Administration (FDA) recently reevaluated the "generally safe and effective" rating for benzoyl peroxide. Although benzoyl peroxide has been used safely for treating acne for about thirty years, a study on laboratory animals caused the FDA to review the product for any possible cancer-causing effects. The decision: Benzoyl peroxide is safe and effective. Since you have your own particular skin type, however, it's a good idea to ask your doctor how you ought to use it.

ACNE

Acne occurs when pores become so clogged that they balloon out underneath the skin. The sebum, dead skin cells, and bacteria that are encased within a whitehead build to the point of bursting. When the pore can no longer withstand the pressure, it breaks open and its contents spread out beneath the surface. Then, what first appeared as a manageable blemish may become an infected papule, a pus-filled pustule, or a cyst/nodule. A stage beyond pimples, papules, pustules, and nodules are swollen red bumps. It's painful to see and to feel these unmistakable signs of inflammatory acne.

"I hope that doesn't happen to me," you're probably saying to yourself right now. Maybe it won't, but over one and a half million teenagers have acne problems. Acne can be inherited, so if your mother, father, brother, or sister has had the condition, you may be next in line. Should your blemishes progress to severe acne, you may only have to deal with the problem for a few months, or a year or two. Usually acne strikes girls at about age fourteen, or around the time of menstruation. Boys are more likely to get acne when they're closer to sixteen. Although it may seem as if acne will never go away, it almost always does. Acne is much more common among teenagers than adults.

Searching for a Cure

Researchers are continually working on the ultimate cure for acne. True, there is no way to clear a blemished complexion overnight, but today there are a wide variety of treatments for fighting the condition. You can take steps to combat the condition yourself, but if you remain unhappy with the way your skin looks, you can turn to a dermatologist for help.

Before you check with a dermatologist, though, try to unclog your pores yourself. As mentioned in the previous section, you can wash twice a day with a gentle soap and buff your skin with a slightly abrasive pad. Black girls should stay away from abrasive soaps or pads, because their skin may lighten or darken where it is irritated. Black skin needs pampering with hypoallergenic soap. If your skin is especially oily, an antibacterial soap may be the best choice. It's not unusual for acne to spread, and a back brush can help fight blemishes that are appearing on your neck, back, and shoulders. Oily hair can contribute to blemishes on the neck, forehead, and face, so frequent shampooing (experts recommend washing hair every day) helps. The object is to keep the affected area as free of oil as possible.

Since hormonal changes increase the amount of sebum, or natural oil, that your body is producing, you may find that your worst skin problems occur in the last half of your menstrual cycle, about a week or two before your period. These regular outbreaks are connected to the shifting balance of your sex hormones. If you can count on getting pimples during those days, think about scheduling an intense cleansing program at that time of the month. Along with twice-daily washing and buffing, wipe your face with skin care products of 5 percent benzoyl peroxide.

Acne can be battled, and here are a few more tips for putting up a good fight:

• **Try not to touch your face.** Bacteria may be on your fingers, and you can inadvertently spread infection by touching or rubbing the acne on your face.
• **Avoid the foods that you think may contribute to acne blemishes.** While some girls do not feel that food aggravates their condition, others can see a direct link between what they eat and how they look. Foods high in iodine, such as seafood and iodized salt, stimulate the oil glands. Chocolate, certain sharp cheeses, nuts, colas, and fried foods may give you trouble. Be your own de-

tective. If you notice that you break out after eating a certain food, eliminate it from your diet.

• **Vitamins** are not considered very helpful in treating acne, but I believe that certain vitamins promote the good health of skin. I recommend daily doses of vitamin A, 5,000 to 10,000 International Units (IU); vitamin C, 500 milligrams (mg) two or three times a day; zinc, 50 mg two or three times a day; vitamin B complex, 100 mg; and vitamin, B_6, 200 to 300 mg. These large doses may be helpful weapons in the war you're waging.

Not only are your pores clogging more now than when you were younger due to your hormonal changes, but environmental grime and industrial pollutants are doing their share to cause acne. So remember to wash, buff, and use an over-the-counter exfoliant, a product that removes dead skin cells. If you feel that you've tried everything and your complexion still isn't showing signs of clearing, it may be time to consult a dermatologist.

WHEN IT'S TIME TO SEE A DERMATOLOGIST

A dermatologist will look at your health history and set up a treatment program based on your skin's sensitivity. Among the remedies a dermatologist may recommend are the following.

Lotions, ointments, and gels by prescription may include greater strengths of benzoyl peroxide than are available over-the-counter, or they may contain antibiotics. Clindamycin phosphate (Cleocin T) and erythromycin are antibiotic preparations that are applied to the skin. The advantage of using antibiotic lotions or creams is that the medicine can seep into a clogged pore and fight inflammation on the spot, whereas an antibiotic pill may affect your entire system.

A doctor may also prescribe **tretinoin (Retin-A)**, made from a synthetic vitamin A, which is the latest "wonder drug" for acne. It was originally used for clearing blackheads, but recently it has been discovered that Retin-A can remove fine lines and rejuvenate damaged skin. It must be used under close supervision of a doctor, however. Retin-A makes some people particularly sensitive to sunlight and may cause skin irritation if it is not used properly. Ironically, Retin-A is effective because it acts by peeling away dead, damaged skin. (Your doctor may suggest that you use it along with benzoyl peroxide.) Also, Retin-A may cause birth defects, so if you are pregnant or are planning to conceive you should not use it.

Antibiotic pills for acne may be prescribed by a dermatologist who feels that you need more intense treatment. These pills reduce the amount of sebum produced by the oil glands and prevent infections from taking hold within clogged pores. Tetracycline and erythromycin are antibiotics that are frequently prescribed for acne, but others have also been used successfully. Often, even though you're taking pills for your condition, your doctor will continue to prescribe lotions or creams, so you'll be fighting inflammation and infection on all fronts.

Birth control pills for acne are prescribed less frequently than they were in the past, since girls are more leery of the Pill today. Still, the birth control pill remains one of the methods of treating acne. (See Questions About Hair And Skin for more about the Pill and acne.) Your dermatologist can work with your gynecologist to find the pill with the right hormonal contents to clear up your acne, but it's a balancing act. Sometimes the hormones in the Pill can aggravate acne.

Isotretinoin (Accutane) may be given when acne is

particularly advanced, and cysts or nodules are bulging out beneath the skin. Accutane is the only real cure for acne because it stops the production of sebum. However, it can cause a number of serious birth defects. If you are on Accutane, you must not become pregnant while you are on the drug. Your doctor will ask you to sign a consent form stating that you will use effective contraception while on Accutane and for one month after treatment. The treatment is so strong that you must take Accutane every day for eight weeks, then give your body an eight-week rest. You can resume another eight-week treatment if your acne hasn't responded. Your dermatologist will closely monitor you while you are being treated with Accutane.

VICTORY CAN BE YOURS

One day you'll realize that you haven't had a pimple in a while, or you're only breaking out a little bit before your period, and you'll know that your bad-complexion stage is over. Until that day comes, try not to let your blemishes get to you and interfere with your self-confidence. Fight blemishes, and believe in your inner and outer beauty. To believe in yourself in the face of adversity, of course, takes personal strength and maturity. Strive for these qualities, and they'll bring you success now, and long after you've improved your complexion.

QUESTIONS ABOUT HAIR AND SKIN

WHAT CAN I DO ABOUT ALL MY DANDRUFF?
I love wearing black clothes, but I have a big dandruff problem. No matter how much I wash my hair, I still see flakes on my

shoulders. I'm constantly brushing my clothes and I can't stand it! I'd like to know what causes so much dandruff, but even more, I want to know how I can get rid of it for good.

Lisa V., age 16

Some flaking from the scalp is normal—skin cells are constantly being shed all over the body—but Lisa obviously has problem dandruff. Many people think that dandruff is a sign of dryness, but dandruff can be oily. It can exist along with an overly oily scalp. During the teen years, hormonal changes, which can be intensified by stress, can cause the body's oil glands to produce a lot of the natural oil, or sebum, connected to acne. It's the same pore-clogging sebum that leads to acne, however, that creates an oily scalp.

The oil will be absorbed by the flakes and bits can fall off. Lisa might be able to control her dandruff with an over-the-counter antidandruff shampoo, but some girls find these products rather harsh. An alternative treatment is washing with a mild shampoo and conditioner, then applying an astringent made of equal parts of an antiseptic mouthwash, such as Scope or Listerine, and witch hazel. Lisa should part her hair and use a cotton ball to dab the solution onto her exposed scalp. She can section her hair until the entire scalp has been treated. The scent of the mouthwash disappears in about ten minutes.

Lisa should wash her hair every day, take a daily B complex vitamin, and try to reduce the stress in her life. As final exams approach, she might exercise, or set aside time to dance to her favorite music group, to release tension. If her dandruff does not go away, she may have a chronic, scaly skin disorder, such as eczema, psoriasis, or seborrheic dermatitis. A dermatologist could diagnose her problem and treat her with the appropriate shampoos and medications.

DOES HAIR DYE CAUSE CANCER?
I've heard that you can get cancer from the chemicals in hair dye. Is that true?

                                                    Pamela E., age 15

I have been concerned about the chemicals in hair dye in relation to my pregnant patients. Research has shown that the coal-tar chemicals in permanent and semipermanent dyes and rinses can penetrate the scalp and enter the bloodstream. These chemicals have been linked to chromosomal damage. As an obstetrician, I am concerned about birth defects from chromosomal damage to a fetus, so I advise my pregnant patients to stop using coal-tar-based hair dyes during pregnancy, especially during the first trimester when the brain and nervous system of the fetus are developing. Even though there is no solid evidence that any harm might be done to the fetus, I am wary.

Recently, researchers at the National Cancer Institute questioned 426 people with different types of blood cancers. The scientists found a higher rate of non-Hodgkins lymphoma, an uncommon kind of blood cancer, among hair-dye users. Non-users had a 1 percent rate and users had a 1.5 percent rate, which is 50 percent higher. The study is controversial and has not shown a strong link between cancer and the coal-tar chemicals, but girls who are concerned might prefer to use hair-coloring techniques that coat the hair shaft rather than penetrate the scalp. Hair frosting, tipping, streaking, and painting only involve the hair shafts. Permanent and semipermanent one-color processes are rubbed into the scalp. Henna, however, is a natural dye obtained from a tropical plant, and although it sits on the scalp, it doesn't enter the bloodstream in the same way as coal-tar chemicals.

Test your sensitivity to a hair coloring before you use it. Girls have had reactions from rashes to hair loss from products that were too strong for them.

I THINK I'M LOSING MY HAIR.
Lately I've noticed that when I pull my hair back into a ponytail, I have to twist the band around three times. My hair used to be so thick that I could only twist the band twice. I think I'm losing my hair. What am I going to do? I don't want to be bald!

Heather J., age 14

Heather does not mention whether she has been on medication for an illness. Powerful drugs can lead to hair loss, but usually hair returns to normal when the drugs are stopped. Another possibility is that she has recently restyled her hair. Some girls have hair that is particularly sensitive to the chemicals used in bleaching, straightening, and perming. Also, hair that is overly brushed, or worn tightly pulled into a ponytail for a long time, can come out. This type of hair loss is called traction alopecia.

Heather seems genuinely perplexed by her hair loss, however, so she might just be the victim of hormonal changes. Sometimes when girls and women go through hormonal upheavals during such biological events as first menstruation, pregnancy, and menopause, their hair thins. They lose more than the usual fifty to a hundred hairs a day. Heather is understandably anxious, but her worry about her hair may be affecting her hormonal balance, and in turn, causing even more thinning of her thick tresses.

It may be time for Heather to confide in her parents and ask for a consultation with her family physician.

---

*A BOY WHO SITS NEXT TO ME IN SCIENCE CLASS
STARTED TEASING ME ABOUT HAVING A MOUSTACHE.*
*I'm tired of being teased. I have beautiful black hair, which I
love, but I also have dark hair above my lip. A boy who sits
next to me in science class started in on me today. He was
teasing me about having a moustache, and he's not the first
one to mention it. What's the best way for me to handle my
problem?*

Jennifer G., age 13

Most girls have hair above their top lip, but often it's
fine and unnoticeable. Sometimes on women with dark
hair and olive skin those hairs are darker and more visible. As explained in Chapter 2, facial and body hair can
sometimes be darker and fuller if a girl has either a high
level of the hair-growing male hormone testosterone or
an ovarian problem that leads to a hormonal imbalance.
(See the next question for more details about hormones
and body hair.) The hairs on Jennifer's top lip seem natural to her overall appearance.

She can make these hairs much less obvious by applying a bleach that's made to lighten facial hair. A number
of easy-to-use commercial bleaches are sold in pharmacies.
Hair removal with a tweezer is another option.

An over-the-counter depilatory, or hair-removing,
cream or lotion is quite effective, but the hairs may feel
bristly when they start growing back. Waxes that remove
the hair from the root (it grows back in a few weeks) are
also available in drugstores. Jennifer can also visit a salon
for professional waxing, but she should know that sometimes wax removal can sting.

A more permanent way to remove hair is by electrolysis, a technique in which a fine needle is inserted into
the hair follicle. A tiny electrical impulse travels through

the probe and destroys the hair at its root. A girl might feel a slight stinging or tingling when a hair is destroyed. This technique must be performed by a reputable, professional electrologist. Scarring can occur when an inexperienced person uses a probe, misses the hair follicle, and has to repeat the procedure. Jennifer does not have to live with facial hair that insensitive boys turn into a joke.

WHY DO I HAVE TO BE SO HAIRY?

As I'm getting older, I'm getting hairier and hairier. I always had hairy arms and legs, but lately I've grown hair around my nipples and on my stomach. Why do I have to be so hairy? Is this a hereditary condition? My mother has electrolysis for hairs on her face. Could I have inherited hairiness from her? What can I do? I hate being this way.

Tracy S., age 14

Although she doesn't mention her hair coloring, perhaps Tracy's hair is not more abundant than other girls, but only darker and more noticeable. That's one possibility. Another is that the women in her family have a lot of body hair and she simply inherited the family trait.

On the other hand, a hormonal imbalance can lead to a lot of body hair. A hormonal imbalance in the adrenal glands (see Chapter 2) can lead to a surge of the hair-growing male hormone testosterone. There also exists an inherited ovarian problem called Stein-Leventhal syndrome, a hormonally upsetting condition that can cause abundant body hair, irregular or heavy periods, and a tendency to be overweight.

A girl with Stein-Leventhal syndrome has what's called polycystic ovaries, which are slightly enlarged and lead to an imbalance of the hormones estrogen and progesterone. Following this imbalance, brain hormones do not function properly, ovulation is off, the testosterone level promotes hair growth around her nipples, and sometimes hair grows up from her pubic area toward her navel.

A girl who has Stein-Leventhal syndrome may be given a birth control pill to help correct the hormonal imbalance caused by the condition. A doctor may recommend an estrogen-potent pill such as Demulen 1/35 or 1/50.

If Tracy is concerned that her body hair might be caused by a hormonal imbalance, then she ought to consult a gynecologist for an examination and a blood test to check levels of estrogen and progesterone, as well as testosterone, in her body.

If she wants to, Tracy can get rid of body hair with either a razor that cuts the hair at the surface or a cordless Epilady-type rotating shaver that removes hair from the root. (Some women tweeze hairs around their nipple or stomach, if the growth isn't too heavy.) Other hair removal methods, such as depilatories, waxing, and electrolysis are discussed above in the answer to Jennifer's question.

HOW CAN I STOP MY LEGS FROM GETTING IRRITATED AFTER I SHAVE?
Even though I put moisturizer on my legs after I shave them, I still get a red rash on my thighs. What can I do to stop my legs from getting irritated?

Diana L., age 16

What Diana has is "razor burn," a skin abrasion from shaving with a dull razor. First, she needs a new razor, and second, she ought to shave in the shower. A steamy shower opens the pores and expands the hair follicles so that the hair is slightly extended and more easily shaved. Lathering the legs with soap or shaving cream helps to smooth the skin's surface, and gives the razor greater glide. Diana might also try other methods of hair removal, such as waxing, or using a cordless Epilady-type hair remover, which pulls the hair from the root rather than cutting it off at the surface.

IS IT SAFE TO SHAVE MY PUBIC HAIR?
I'm on the swim team and I shaved off my pubic hair. The hair gets in the way of my swimsuit, and it's just easier to compete without it. Is it safe to shave pubic hair? What happens when it grows back?

Marisa B., age 15

It is perfectly safe to shave pubic hair. It will grow back just the way it does anywhere else on a girl's body, although there might be some itchiness. Marisa should not be concerned.

CAN I TAKE THE PILL TO CLEAR UP MY ACNE EVEN THOUGH I'M NOT SEXUALLY ACTIVE?
My sixteen-year-old cousin went on the Pill and her face cleared up really fast. I'm fourteen and not sexually active, but I wondered if I should take birth control pills to make my acne go away. I'll try anything.

Hannah C., age 14

A girl's hormonal changes at the time of her first period contribute to the amount of natural oil, or sebum, that her body produces. A lot of sebum can clog pores and lead to acne, which Hannah has. Since birth control pills contain synthetic estrogen and progesterone, they can sometimes influence the production of sebum. Years ago, when estrogen levels in all birth control pills were quite high, natural oil and acne were affected more. The estrogen levels in today's birth control pills are much lower, but some of the pills can still help to combat acne. A girl cannot be sure how she will respond to the hormonal level in a pill, however. Sometimes birth control pills make acne worse, particularly if they contain a high dose of progestogen (synthetic progesterone), but often they help. The pill that usually works best for girls with severe acne is Demulen 1/35 or 1/50—the numbers refer to the pill's progesterone/estrogen mix.

Although the birth control pill was made for contraception, some girls who are not sexually active take it to regulate their cycles or to alleviate severe menstrual cramps. These girls have often found that while on the Pill, their skin improved. If Hannah has already tried to clear her skin through cleansing programs, by avoiding foods that might make her break out, and by applying over-the-counter and prescription lotions, gels, or creams, she may be at her wit's end by now.

She, her parents, and her doctor ought to discuss her condition, and together they should decide whether she should be placed on the Pill for her skin problem. She might be helped by the Pill for the time that her body is going through its most intense hormonal changes. An oral contraceptive can change the progesterone/estrogen balance in her body and, if the hormonal balance of the pill is carefully selected, it just might improve her complexion. Taking a birth control pill for acne, though, does not mean that a girl should feel a need to be sexually active for the first time. The desire to start sexual activity comes from a girl's sense of her own emotional maturity. The Pill prevents pregnancy, but it doesn't make a girl ready for sex.

ARE THERE ANY SECRETS TO HAVING GREAT SKIN?
I'm seventeen and I think I have pretty good skin right now. I
use sunblock and I don't smoke because I don't want to have
wrinkles when I'm older. I wonder if there's anything else I can
do healthwise. Are there any secrets to having great skin?
                                                    Nicole V., age 17

As a physician, I advise healthy habits for the inside and outside of a body. Nicole can keep her skin beautiful by drinking lots of nonalcoholic beverages and water every day and eating fruits and vegetables high in vitamin A. The How Your Skin Reflects What You Eat and Drink sections in this chapter offer advice on how to treat skin from the inside out. Also, if Nicole is able to sleep soundly at night and to avoid stress as much as possible, her skin will certainly look more radiant.

CONTINUING YOUR HEAD-TO-TOE SURVEY: BREASTS

Every girl's breasts are uniquely hers. The ultimate size and shape of your breasts depend upon the amount of estrogen and progesterone you produce, and how your body responds to these hormones. Heredity and body type also play their parts. The genes that are affecting your breasts, however, may be from your mother or your father's side. Find out what kind of figure each of your grandmothers had, and you'll have some idea of what might be in store for you.

Sometimes a girl's breasts can seem quite womanly when she's only twelve years old, and sometimes a girl can have a small-breasted, boyish figure until she's fifteen, then notice her breasts emerging more fully. The timing of breast development varies, and most girls won't know what the adult shape of their breasts will be until they're between fifteen and eighteen years old.

Generally, at about age eleven, a girl's breast buds become more prominent and start pointing up. Between eleven and fifteen, breasts grow more rounded, and a nipple becomes a part of the breast, rather than a separate mound. Between the ages of fifteen and eighteen, breasts become fully developed. So keep your age in mind when you look at your breasts, because if you're younger than fifteen, your breast size has not yet reached its peak.

WHAT BREASTS ARE MADE OF

Breasts have no muscle, but their deepest inner surfaces combine with the covering of the chest, or pectoral muscles. The size and shape of the breasts depend on how they are supported by the neighboring muscles and fine bands called **ligaments**, which attach each breast to the collarbone, bone of the upper arm, breastbone, and ribs.

A blood supply, a lymph system, and fat are inside a breast. Lymph is a clear fluid found in tissue spaces throughout the body. Also each breast is a highly developed network of nerves and nerve endings that connects the breasts to the hormonal impulses coming from the brain and the ovaries. Fat, however, is the main substance. Within the fatty tissue, milk-producing glands form fifteen to twenty-five lobes, each separate but grouped together. Inside each lobe is a main milk duct.

Imagine that each lobe contains a bunch of grapes with its stem pointing toward the nipple, because that's what the milk ducts and milk glands look like. The milk duct is like the stem leading from the saclike acini, which

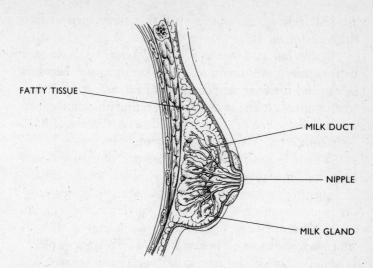

FATTY TISSUE

MILK DUCT

NIPPLE

MILK GLAND

6. Internal Side View of a Breast. The breast is made up of both fatty tissue and milk glands and milk ducts, which funnel into the nipple.

are the grapes. In fact, the word *acini* means "grapes" in Latin. The acini store the breast milk. When a woman is breast-feeding, milk fills the acini and travels down to the main milk duct. Moving along the stem of the milk duct, the milk passes through the breast and out the nipple. A girl might have twenty-five of these "bunches of grapes" in one breast.

A breast begins to grow when the milk ducts and fatty tissue push out a breast bud. When you touch your breasts, you can feel the fatty tissue on the outside, but as you press down you may detect a lumpiness deeper within, as if your breasts were made of cottage cheese. This lumpiness is normal; you are feeling the milk glands, the acini. If you have small breasts, you may feel a bump that seems quite hard and that scares you, but usually you are just feeling a rib. Occasionally, a rib protrudes into the breast area.

In the last two weeks of your menstrual cycle, just before your period is due, your breast tissue becomes more fluid-filled and tender to the touch. Sometimes cysts, small sacs of fluid, form inside the breasts of girls who are prone to benign **fibrocystic breast disease (FBD)**. This condition makes breasts extremely lumpy.

With FBD, a hormonal imbalance of estrogen and progesterone causes the acini and milk ducts to expand and form the cysts, which feel like squishy lumps ranging in size from a pea to a plum. One out of five women, or 20 percent of the female population, might at some time have fibrocystic breast disease. The cysts enlarge gradually during the menstrual cycle and are at their largest and most painful just before the start of the menstrual period. That's why it's better for you to examine your breasts right after your period, when most of the cysts diminish or disappear. At that time, you have a lower level of female hormones, so your breasts are not retaining fluid, and are less lumpy and tender. (See the questions section, "What makes my breasts so sore?" and "My breasts always feel lumpy to me," for more about FBD.)

Although breast cancer is rare among teenagers, it's never too soon to become familiar with the look and feel of your breasts. The How to Examine Your Breasts section offers instructions for breast self-examination. You should not be shy about touching your breasts and telling your mother if you see or feel anything out of the ordinary. If you examine your breasts after your period and notice an outstanding lump, you should not ignore it. In general, the lumps of fibrocystic breast disease are soft and tender to the touch, whereas the lumps of breast cancer are hard and painless. A doctor can often tell right away if the lumps you are feeling are cause for concern.

ALL BREASTS ARE NOT ALIKE

Sometimes when you're naked with another girl, say you're changing in a locker room or sleeping overnight at a friend's house, you can see the difference between your breasts and someone else's. Don't worry if your breasts don't look anything like the girl's you happen to see. There is no standard.

Take the **areola,** for instance. The areola is the pigmented area around the nipple. As your breasts begin to protrude, the areola will widen and darken. Your nipple will also become darker and more prominent. When you see another girl's breasts, you may notice that her areola is not the same color or shape that yours is, and that's fine. The areola on a breast may be various shades of pink, tan, or brown. Girls with darker complexions tend to have darker areolae. Also, one girl's areola may occupy a small area at her breast's tip, while another girl has an areola that substantially caps the end of her breast. Heredity influences the features of each girl's breast.

Breasts may be small and separated, or wide and close together. They may be round, egg-shaped, or conical. Nipples may project a lot or hardly at all. Each breast is one of a kind. You can notice a slight difference between your breasts, and no pair of breasts ever matches another.

QUESTIONS ABOUT BREASTS

---

*I THINK ONE OF MY BREASTS IS SMALLER THAN THE
OTHER. WILL I BE LOPSIDED?*
*I was getting dressed the other day and I happened to glance
in the mirror. I think one of my breasts is smaller than the
other. Is it possible that they're not growing at the same rate?
Will I be lopsided?*

Elizabeth N., age 14

I doubt that Elizabeth will have to buy a bra with
cups of different sizes. There's often a slight asymmetry
between breasts. Usually the left breast is slightly larger
than the right one, due to an enriched blood supply from
the main artery on the left side of the body. Coinciden-
tally, a boy's left testicle is often larger than the right one!

Elizabeth may always have a slight difference between
her breasts, one that only she will notice. If Elizabeth
goes through pregnancy, childbirth, and breast-feeding
someday, her breasts will change so radically that the size
difference that bothers her now will seem insignificant.

I think she should only be concerned about the difference between her breasts if it is causing her clothes to
fit improperly. Then, she ought to confide in her mother,
and perhaps, a family physician. A lined bra with a soft
padding may make the difference completely disappear.

---

*IF I EXERCISE ALL THE TIME CAN I MAKE MY BREASTS
BIGGER?*
*I'm so small-breasted that I'm embarrassed to change in front
of other girls. I don't want them to see how flat I am. I know
I should be happy with what I have, but I want more. I want
my breasts to grow, and I'm also afraid that they may have*

stopped growing. If I exercise all the time, can I make my breasts bigger? Please don't tell me there's nothing I can do!

Martha O., age 15

Exercises for the upper body, which strengthen the chest's pectoral muscles, can sometimes make the breasts look bigger. As the muscles build, they support and lift the breasts on the chest wall. Martha might try the pectoral squeeze: With elbows down, palms up, stretch arms straight out to the side at shoulder height. Bend arms at a right angle and bring the elbows together in front of the body. Squeeze the elbows together and slowly return the right-angled arms to position. With shoulders pressed down, repeat the pectoral squeeze eight times twice.

No exercise can build up the breast itself, however, and the "breast-enlarging" devices that Martha may see advertised in magazines do not work.

Sometimes when a girl starts on a birth control pill her breasts swell somewhat in response to the hormonal changes brought on by the contraceptive. Even without the Pill, though, breasts may seem a little bigger just before a girl's menstrual period, because that's when the hormone progesterone is high. Breast enlargement during pregnancy is due to progesterone, too.

Martha's breasts may still be developing, however. Whatever nature has in store for her, she should know that breasts of any size are beautiful.

WHEN WILL MY BREASTS STOP GROWING?

I can't believe how big my breasts are getting. I'm sixteen and they have ballooned very fast this year. I wear loose clothes because I'm so self-conscious about them. Do you know when they'll stop growing?

Paula Y., age 16

A girl's breasts can grow until she's in her early twenties, when her entire body takes on a new look. Paula doesn't know how her figure will ultimately appear. I once knew a girl, whom I'll call Karen, who was so concerned over her large breasts that she underwent a surgical reduction at age eighteen. Karen was beautiful and talented, but she knew that the kids in school referred to her as the girl with "big boobs." She desperately wanted to be recognized for other qualities, and breast reduction surgery seemed a way to make a positive change. She acted too hastily, though. Karen had her breasts made smaller when she was eighteen, but at age twenty-one she slimmed down and lost a lot of fat tissue naturally. She panicked. Her breasts became so small that she consulted a plastic surgeon again, and this time she had her breasts enlarged with silicone, manufactured gel implants, which today are not recommended. While both silicone and saline (salt solution) implants are still being evaluated by the Food and Drug Administration and medical researchers, silicone has been especially singled out for its possible health hazards.

That a girl should have breast reduction to make her breasts smaller and then have possibly health hazardous implants to make her breasts bigger is tragic. I tell Karen's story to girls like Paula who seem unhappy with their bodies. Even at age sixteen, Paula has physical changes ahead. A girl's body will not settle into its female figure until she has reached her mid-twenties. If Paula dressed to feel good, rather than to hide her breasts, she could draw attention to her overall beauty—her smile, eyes, hair. The comments about her breasts can be silenced by her self-confidence.

WILL MY BREASTS SAG IF I DON'T WEAR A BRA?

I have medium-size B cup breasts and I don't always wear a bra. Some of my friends have said that my breasts will fall someday. I've heard that it's good to wear a bra for jogging or sports, although I'm not exactly sure why, but I don't believe that I have to wear a bra all the time. Who's right? Will my breasts sag if I don't wear a bra?

Caitlin Q., age 18

While she is young, Caitlin's breasts won't sag, but when she reaches middle age, her breasts will sag to some degree regardless of whether she wears a bra today. Every woman's breasts drop a little with age.

As she gets older, Caitlin can work to keep her breasts from drooping by firming her pectoral muscles. (See directions for the pectoral squeeze in the question, "If I exercise all the time, can I make my breasts bigger?") She should also remember not to fasten her bra too tightly or to pull her bra straps so that her breasts are high. A tight, high bra prevents movement of the pectoral muscles in the chest, and movement is desirable because it is muscle-strengthening. Strong pectoral muscles help to lift the breasts. For jogging and strenuous exercise, a bra is recommended strictly for comfort.

WHAT'S WRONG WITH MY NIPPLES? ONE OF THEM STICKS OUT, BUT THE OTHER ONE DOESN'T!

I'm freaking out! One of my nipples sticks out, but the other one doesn't. It's sort of flat and inside my breast. What's wrong? Is there anything I can do to make my nipple pop out? Will I be able to breast-feed when I'm a mother? I'm really worried.

Alison P., age 16

Alison has what's called an inverted nipple, and she may have inherited this trait. I've seen many inverted nipples on teenage breasts; sometimes a girl has two. What happens is that a bit of internal scar tissue pulls on the breast tissue and draws the nipple inward. As a girl gets older, the nipple sometimes grows out on its own.

A girl can help to make her nipple protrude, however, by doing a daily exercise that aims to break up the adhesions pulling on the nipple. She first places a thumb and forefinger at the right and left edges of her areola and then presses back toward her ribs. She then squeezes these two fingers together behind the nipple. Repeating the press-and-squeeze, she should work her way around the outside of the areola for ten to fifteen minutes. This is an exercise usually used by pregnant women who have inverted nipples. It prepares them for breast-feeding.

Alison can perform this exercise now if she likes, or when she is pregnant. She will definitely be able to breast-feed. Any woman who has an inverted nipple just has to work a little harder to make her milk available. And often, after a woman breast-feeds, the scar tissue disappears and her nipple permanently points outward.

WHAT MAKES MY BREASTS SO SORE?
I know that it's normal for my breasts to be tender just before my period, but sometimes they hurt so much. What makes my breasts sore? Sometimes I wonder if I'm getting breast cancer because I can hardly touch my breasts for weeks. Do I have a problem?

Carrie B., age 15

Carrie's right; it's normal for breasts to be somewhat tender before the menstrual period. The rise in estrogen and progesterone levels in the second half of the menstrual cycle can lead to greater tenderness in her breasts. This discomfort usually passes with the beginning of menstruation. Since Carrie's soreness lasts for weeks, she could be having "growing pains." As a girl's body changes during her teens, joints and muscles can actually hurt from time to time. Carrie does not say whether she has put on a few pounds recently, but weight gain can also bring on soreness. Since estrogen can be converted from fat cells, sometimes when a woman gains weight, the fat-converted estrogen, which is new to her body, makes her breasts hurt.

On the other hand, Carrie could be experiencing symptoms of benign fibrocystic breast disease (FBD). If a breast continues to feel sore and tender after menstruation, a girl may have FBD. A hormonal imbalance in the estrogen/progesterone ratio can cause the acini (the grapelike clusters of milk glands) and the milk ducts in the breast to expand and form cysts (fluid-filled sacs). A cyst can pull on the nerves that encircle the breast tissue and cause pain. A cyst is always tender to touch, while a cancerous lump is generally hard and painless.

Changes in hormone levels are unpredictable in the teens, and girls who do not yet have regular periods may suffer from cystic breasts. Breast cancer is rare among teenagers, and I don't think Carrie has to concern herself with this disease. If her breast tenderness is unrelenting, however, she might want to consult a gynecologist about a breast examination. The doctor may suggest further tests, such as a thermogram (which measures heat to create a picture), a sonogram (which uses sound waves to create a picture), or a mammogram (which uses X rays). I recommend the first two types of tests for young women. Sometimes a biopsy is also necessary.

Carrie can take steps to reduce her soreness herself,

however. Caffeine has been linked to fibrocystic breast disease, so she might limit caffeine by cutting back on coffee, tea, and cola, and eating less chocolate. Also, daily vitamin E (400 to 800 IU) and vitamin B complex (100 mg) sometimes help hormonal balance and may reduce soreness. As a girl's hormones change, the cysts of FBD often disappear by themselves, and that lingering breast tenderness simply goes away.

IS IT NORMAL TO HAVE LUMPY BREASTS?
I don't like the idea of doing a breast self-examination because my breasts always feel lumpy to me. It scares me to feel them. I always worry that something is wrong with them. Is it normal to have lumpy breasts?

Stephanie G., age 17

Every girl's breasts are slightly lumpy, especially in the middle of the breast, where the milk glands are. The feel of these milk glands has alarmed many young women who examine their breasts just before their periods. *Before* a period, the milk glands have a lumpiness that disappears afterward. The lumpiness comes from the rise in estrogen and progesterone levels during the last two weeks of the menstrual cycle. That's why it's always recommended that you examine your breasts a day or two *after* you have finished menstruating. (See How to Examine Your Breasts in this chapter.)

Stephanie may have felt her breasts during the last half of her cycle when her milk glands were particularly swollen. On the other hand, if she has a hormonal imbalance, which sometimes happens, she might instead be feeling the fluid-filled cysts of benign fibrocystic breast disease (FBD). The hormonal imbalance causes FBD's cysts to form, and they feel like squishy lumps. The steps a girl can take to eliminate these cysts are described in the preceding answer. (Sometimes an imbalance of the hormone prolactin from the pituitary gland [see Chapter 2] also brings on cystic breasts.)

Another possibility is that Stephanie may be feeling a hard lump. While a cancerous lump is usually hard and painless, there is another type of hard, painless lump called a **fibroadenoma**, which is not cancerous. Usually, a fibroadenoma feels the same throughout the menstrual cycle.

Since breasts do have a lumpy quality, a breast self-examination can be confusing. The only real way to know if a lump is normal or not is to ask a doctor, which Stephanie might do. She's maturing into a woman, her breasts are changing, and it's time she had a sense of their healthy "feel." If a lump is suspicious, the doctor may suggest further tests, such as a sonogram or a mammogram. (For a teenager, I usually recommend tests that do not use radiation, but sometimes a mammogram is needed.) Teenage girls usually don't get breast cancer, but the rare possibility does exist, and a doctor can give Stephanie peace of mind.

SOMETIMES I SEE DRIED-UP WHITE FLAKES ON THE TIP OF MY NIPPLE. AM I LEAKING MILK?

I didn't think that breasts made milk until a woman had a baby, but sometimes I see dried-up white flakes on the tip of my nipple. It looks as if a little milk came out and then dried up there. It seems incredible, but am I leaking milk?

Megan R., age 13

It's possible that Megan is leaking, and no leaking should be ignored. When milk leaks from the breast of a girl who has not been pregnant, she should consult a gynecologist to find the reason why. Sometimes a noncancerous pituitary tumor can cause the milk-producing hormone prolactin to be triggered. If Megan hurt herself or was injured, a cyst could have ruptured in her breast and caused leakage. I doubt that Megan is on the birth control pill, but for some women, certain oral contraceptives bring on milk flow.

While it's normal for a woman who has given birth to notice leakage from her breasts, a girl like Megan is right to be concerned. She ought to confide in her mother and visit a doctor for an examination and a diagnosis.

HOW TO EXAMINE YOUR BREASTS

While teenage girls are hardly ever afflicted with breast cancer, one out of eight will develop it when they're older. By learning how to examine your breasts once a month, you can form a healthy habit that someday might save your life. When breast cancer is detected early, there's a good chance of conquering it.

The best time for a breast self-examination is about a week after your period ends, when your breasts are no longer tender or swollen. You can become so familiar with the feel of your breasts that you're able to detect a lump right away. (For more information about how a breast feels see the question, "Is it normal to have lumpy breasts?") A lump that may be cancerous is usually hard and painless to the touch, while a fluid-filled, benign cyst is a soft, squishy lump that hurts when you press it. If you feel anything suspicious during an exam, consult a gynecologist.

What to do:
1. You can examine your breasts while standing in the shower or while lying down, whichever you prefer.

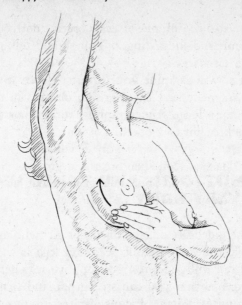

7. Breast Self-Examination. Examine the right breast with
your left hand, as described in steps 3 through 6.

If you are lying down, put a pillow under your right
shoulder to distribute the breast tissue evenly.

2. Start by placing your right arm behind your
head.

3. With your left hand, fingers flat, press the pads of
the three middle fingers at the 12 o'clock position on the
outermost part of the right breast.

4. Move to one o'clock, and so on, around the circle
back to twelve. (See illustration.) A ridge of firm tissue
in the lower curve of each breast is normal.

5. Now move in an inch toward the nipple for another circle.

6. Keep circling to feel every part of your breast, including the nipple. It may take four or five circles.

7. Repeat on the left breast. (If you are lying down,
move the pillow under your left shoulder.)

8. Squeeze the nipple of each breast gently between your thumb and index finger. You should tell a doctor about any discharge.

9. After you examine your breasts, glance at them in a mirror to make sure there are no changes in the way they normally look. Any dimpling, redness, or swelling should be brought to a doctor's attention.

FIRM BUTTOCKS AND TONED LEGS FOR EVERY BODY

Short or tall, delicate or big-boned, the girl who improves the muscle tone of her buttocks and legs is creating a strong, beautifully contoured support for her body. This is an area that you can strengthen and shape with fifteen minutes a day of concentrated exercises. New York choreographer and fitness expert Liz Milwe suggests three warm-up stretches, followed by three buttocks/leg toners.

Warm-Ups

Warm-Up 1. Sit on the floor. Bend your knees and bring your legs close to your chest. Slip your arms between your legs, and loosely hold on to your ankles. Relax your legs and let your knees fall to the sides. Allow your head to fall forward and completely relax your neck. Relax your entire body. Let your body weight naturally round your back and shoulders. With your soles still facing each other and your hands still on your ankles, hold this pose for twelve counts. This position stretches your thigh muscles.

Warm-Up 2. Unroll your body from the Warm-Up 1 position. Keep your back, neck, and head in a straight line, and extend your legs out in front of you.

8. Warm-Up 1.   9. Warm-Up 2.

10. Warm-Up 3.

11. Buttock Booster.

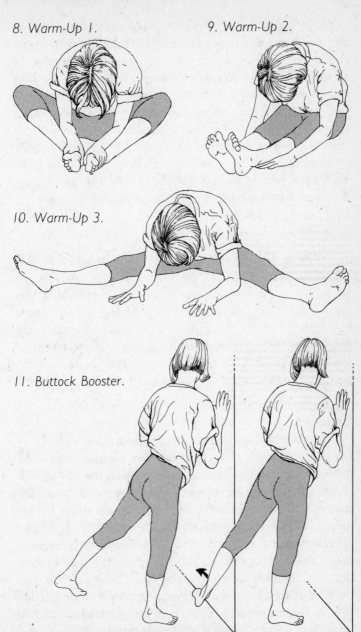

Legs are together with knees slightly bent. Your feet are relaxed. Arms and hands are relaxed alongside your body, and your hands are palms down on the floor. Bend your upper body down toward your legs. Bend from the hips and let your natural body weight move you toward your knees. Don't force yourself to get closer than your natural body weight will allow. Hold this position for ten counts, but as you become more flexible, gradually work up to holding the position for sixteen counts. Your hamstrings are getting a good stretch. Gently roll up and feel the energy moving from the base of your spine, up your back, neck, and head.

Warm-Up 3. Coming out of Warm-Up 2, still seated on the floor, separate your legs at a comfortable angle and slightly bend your knees. Do not strain. Rest your hands palms down between your legs. As in Warm-Up 2, bend from the hips and let your natural body weight move you toward the floor. Hold this position for twelve counts. Do not bounce or make an extra effort to press your upper body closer to the floor.

Toners
Buttock Booster. Stand about two feet away from a wall with your legs and feet parallel. Press the palms of both hands flat against the wall, bend your elbows, and lean toward your hands as you lift your left foot off the floor. Stretch your left leg back about twelve inches behind your right leg. With your left leg in the stretched-back position, flex your left foot and rotate your entire leg, from buttocks to toes, out to the left and count one, and then forward and count two. Your pelvis is also rotating. Complete eight 2-count sets with your left leg and eight 2-count sets with your right leg. Gradually work up to sixteen sets on each leg for firmness.

12. Bent Leg Lifts.

Bent Leg Lifts. Lie on the floor on your right side. Your right arm is outstretched and your hand is palm down on the floor. Your head is resting on your right arm. Your left hand is flat on the floor about a foot away from your body, for balance. Bend your legs. Your left leg is your top leg. With your left foot completely relaxed, lift your entire left leg about five inches above your right leg. Lower your left leg to the right leg but do not allow the left leg to rest. Raise and lower your left leg sixteen times, then roll over to your left side and raise and lower your right leg sixteen times. Bent leg lifts tone your buttocks and outer thighs. (For extra toning of the thighs, stay in the bent-leg position on your side. Flex your foot, bring your knee in toward your chest, then extend it straight out at a 90° angle to your body. Begin with eight leg contraction/extensions and gradually work up to sixteen on each side.)

Prone Leg Lifts. Lie face down on the floor with your forehead resting on your hands. Press your hip bones to the floor. Point your toes and without moving your hip bones lift your left leg as high as it can go, usually about four inches off the floor. You should not feel any pressure on your lower back. If you do feel pressure, you're lifting too high. Lower your leg to the floor, then quickly lift again. Lift the left leg eight times, and then

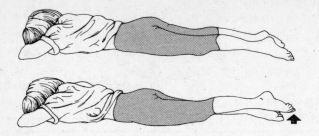

13. Prone Leg Lifts.

the right leg eight times. As you become more accomplished, increase your leg lifts to sixteen on each leg, and when sixteen are a snap, aim for twenty-four.

BELOW THE WAIST: SEX ORGANS YOU CAN SEE

The Mons Pubis and the Vulva

The area well below your navel, where a triangle of wiry pubic hair is growing, is called the **mons pubis**, or "the mound above the pubic bone." Its other name is the **mons veneris**, or "the mountain of Venus." As you mature into your teens, extra fat settles into this area, and makes the mons more prominent and protective. Your body is announcing its sexuality. The springy pubic hairs keep dirt and germs away from the sexual organs between your thighs.

By holding a small mirror between your legs, you can see what your external sexual organs, or **vulva**, look like. Every girl's vulva has labia, or lips, a clitoris, a vagina, and a hymen, but the appearance of the vulva changes from person to person.

The Labia

At the base of the mons, you will see the most obvious part of the vulva, the labia, which is Latin for lips. There are two pairs of labia: **labia majora**, or "big lips," and **labia minora**, or "little lips."

Before puberty, the labia majora, or big, outer lips, are not defined, and the space at the base of the mons is slightly parted. During the teen years, the big lips grow in fat and flesh; they extend outward and meet. Depending on your coloring, they may be pinkish, reddish, brownish, or blackish. They are covered by pubic hair on the outside and are rather wrinkled-looking. On the inside, they're hairless, soft, moist, with an uneven surface from oil glands that moisten the area and prevent the lips from rubbing and irritating each other. Although sometimes a girl may have small lips that protrude beyond her big lips, most of the time the big lips conceal the other external sexual organs. If you angle a mirror with one hand, you can use the fingers of the other hand to part the big lips. It is only with the big lips separated that you are able to see the rest of your visible organs.

The labia minora, or little lips, are two thin, soft, hairless folds of skin between the labia majora. The tissue of these lips is very sensitive. When the small lips are stimulated by the touch of a finger, mouth, or penis during sex, they can become so engorged with blood that they deepen in color, enlarge, and harden. They also grow moist as the many oil glands in the labia minora lubricate the tissue. Under normal conditions, the oil from the little lips' glands, together with secretions from the vagina and sweat glands, shield the vulva against possible contamination from bacteria, urine, and menstrual flow.

After identifying the labia minora, you can follow these lips toward the mons, where they meet and often form a hood over a tiny nub called the clitoris.

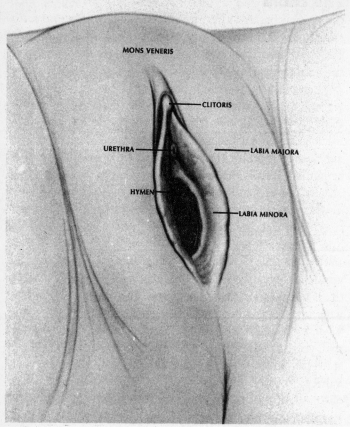

MONS VENERIS

CLITORIS

URETHRA

LABIA MAJORA

HYMEN

LABIA MINORA

14. External Female Sexual Organs, Also Called the Vulva.

The Clitoris

From the Greek word meaning "key," the clitoris is a small organ at the front of the vulva, about the size of a pearl. It may be hidden by the folds of the labia, or it may be either partially or completely visible. Rich in responsive nerve endings, the clitoris is similar to the highly sensitive head of a boy's penis. This is a girl's main erogenous, or sexually sensitive, zone. When a girl is sexually excited, her clitoris grows in size and prominence.

Masturbation is the rubbing or stroking of the clitoris or penis for the experience of being sexually excited. Both girls and boys masturbate for the pleasure they feel, and although slang expressions such as "playing with yourself" or "jerking off" have made masturbation seem dirty, it is a normal activity. (See Chapter 6, *Understanding Your Sexuality*, for a further discussion of masturbation.)

The Vagina

If you follow an imaginary line down from the clitoris, you will see a raised dimple that is the **urethra**, or urinary opening. The urethra is the tube through which urine passes from the bladder out of your body. Below the urethra, along that same line, is the opening to the **vagina**, or birth canal.

The vaginal opening may be ringed or partially covered by a thin tissue called the **hymen**, which is explained more fully in the section below. Beyond the hymen, the vaginal walls touch, so you can't see into the vagina, a three- to five-inch channel that travels up to the **cervix**, the mouth of the uterus.

An amazing organ, the vagina is so narrow that you can hardly fit a finger into it during your self-examination. During sexual excitation, however, the vaginal walls expand to allow a penis to enter, and during childbirth, they stretch wide enough to permit the passage of an infant. The vagina is also the way in which menstrual blood leaves the uterus and exits the body. A vagina is incredibly elastic. It will stretch but it will not break, and after it is through expanding, it will return to its normal size.

The Hymen

The hymen, a thin tissue that covers the vaginal opening, looks very different on different girls. A girl may have a hymen that barely surrounds the vaginal opening, while another girl's hymen may completely cover it. A hymen may be unbroken, have several holes in it, or consist of strips of tissue that make it seem as if it hardly exists. (See illustration.)

As a baby girl takes shape in her mother's uterus, tissue from above and below the vagina that is forming meets to create the structure of the hymen. Referred to in slang terms as a "cherry," the hymen has more significance in folk customs than in medicine. In some cultures the unbroken hymen gained a reputation as the mark of a virgin. Since sexual intercourse can sometimes tear a hymen and cause slight bleeding, in certain countries a new bride was expected to air a bloody sheet to her family the day after her wedding. This showed that her marriage had been consummated, and it "proved" that until her wedding night, she was a virgin. Yet a hymen, whether broken or unbroken, has nothing to do with virginity.

OPEN HYMEN   DIVIDED HYMEN   HYMEN WITH
                                           STRIPS OF TISSUE

15. The Hymen. These drawings show how a hymen varies dramatically from girl to girl.

First of all, a girl may not have even been born with a hymen, and second, even if she has one, it may have been torn during activities like horseback riding or cycling. Also, some hymens are particularly thick and are not broken during intercourse. If a girl has a thick hymen, by the way, she may have difficulty using a tampon, but most of the time the tissue of the hymen is thin and a girl can comfortably insert a tampon during her menstrual period.

Not every girl wants to use a tampon, but if you do, try to gauge the width of your vaginal opening before insertion. If you can fit a finger into your vaginal opening, you will be able to use a tampon. A girl who does not have a finger-wide opening should not use a tampon. It's when you try to push a tampon into a tiny vaginal opening that you risk breaking the hymen.

WHEN IT COMES TO BODY IMAGE, SET YOUR OWN STYLE

The teenage magazine *Sassy* reported that in a study of 700 ten- to eighteen-year-olds, girls were twice as prone to depression as boys, and one big reason—their number one concern—was that most of them hated their bodies. Even girls who were normal height and weight couldn't stand the way they looked. This is more proof that too many girls are focused on having the "perfect body," when there is no such thing.

The very thin female body image has nothing to do with the way real girls and women are built. Thanks to improved nutrition, real girls and women have even become a little heavier than they used to be. In 1960, for instance, a medium-boned woman between eighteen and twenty-five years old weighed 127 pounds, while in 1980, the same woman weighed 134 pounds.[2] Add to this picture the fact that teenage girls need extra weight to grow and mature. A girl won't menstruate unless she has at least 16 percent body fat. Perhaps it's time for each teenage girl to create her own image of beauty.

The body reflected in your mirror is yours to care for and respect. No matter what your waistline is, the healthier you keep your body through exercise and good nutrition, the stronger and prettier it will look to you and to everyone else. So set your own style.

---

[2]Figures provided by the National Center for Health Statistics, National Health and Nutrition Examination Series #11.

BOYS ARE DEEPLY CONCERNED WITH THEIR LOOKS

It's true that boys are distracted by girls' looks. Breasts, waist, behind, legs—the shape of the female figure intrigues males of any age, but in the looks department, boys are also thinking about themselves. Young men are deeply concerned about the shape of their own bodies. At Madigan Army Hospital in Tacoma, Washington, researchers who surveyed almost 900 boys from twelve to twenty-two years old found that 42 percent of them were unhappy with their weight. Why? They wanted to gain, to be larger. Girls are almost always worried about not being thin enough, but boys have the opposite problem. They worry that they won't be big enough. They have an "ideal" body image of a broad-chested, muscle-armed guy. They think that girls want them to have lots of muscles.

A girl can help a guy build his self-confidence by admiring him for more than his pectorals. Sometimes girls don't realize that boys are also insecure about their bodies during their teens. Boys have to cope with being the shorter sex for a while, since the growth spurt girls have between nine and twelve years old is not felt by males until later, between twelve and fourteen. Add acne or braces to the too slight, too short image, and you have a typical male in his early teens.

As a girl approaches eighteen, of course, boys pass her by in height. The median height for eighteen-year-old girls is five feet four and a half inches; for boys, it's five feet ten inches. Older teenage boys can also appear to have traded their insecurity for a certain toughness, which is why a "sensitive" guy holds appeal. He's different from the rest. Yet most boys are only trying to adjust to the changes going on in their bodies.

While your changes are obvious, you can't see a boy's

CHAPTER FOUR

What Boys Are Going Through

Girls want to know what guys are thinking, while boys are thinking the same thing about girls.

Girls say that boys drive them crazy, make them laugh, aggravate them, and turn them on.

Boys say that girls drive them crazy, make them laugh, aggravate them, and turn them on.

The sexes have similar feelings about each other. Here are a few girls describing what they like most about their boyfriends:

He's honest with me and I'm more comfortable with him than anyone else. We have a lot of fun together, even if we're just talking.

Lori, age 16

He has a great sense of humor. He's sensitive and

willing to talk about anything. He makes me like myself more and he gives me confidence and happiness.

Margaret, age 16

He listens to my weird idiosyncrasies and enjoys my messed up sense of humor. I like his sensitivity—this seems to be lacking in a lot of my male friends.

Vanessa, age 18

He has a great personality, he's sensitive and isn't afraid to express his feelings.

Jennie, age 15

When girls describe what they're looking for in guys, they speak in one voice: We want a caring boyfriend, a guy who is sensitive, open, supportive, funny, and who makes us happy to be with him. When boys describe what they're looking for in girls, they say similar things.

Here are how boys in relationships explain what they like about their girlfriends, and how guys who don't have regular girlfriends feel.

First, the boys who are already involved:

She's really fun to be with. I can talk to her about anything, how I feel about other people, etc. She's also very pretty, and very nice.

Mark, age 15

She's nice. She has a sense of humor. She's pretty, not necessarily beautiful, but pretty. I guess that niceness and a sense of humor are most important.

Alex, age 16

And then, the guys not in relationships, a looking for in a girlfriend:

The things that I value most in a relati ing, understanding, and spontaneity, basica person.

Chris

I look for a sense of humor.

I like a girl's spontaneity and fun-lovin don't feel I have to do anything other than

A sense of humor and lots of understand

Jer

In my one long-term relationship what I was that she was a support system for me.

I

There are a few differences. Girls emphasi ity more than boys do, and guys talk about l than girls do, but both sexes have their sight sense of humor. This is your common ground trying to crack the mystery of the male, just laugh.

The last count from the U.S. Census Burea 11,929,000 teenage girls and 12,467,000 teenage this country. There are more of them than the you, so you might as well do your best to ur them, and since the odds are in your favor, yo good chance of finding at least one whom you be around.

sexual development. Your breasts grow, your waist gets slimmer, your hips widen, and your period comes on a regular schedule. A boy's sexual organs are changing, growing in size and becoming hairier, but the shape of his body is not so different. A deeper voice, a broader chest, a slight shadow of a beard can let you know he's changing, but sometimes you still have to remind yourself. The five stages of development of a boy's sexual organs are described below. Most of the boys you know are likely to be in one of these five stages right now.

AS A BOY ENTERS MANHOOD

Any time between the ages of nine and fifteen a boy's pituitary gland, as described in Chapter 2, sends out its hormonal messengers, the follicle-stimulating hormone (FSH) and luteinizing hormone (LH), to the testicles, also called testes, which are two egg-shaped organs within the scrotum, a skin sac underneath the penis. (As you can see from the drawing, a boy's visible sex organs are his penis and his scrotum.) When the testicles get the hormonal messages, they respond by releasing the male sex hormone testosterone, which stimulates the growth of a boy's sex organs. You don't notice a boy's penis getting bigger, the way you can your breasts, but a lot of action is taking place. Here's what all boys see.

Stage 1: Preteen

This is the boyhood stage, before a boy's penis and scrotum begin to grow. Testosterone, the male sex hormone, will soon start to stimulate change.

Stage 2: Age Twelve or Thirteen

A boy may be in stage 2 any time between the ages of nine and fifteen. This is the time when the testicles

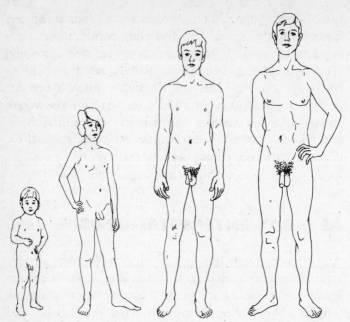

16. How a Boy's Body Changes to a Man's. The male body
at ages 4, 8, 12, and 16.

inside the scrotum are enlarging and causing the scrotum
to get bigger, too. A boy's penis doesn't grow, but his
scrotum gets baggier and hangs lower. The skin on the
scrotum appears to be more wrinkled, and its color deepens. Any pubic hair is straight right now. The areolae,
the dark circles surrounding the nipples on a boy's chest,
also widen and darken during this stage.

Stage 3: Age Thirteen or Fourteen

It's perfectly normal for a boy to enter stage 3 when
he's between eleven and sixteen years old. The main feature of stage 3 is that a boy's penis begins to grow in
length. While his penis is extending, his testicles and scro-

tum continue to get larger, and one testicle begins to hang lower than the other. This positioning prevents the testicles from getting squeezed when a boy is moving around. In most males, the left testicle is the lower one. As a boy looks at his naked body, he can see coarse, curly pubic hair filling in at the base of his penis and spreading around his groin area. From her perspective, a girl sees a boy whose shoulders seem a little broader, hips a little narrower, and voice a bit deeper.

Stage 4: Age Fourteen or Fifteen

Stage 4 can take place between the ages of eleven and seventeen. The penis of a boy in this stage has grown longer and wider, and is generally more developed. The testicles and scrotum have grown large, and all organs have deepened in color. Curly pubic hair covers a broader area, and grows upward toward the navel and outward between the thighs. Underarm hair sprouts, as do whiskers on a boy's chin and upper lip. Skin is oilier, and a boy's voice is more masculine. He may have his first **ejaculation** during this stage, and that's when he can theoretically get a girl pregnant. (To have an ejaculation, the muscles of a boy's penis must contract to pump out sperm from the testicles. The microscopic sperm, which are long-tailed reproductive cells, travel in a thick, white, creamy fluid called **semen**. The sperm-carrying semen moves along the **urethra**, the hollow tube inside the penis, to the **glans**, or head of the penis, where it spurts out. That spurt of semen is called ejaculate or in slang terms, "come.")

Stage 5: Age Sixteen

A boy is now in a man's body. His testicles are about an inch and three-quarters long, and his penis is generally three to four inches long. Whatever the length of a male's penis, though, it will expand to five to seven inches during an **erection**, when his penis will fill with blood and become hard. These measurements are only approximations, however. Just as girls' breasts come in different sizes, so do boys' penises, and just as bust size has nothing to do with a girl's femininity, so the "bigness" of a penis has nothing to do with a guy's masculinity.

WHAT GIRLS WANT TO KNOW

Sometimes I find that girls wonder more about boys' bodies than they do about their own. More than once I've been asked if a penis has a bone that makes it rise during an erection. (There are no bones in a penis!) Here are more questions many girls, and perhaps you, too, want answered.

CAN A GUY GET AN ERECTION JUST BY LOOKING AT A GIRL, WITHOUT HAVING ANY PHYSICAL CONTACT?

Yes, he can. A boy's penis is made up of spongy tissue through which many large blood vessels flow. Blood constantly travels in and out of a soft, floppy penis. When a boy has an erection, the blood rushes into the vessels. Muscles at the base of the penis tighten; valves in the blood vessels close under the pressure, and blood is trapped inside. The spongy walls of the penis enlarge and harden due to the entrapped blood. A penis gets longer, wider, and darker in color. In its erect position, it points anywhere from 90° to straight up. During sexual intercourse, an erect penis easily fits into a vagina, but an erection can occur without sexual intercourse ever being part of the event.

Naturally, a boy will experience an erection when he

is sexually stroked or touched, but sometimes boys have spontaneous erections. A boy's clothing may rub against his penis while he is walking and an erection may occur. A few sexy thoughts might cause an erection, as may a girl in body-hugging jeans. He may only have to watch her stroll down the street, and his penis will respond to his thoughts. Yet a girl shouldn't worry that a boy will be overcome with a need for sexual fulfillment when his penis is erect. Most of the time, a boy is embarrassed by the suddenness of a spontaneous erection and just hopes that it will go away quickly. Sometimes a boy can be thinking of nothing in particular, just heading for his next class, and an erection appears out of nowhere. The unpredictability of his penis can certainly unnerve a boy, but usually unwanted erections disappear swiftly.

ARE SPERM AND SEMEN THE SAME THING?

When a male ejaculates, a sticky fluid spurts from his penis. Although that fluid is actually a mixture of sperm and semen, the word *semen* alone has become an accepted term. The sticky fluid also is called ejaculate or in slang, "come," and only 10 percent of it is sperm. The other 90 percent is the semen that the sperm needed to move through the penis. Here's how the two get together.

First, microscopic sperm, cells which look like tadpoles, are produced in the testicles encased in a boy's scrotum. (See illustration.) As the sperm mature, they travel to the **epididymis**, which is a coiled-up tubing located directly above a testicle. Inside the epididymis, the sperm ripen for four to six weeks, and then move along the outer tubing, the **vas deferens**. The sperm travel inside the tunnel of the vas deferens to the base of the **seminal vesicles**, where they are stored at a duct called the **am-**

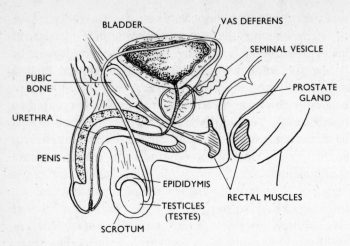

17. The Male Internal and External Sexual Organs.

pulla. The seminal vesicles are small sacs that release the fluid semen into the ampulla. The semen, in effect, wakes up the sperm and gets them moving. The **prostate gland** also adds fluid to the mixture to help the sperm make it through the **urethra**, a tube that runs down the middle of the penis to its tip. In all, it takes about seventy-two days for a sperm to go through the whole cycle. When a male ejaculates, as mentioned before, the white, sticky, gluelike fluid that comes out the tip of his penis is 10 percent sperm and 90 percent semen. Still, that 10 percent may contain as many as 200 million sperm!

Sperm Counts. A curious fact is that the time of the year may affect a man's sperm count. (Sperm can be counted under a microscope. A count of 20 million or more sperm in a cubic centimeter [cc] is normal; a low sperm count would be under 10 million/cc.) Studies have shown that sperm counts are higher in the cool days of winter than during summer's sizzle. Sperm die out if they get overheated. That's why sperm-storing testicles are located outside the body, in the scrotum. The testicles must be one degree cooler than the rest of the body for sperm to be healthy and fertile.

Sperm counts show that the average amount of ejaculate for a man is 3 cubic centimeters (cc) or about one-half of a teaspoon, but that is the middle range. A man may ejaculate between 0.5 cc to 5 cc of semen at a time. Each ejaculate usually has an average 60 million sperm. Some sperm counts are lower, and some may go as high as 200 million.

An egg in an ovary seems quite defenseless when you consider the onslaught of millions of sperm, but most of the sperm are wasted. It's estimated that out of all those sperm, only about 400 make their way through a woman's uterus and Fallopian tubes, and only about 40 of those ever get near an ovary. Yet only one sperm is needed to make a pregnancy, so the odds are still on the side of the sperm!

IF A BOY MASTURBATES A LOT, CAN HE USE UP HIS SPERM BEFORE HE'S THIRTY?

No. If a boy masturbates several times in the same day, eventually he'll be masturbating fluid with few or no sperm in it, but his testicles will continue producing sperm. A boy's testicles will produce new sperm every day for the rest of his life, no matter how often he ejaculates during masturbation or sexual intercourse. Although the average sperm count for an adult male is 60 million per ejaculate, a male is at the peak of his production when he's around eighteen. From that point on, as a man ages, sperm production goes into a slow decline. A healthy man, however, still has plenty of sperm at age thirty, and he will constantly replenish his supply.

DURING SEX, DOES URINE EVER COME OUT INSTEAD OF SPERM?

If urine is in the urethra and a young man has sexual intercourse, a few drops may unexpectedly leak out. Basically, though, a man cannot urinate and ejaculate at the same time. Sperm travel through the urethra, which is the same route that urine takes, but during ejaculation, muscle contractions close down a valve in the bladder, preventing it from emptying while sperm are passing through.

IS IT BETTER FOR A BOY TO BE CIRCUMCISED?

Lately, more and more people believe in the saying, "Don't fool around with Mother Nature," and parents ask doctors not to circumcise their baby boys. Yet other parents want their sons to be circumcised. Although the wisdom of circumcision is often debated, it is not a medical necessity. In fact, the majority of men are uncircumcised—a great many Europeans, Indians, Asians, Africans, and even Americans are uncircumcised.

A boy is born with a foreskin, a thick, tight layer of skin, completely covering his penis. (See illustration.) As he grows, the foreskin loosens and can be pushed back. When a boy has an erection, in fact, the foreskin of an uncircumcised penis automatically slips back so that you cannot tell the difference between it and the circumcised penis.

When a circumcision is performed, which is usually when a boy is a newborn in the hospital, the foreskin is cut back to expose the head of the penis. Jewish and Mos-

CIRCUMCISED PENIS

SEMI-CIRCUMCISED OR
UNCIRCUMCISED PENIS
WITH NATURAL
SHORTENING OF
THE FORESKIN

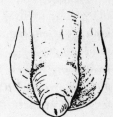

UNCIRCUMCISED PENIS

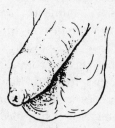

18. Circumcision. Views of circumcised and uncircumcised penises.

lem boys have traditionally been circumcised in accordance with their religious beliefs. A Jewish boy is ceremonially cut at a "briss" when he is eight days old.

For a while, doctors felt that circumcision helped to lower the risk of developing infections and certain cancers later in life. The practice was becoming commonplace in hospitals until some parents and physicians questioned whether circumcision actually offered a health advantage. Studies have now found that circumcision is not necessary. It does not improve a man's health, sex drive, sexual pleasure, or fertility. Some doctors believe that the foreskin has a purpose, that it enables the penis to stretch more easily and supports an erection. Today parents are more frequently deciding against circumcision for their newborn sons.

ARE GIRLS CIRCUMCISED, TOO?

In more than twenty African countries, girls are regularly circumcised to protect their virginity and to discourage them from having sex outside marriage. In many tribes, once a girl starts menstruating, it's time for her to be circumcised. It's a ritual that her family wants for her, and she wants for herself. A local woman will take her to a nearby river early in the morning when the water is at its coldest. The cold will numb the area and keep the bleeding down, and the woman will cut or remove the girl's clitoris.

Female circumcision affects from 20 million to 70 million women today, in spite of the laws forbidding it. It is a painful mutilation of a young woman that leaves her with little opportunity for sexual pleasure, and sometimes kills her. The cutting can lead to bleeding and infections that permanently damage a girl's reproductive organs and make her infertile or are so severe that she dies. Yet this practice is so deeply rooted in African culture that the women are keeping it alive just as much as the men.

WHAT EXACTLY HAPPENS DURING A WET DREAM?

Often the first time a boy ejaculates and releases an abundance of white sticky sperm-filled semen is in his sleep. A boy has to be asleep to have a wet dream (or **nocturnal emission**), but he does not have to be dreaming. Sometimes a boy wakes up and is completely surprised and embarrassed by the pasty substance on his sheets. On occasion he may connect his emission with a sexy dream, but he may not recall having dreamed at all.

A wet dream eases the pressure of sperm buildup on the testicles. If a boy masturbates a lot, he may have fewer wet dreams. The first time a boy ejaculates he usually feels a sense of power and maturity, much as a girl does when she sees her first menstrual blood.

ARE THE NIPPLES ON BOYS' CHESTS AS SENSITIVE AS THE NIPPLES ON GIRLS' BREASTS?

A boy has the same nerve endings in his breasts that a girl has in hers, and if sexually stroked, a boy can get a nipple erection, just the way a girl can—it's all a matter of degree. The breast is an erogenous zone for a boy, but although he is sensitive in this area, a girl has greater sensations. She'll be more turned-on by nipple stimulation.

Girls might not know that boys' breasts often hurt. A boy has female as well as male hormones, and as these hormones change during puberty, he may have breast tenderness for weeks or months. Since a boy does not have the same amount of the female hormone estrogen that a girl has, his breasts will never grow to the size of hers.

HOW DO I GET A GUY INTERESTED IN ME?

Most young men are unsure of themselves around girls. Ever notice how a boy may ask a girl if her best friend likes him? Usually the boy wants to ask the best friend out, but he's afraid he may be rejected. Better to check first, he thinks.

A girl who is interested in a particular boy just has to smile and say "Hi" to him, and she has made a connection. If a guy thinks a girl has noticed him, he's sure to be flattered and to notice her the next time. Friendliness is key.

HOW DO I END A RELATIONSHIP?

I have found that the problem many girls have is not how to keep a guy around but how to end a relationship. Many girls think that they want to be with a certain young man, but after getting to know him better, they realize that the "chemistry" is not working, or that he's not the person they thought he was. Then the problem is "How do I end the relationship?" I find myself again and again asking girls to do a little research and find out if a boy is the kind of person they'd like to spend time with before they become involved, because there is no easy way to end a relationship.

My best advice is to be honest and direct, to tell your soon-to-be-former boyfriend that your feelings have changed. The words you use should be conveyed with kindness and compassion, because he may be hurt and confused. Do not be surprised if you are emotionally stressed while you are telling him. It is just as difficult to say you want a relationship ended, as it is to hear it.

IF I KISS A GUY WHO HAS ACNE, CAN I CATCH IT?

Kissing a boy who has a few blemishes should not be a problem. If a boy has inflamed acne or a skin infection, however, a girl may pick up the bacteria. A staph germ can get on her skin and spread infection.

Kissing can be risky business. Mononucleosis, a flu-like illness that can leave you weakened, is called "the kissing disease" because it spreads so rapidly between intimate couples. A strep throat is also highly contagious.

If a girl knows that her boyfriend is sick, or has a severe acne problem, she ought to encourage him to see a doctor for treatment. She will be helping herself while she's helping him.

WHAT ARE A MALE'S LESS OBVIOUS EROGENOUS ZONES?

The most obvious erogenous zones, of course, are around the inner thighs and the area of the penis, but other areas are behind the ears, where kissing is a turn-on, and the chest, back, and legs, where touching can give great pleasure. Some boys love to have their feet massaged, but others can't stand it. By knowing someone's less obvious erogenous zones, you can share a loving relationship, without having sex.

CAN A FOURTEEN-YEAR-OLD BOY ALREADY KNOW THAT HE'S GAY?

Some homosexual men have said that they knew when they were very young that they were "different," but other men have married women, become fathers, and lived heterosexually for many years before they understood or acknowledged their sexual preference for men. There's no clear answer to this question. Also, there are always scientific debates going on about whether homosexuality is a psychological or a biological leaning. Does a boy become homosexual because he is influenced by his environment, by his genes, or are both affecting him? A teenage boy may be confused about his sexuality.

If a girl is interested in a boy whom she feels is shy around her, she should try to be sensitive to him. He may be sorting out his feelings about girls. Also, many boys are simply not ready for a "girlfriend" situation; they need time to mature. Aware young women can appreciate the friendship of young men, and give them room to grow.

THE BOTTOM LINE

Most boys your age are worried about their looks, and concerned about the opposite sex—in their case, girls—just as you are. Consider your similarities, and you can be great friends.

CHAPTER FIVE

Once a Month:
What Really Happens!

Many more girls today are experiencing menarche (the onset of menstruation) when they're ten or eleven, instead of twelve, thirteen, or even older ages more typical for first periods. Also, once begun, menstruation extends longer in life than it used to, and it is not uncommon for menopause (the end of menstruation) to be delayed until a woman reaches her late fifties.

Doctors think that two of the main reasons for these menstrual changes are better nutrition and increased average weight gain. In spite of junk foods—french fries, burgers, and sodas—most girls have become more health conscious and are eating nutritious foods and taking vitamins. As a result, menstrual cycles are reacting to healthier diets. Today's teenager is likely to experience a more regular menstrual pattern than a girl her age from a previous generation. Yet there is no "perfect" cycle.

Most girls do not have an exact twenty-eight-day menstrual cycle, although every time you learn about menstruation, twenty-eight is mentioned as if it were some sort of magic number. In reality, the days in a cycle vary from person to person and often from month to month, at least at first. Some girls have their periods in fewer than twenty-eight days, while others have cycles that may take thirty, thirty-one, or thirty-four days from start to finish. Once your period takes on its own pattern, you'll know what's "normal" for you.

As explained in Chapter 2, menstruation is the result of a dialogue between the brain and the ovaries. Hormones from both act and react to each other, showing the close connection between mind and body. You may feel that you understand how hormones affect your menstrual cycle, because menstruation was much discussed in health class. You may not know about mucus changes, however.

The cervix, the mouth of the uterus, which is located at the upper, inside end of the vagina, produces different types of mucus throughout a cycle. This changing mucus is a visible sign of hormonal flows, so you can actually check the state of your hormones, and your most fertile time of the month, by checking the mucus. Mucus checks offer you a good way to know your most fertile time of the month—the time when you are more likely to get pregnant.

With your index finger and thumb inserted a short way into the vaginal opening, you can feel the mucus, then look at a sample of it on your fingertips. Here, with a review of the menstrual cycle from Chapter 2, are the times when it's best to check for changes in cervical mucus.

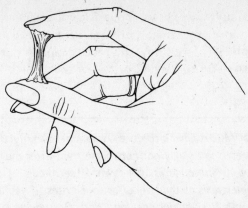

19. Cervical Mucus Check. By inserting a thumb and index finger into the vagina, you can check for the "stretchability" of the clear cervical mucus. Called spinnbarkeit, this stretchability indicates that you are ovulating and at your most fertile time of the month.

THE MENSTRUAL CYCLE AND MUCUS CHECKS

A few days after you begin menstruating, as the blood flow lightens, the hypothalamus of the brain, which controls the menstrual cycle, sends its hormonal message to the pituitary gland. The message doesn't have far to go because the pituitary is located just below the hypothalamus.

The pituitary then moves the follicle-stimulating hormone (FSH) into the bloodstream, where it follows a course, through the blood, to the ovaries. When the FSH arrives at the ovaries, the action begins.

A crop of little follicles, the potential egg cells in the ovaries, begin to grow and increase the production of the female hormone estrogen. Hormone-producing ovarian tissue also adds estrogen to the buildup. As estrogen climbs, your skin is at its best. Blemishes disappear and your complexion glows. Your natural fragrance also becomes more appealing, and your breasts may take on a new fullness. Here's how the mucus appears during these early days—up to Day 12 or so—of the cycle:

The First Mucus Check (Before Ovulation): The mucus secreted by the cervix is usually not noticeable right after menstruation; it makes its presence known toward the middle of the cycle. Mucus increases as the level of estrogen rises. If you insert your fingers into the vaginal opening right after you stop bleeding, you will sense a dryness. Near the middle of your cycle and ovulation, though, you will find a gooey mucus that looks and feels like raw egg white.

One of the follicles that started the estrogen build-up, for some unknown reason, grows faster than the rest. That one egg cell, called the Graafian follicle, swells out, making a bubble on the outside of an ovary. Inside the bubble, the egg continues to develop. Estrogen is going up and up, and halfway through the cycle (usually about Days 13 to 16), the pituitary responds to the abundance of estrogen by slowing down its release of FSH. As estrogen reaches a certain level, it stimulates the pituitary to send out luteinizing hormone (LH), which is designed to promote the escape of the monthly egg.

The presence of the LH makes the Graafian follicle burst its bubble and eject the mature egg-of-the-month. This ejection of an egg is ovulation. This is the time of the month—about fourteen days into the cycle—when you would be most likely to conceive.

The Fallopian tubes, which extend out from either side at the top of the uterus (see illustration), resemble long, thin arms with fingers at the ends. The fingers, or tentacles, on the end of a Fallopian tube are called fim-

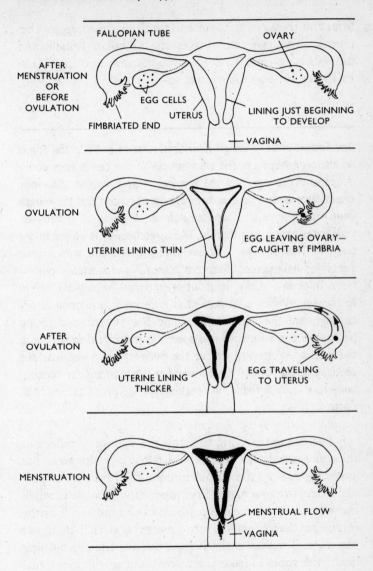

20. *The Journey of an Egg from Its Release from the Ovary, Through the Fallopian Tubes and into the Uterus, During Different Stages of the Menstrual Cycle.*

bria, and they reach down and catch the freed egg-of-the-month. The egg then leaves the Graafian follicle and moves along on a five- to seven-day journey inside the Fallopian tube to the uterus.

The Second Mucus Check (During Ovulation): When the egg is about to be released, the clear mucus in the cervix is in abundance and you can feel the wetness in your vagina. You may even notice a clear to cloudy discharge. You can feel the mucus with your fingers and even stretch out a string of it between your index finger and thumb. This stretchability is called spinnbarkeit. This change, and everything about the way mucus starts out nonexistent, becomes plentiful and stretchy, and finally, thick and sticky, is about pregnancy—helping the sperm to the egg. When spinnbarkeit is happening, ovulation is occurring, and the cervix, which had been closed and facing backward, turns forward and opens. Sperm can slide right into the uterus. When you are at the peak of your wetness, the cervix is open and you have arrived at the moment for conception. Your body is ready for pregnancy, if you aren't using birth control.

The egg is traveling through the Fallopian tube, but the scar tissue that it left behind when it broke away has a job. It becomes the corpus luteum, the producer of progesterone, the pregnancy hormone. Progesterone is called the pregnancy hormone because it causes the lining of the uterus to change into a soft, spongy nest rich in blood vessels, and makes it the perfect bed for the egg coming down the tube. During the second half of the menstrual cycle, from about Days 17 to 28, progesterone is readying the uterus for a possible pregnancy.

If you do not have sexual contact, or are sexually active but use birth control, the egg will pass into the

Fallopian tube and disintegrate. If you are not using protection, an egg traveling toward the uterus can meet a sperm coming in the opposite direction. Sperm and egg get together and fertilize—a new life begins. The fertilized egg then moves into the uterus, where progesterone has transformed the uterine lining into the thick, cushy endometrium, the perfect place for a fertilized egg to call home.

If you get pregnant, and the fertilized egg settles into the endometrium, then the hormones estrogen and progesterone stay at high levels. Most of the time, though, you are not having sex or getting pregnant and this whole process never happens. The pituitary does not get a hormonal message to keep the corpus luteum, the producer of progesterone, going. Without a signal from the brain, the corpus luteum shrivels away, estrogen and progesterone drop, and levels of prostaglandins, hormonelike substances in the soft, blood-rich endometrium, rise. Prostaglandins start small contractions in the uterus, which help it to shed the endometrium. The cycle winds down.

The Third Mucus Check (After Ovulation): After the egg-of-the-month sets off on its journey, progesterone enters into the cycle. This hormone makes the mucus more of a paste. What was clear and stretchy becomes cloudy white and thick. In this part of the cycle, the mucus stays around the cervix like a protective shield. It guards the entrance of the uterus and doesn't let germs pass through. The mucus helps keep the environment clean, should there be a fertilized egg inside.

Your body readies itself for pregnancy each month, no matter what you might want. When there is no pregnancy, the body gets rid of everything that's no longer needed. The endometrium separates from the uterus and leaves the body as menstrual blood. Meanwhile, your body is already gearing up for a new try for pregnancy during the next monthly cycle.

WHAT IT'S LIKE IN REAL LIFE: YOUR BODY DAY BY DAY

It's one thing to sit through health classes or read books that explain the menstrual cycle, and go on about hormones and mucus, but quite another to be female and live with a menstrual cycle every month. How much of your body's changes do you actually feel? Here's what real life is like, once you start having periods.

Day 1: You realize that you have your period. If it came on the same day the last two times, you may have expected it. Some girls become regular right away, and a week ahead of time they can name the day their periods are going to start. Other girls aren't so sure because their cycles haven't settled down yet. Usually, by the time a girl is in her late teens, she has a good idea of what her pattern is.

Many girls find that aside from bleeding, they hardly notice the arrival of their periods. Suddenly, it's Day 1, but they weren't forewarned by cramps or any other menstrual signals. You may be problem-free, or you may find that Day 1 arrives with cramps. The level of prostaglandins rises and causes your uterus to contract and push out the rich, blood-filled lining that your body created as a nest for a fertilized egg. All that activity can bring on different degrees of cramping.

As the lining leaves your body as blood, it tears from the walls of the uterus and the uterus itself bleeds. Whether you notice cramps or not, you may grow tired, feel an overall heaviness, and sometimes have pressure on your legs, a headache, or a backache. The hormonal readjustment that the body undergoes—because it got ready for a pregnancy that didn't happen—can be quite uncomfortable, even painful. Consider yourself lucky if your periods are marked only by the inconvenience of changing pads or tampons.

Days 2–5: You're still bleeding. You may be feeling more like yourself by Day 2, or you may have breezed through Day 1, only to find that Day 2 brings you down. Whatever your pattern, once you get past the initial effects and into your period, you spend about five days bleeding. Usually, a girl has a heavy flow from one to three days, when it's a good idea to take vitamins B complex, B₆, C, and iron to strengthen blood count. After Day 3, the bleeding slows and trickles off to a stop. You may stop on Day 4, 5, 6, or 7—five days is average—and not give another thought to your period.

Days 6–12: You're looking good. The female hormone estrogen is rising and as it goes up, so does your radiance level. These are the best days of the month. You're energized and feel the power.

Days 13–15: A slight abdominal twinge lets you know you're ovulating. At some point during these middle-of-the-month days, the egg-of-the-month is going to pop out of its bubble and if you're alert, you'll feel a tiny twinge in your abdomen. (Sometimes you may not have a "typical" cycle with ovulation in the middle of the month. See Reasons for Unpredictable Periods.) This twinge is called **mittelschmerz,** from the German "middle pain," but what you feel is more like a quick pinch than an actual pain. Sometimes when ovulation occurs, you may also see a light spot of blood on your underpants

and think you're getting your period. You rush for the
pads or tampons, but the bleeding never gets going. That
spot is only a passing sign of ovulation, not a full-fledged
period.

As mentioned earlier, your cervical mucus changes at
ovulation, but do you know that your body temperature
changes, too? If before you got out of bed, you took your
morning temperature, it would be 97.5° in the days before ovulation. After ovulation, it jumps one degree to
98.5°. Just before your period starts, it drops back down.

The day your temperature changed is the day that
you ovulated, the day that you're most likely to become
pregnant. Your freed egg is beginning its trek through
the Fallopian tube to your uterus. Should it meet up with
sperm on its first day out, you'll conceive a new life.
Your body is setting itself up for conception every month,
but it's up to you to take charge of your days, in spite of
what your body is doing. Unless you want to be pregnant, you'll stop sperm and egg from running into each
other. (See Chapter 7, *When You're Ready for Sex, What
Birth Control Is Safe?*)

Days 16–19: You're feeling fine. The egg-of-the-
month is moving through the Fallopian tube, but it probably won't have a very long trip. An egg can only be
fertilized by a sperm for the first twenty-four hours after
it separates from the ovary—that's during the day you
ovulate, the day you can become pregnant. If egg and
sperm don't meet during that day, the egg dies in the tube
and disappears. If an egg becomes fertilized, it takes four
to six days to travel through the tube. An egg is microscopic, so you don't feel it breaking away from the ovary
and entering the tube. Aside from the twinge of mittelschmerz, its movement doesn't bother you at all.

The corpus luteum, the scar tissue that the egg-of-the-month left behind in the ovary, begins to produce the female hormone progesterone during these days. At this point, your progesterone level is low; it gets higher as the days of the cycle build to the end. Progesterone uses its hormonal influence to convert the endometrium, the uterine lining, into a nourishing bed for that liberated egg, just in case it gets fertilized by sperm. Blood and nutrients build up in the lining. Your body wants to be ready to support a pregnancy and is always prepared.

Days 20–28: **You may feel bloated and your breasts may be a little sore.** While progesterone is at work on the endometrium, the combination of estrogen and progesterone can lead to water retention and make other areas of your body expand, too. Since the Pill contains estrogen and progesterone, sometimes girls on oral contraceptives are more susceptible to bloating, as are girls who have slight hormonal imbalances. You may never have any signs of water retention, but if you tend to retain water, you may notice a slight swelling around your feet and fingers. Sometimes a ring that normally fits perfectly gets stuck because your finger is a little bigger.

Female hormones can also enlarge your breasts and make them tender to touch. In addition, these are the days when **premenstrual syndrome (PMS)** may strike. Not every girl experiences PMS, but if you do, there are an assortment of symptoms that may descend upon you. For instance, you may feel uncoordinated and notice that you drop things. You might be in a bad mood and ready to pick a fight. Then the cravings may come! You might not be able to pass by a candy counter without reaching for a Snickers one minute, and a bag of potato chips the next. If you're a PMS sufferer, right now you'll want your period to start so you can get back to normal. Finally it happens. Your body gives up its focus on pregnancy and gives you a break. Prostaglandins increase and a slight cramping is a sign that your uterus is trying to shed its lining.

Day 1: You realize that you have your period. The cycle begins again.

QUESTIONS ABOUT YOUR PERIOD

I know from the teenage girls I see in my practice that girls usually have a lot of questions about menstruation. I am probably asked more questions about menstrual periods than anything else. I'm sure you have questions yourself, so here's what I've done. I've presented the questions I've been asked most frequently and answered them here. If your question is not among them, please feel free to write to me. (My address is mentioned at the end of Chapter 1.) I'll answer your question and save it for future books.

I'M A VIRGIN. WILL IT HURT ME TO USE A TAMPON? WILL I LOSE MY VIRGINITY?
I got my first period a few months ago and I've been using pads. I feel like I'm wearing a diaper. I want to try a tampon, but I'm afraid. I'm a virgin. Will it hurt me to use a tampon? Will I lose my virginity?

Kerry P., age 13

No one knows when the first woman rolled up a material like grass or cloth to absorb her menstrual flow internally, but women have been doing this throughout history. Today's manufactured tampons are rolls of compressed cotton and rayon. The best-known tampons, such as Tampax and Playtex brands, come in cardboard (more environmentally sound) and plastic tubes for insertion. With others, like o.b., you just push the tampon in with your fingers. All tampons have a string hanging out the end, so you can pull them out.

Like Kerry, most girls use sanitary pads when they begin menstruating because they don't like the idea of putting something inside their bodies. Eventually, though, the bulkiness of a pad starts to bother a girl and she begins wondering whether she could use a tampon. Some girls find that their mothers discourage them from using tampons. I've heard many mothers say that they didn't want their daughters using tampons while they were still virgins. I know, though, that every girl decides for herself. Kerry's personal comfort will help her decide whether to use a tampon or not.

Here's the best way for Kerry to find out if she can easily use a tampon: She should part the lips covering her vaginal opening with the fingers of one hand. Then she should slowly insert the index finger of her other hand into her vagina. Can she easily slide her finger in up to the second knuckle? Or does she feel that her finger is hurting her? Or is her hymen blocking her finger? (See Chapter 3 for descriptions of different hymens.)

If Kerry can easily slide her finger in, then she should have no trouble using a small-size—slender or junior—tampon. (See box, Getting a Tampon In and Out.) On the other hand, if she has any difficulty, especially if inserting her finger hurts, I think she should forget about tampons for now and use pads. A girl may have a tight vaginal opening, or a thick hymen, and a tampon would cause her discomfort. A girl who has not used a tampon before often finds that she is comfortable with one after her hymen has been broken by a physical activity such as horseback riding, or after she has experienced sexual intercourse.

A tampon will not make a girl "lose her virginity." A girl can only lose her virginity when she has sexual intercourse. Also, if Kerry can easily insert her finger into her vaginal opening, a tampon will not break her hymen. As explained in Chapter 3, a hymen is often pliant, with wide openings, and it's not likely to rupture.

CAN A TAMPON EVER GET LOST OR STUCK IN THERE?

I got my first period a few months ago. My girlfriend keeps telling me to try a tampon, but I've heard stories about girls losing their tampons inside them. Is this true? Can a tampon ever get lost or stuck in there?

Christina L., age 13

A tampon cannot get literally "lost" because it sits inside a confined area: the vaginal canal, which is several inches from its outer opening to its inner end at the cervix. While it's true that the cervix also has an opening, that opening is just a tiny slit, about the size of a flat match head. (The cervix only widens when a woman is about to give birth.) A tampon is too big to float through the cervical opening and get "lost" in the uterus. It stays in the vagina.

A girl can forget that she has inserted a tampon, however. On rare occasions, the string from the tampon can break off or get caught inside the vagina, and a girl can forget that she used a tampon at all. Sometimes she can try to insert a new tampon when she hasn't removed the old one. The body lets you know, though. It tries to break down the tampon and in doing so, it causes the tampon to give off a strong, foul odor.

I often remove tampons that girls either forgot about until they smelled something "funny," or had trouble pulling out. At the end of her period, a girl can have a hard time withdrawing a tampon. That's when there's not much blood, and a tampon can absorb all the vaginal fluid and expand. A girl may have to give the string a real yank because her vaginal canal is dry and the tampon has widened to the size of the space it occupies. If the tampon doesn't budge, or the string breaks, she should never be embarrassed to ask her doctor for help. Gynecologists are used to such requests, and can quickly remove a troublesome tampon.

All that said, the chance that a tampon will be "lost" or "stuck" is a slim one. If Christina feels comfortable wearing a tampon, she shouldn't worry.

CAN I GET TOXIC SHOCK SYNDROME FROM KEEPING A TAMPON IN OVERNIGHT?

I've heard that you shouldn't use a tampon for more than six hours because of toxic shock syndrome. I haven't known how to handle this at night. When I have my period, I keep a tampon in while I'm sleeping, which is about eight hours. Is this safe? Can I get toxic shock syndrome from keeping a tampon in overnight?

Tamara S., age 16

Toxic shock syndrome (TSS) starts with a toxin released by the very potent and dangerous *Staphylococcus aureus (Staph. aureus)* bacteria. This is a rare disease, but it can be treated. The symptoms of TSS can at first seem to resemble the flu. Within five days of menstruation a girl may have a sudden, high fever of at least 102° accompanied by vomiting and diarrhea. Dehydration can begin, along with dizziness and a drop in blood pressure. There is also a fine, sunburnlike rash that is most prevalent on the palms of the hands and the soles of the feet.

About one to two weeks after the onset of the disease

GETTING A TAMPON
IN AND OUT

For girls who feel they will be comfortable using tampons:

• Choose the smallest size, such as "slender" or "junior." The vaginal opening can stretch wide enough for a baby to pass through, so it can certainly accommodate the narrowest tampon. (Eventually you'll graduate to the tampon size that feels right for your flow and your comfort.)

• Allow yourself enough room to lean back slightly as you sit on the toilet seat. Part your legs and relax. If you're tense, your vaginal muscles can tighten up and it will seem as if you'll never be able to get the tampon in.

• With the fingers of one hand, separate the lips of your vulva. Hold a small mirror to the area with the other hand, so you can see your exposed vaginal opening. Now you know where you're heading with the tampon. Now you're ready.

• Your vagina is slightly angled toward the small of your back, so angle the tampon the same way. If you're using a tampon with a cardboard or plastic applicator, grip the grooved edge of the applicator with your middle finger and thumb. Gently slide and rotate the applicator into your vagina until your fingertips are touching your body. (If you have trouble getting a tampon in, you may want to moisten the tip of it with saliva or water-soluble K-Y jelly. Moisturizer or body lotion can have irritating chemicals, and Vaseline is too greasy.)

• While still holding onto the grooved edge of the applicator, press the plunger with your index finger. (For tampons without applicators, you push the tampon inside with your fingers.) You are sending the tampon up into your vagina, where it's secure. You want to get the tampon well beyond the muscles that are at the vagina's entrance. (If a tampon is sitting right at the opening, the muscles will close around it and you'll feel as if there's a wad between your legs that's about to fall out. To get the tampon positioned beyond the muscles, push it in a bit deeper with your fingertips, while keeping the string visible and handy.) When a tampon is resting at a comfortable angle within your vagina, you won't even know it's there.

• Slowly withdraw the applicator and look for a string to appear outside your vulva. The string is attached to the tampon. When it's time for a change, you'll gently pull on the string. While applicators should always be thrown in a wastebasket, a used tampon can be flushed away. The average time for changing tampons is every four to six hours, but your flow may demand more frequent changes.

• A tampon is not a challenge. If you feel you can't get comfortable with it, switch. Some girls prefer adhesive-backed pads that adhere to their underpants. The choice is yours.

the skin will begin to scale and peel on the palms and soles especially, but at the beginning a rash is the symptom to notice and so is a strawberry-red tongue and vagina. There might also be a sore throat, headache, and muscle pain. The good news is that *TSS can be treated*, but it must be caught early. A victim should be rushed to the hospital within the first forty-eight hours of the disease to receive intravenous fluid and antibiotics. A girl who does not get immediate care can lapse into a coma, her body can go into shock, and the shock can lead to death. When TSS was at its height in 1980, thirty-five women died in the United States. No recent deaths have been reported.

In 1980 a link was found between the *Staph. aureus* bacteria, menstruation, and—possibly—tampons. Yet TSS always was, and still is, a rare illness. In 1980, when the TSS scare reached its peak, 890 cases were reported out of about 52 million menstruating women in the United States. (Victims of TSS, by the way, have included non-menstruating women, children, and men. Menstruating women have not suffered alone.) Today, the risk for girls between fifteen and nineteen years old—an age group at greater risk of developing TSS—has dropped from about 10 in 100,000 a decade ago to 1.5 in 100,000, thanks to less absorbent tampons.

In 1980 toxic shock syndrome seemed to increase with the introduction of new, superabsorbent tampons. A brand called Rely, made of polyester foam and carboxy-methylcellulose, unfolded in the vagina and was so super-absorbent that it needed to be changed less frequently than other brands. A number of patients who were admitted to hospitals with toxic shock were, indeed, using Rely tampons.

Researchers theorized that the tampon created an air-tight culture medium in the vagina in which the bacteria could flourish and the toxin could develop. The makers of Rely withdrew their product from the market, but scientists also said that even a different brand and size of tampon that remained in the vagina for many hours might irritate the fine lining of the vagina and cause sores that encourage bacterial growth. Manufacturers responded by producing less absorbent tampons of cotton and rayon, and today's products are much less likely to promote the spread of bacteria.

So, is it safe to wear a tampon overnight? The answer is that there is no risk for TSS if you switch to a pad before going to bed. Since the suggested time limit for wearing a tampon is six hours, there might be only a tiny risk if a tampon is left in for eight hours. It's important to know, however, that if you get a high fever and watery diarrhea during your period, you should be examined by a doctor to rule out the remote chance of TSS.

WHAT'S THE BEST WAY TO DEAL WITH CRAMPS?
Lately I've noticed that I get cramps the day before my period. I've had my period for three years and the cramps only began about two months ago. One friend told me to take Advil, and another said Midol is better. What do you recommend? What's the best way to deal with cramps?

Sharon D., age 16

Cramps are caused by prostaglandins, hormonelike substances that are normally held in check by the female hormone progesterone. At the end of the monthly cycle, however, just before menstruation occurs, levels of progesterone drop and prostaglandins rise. It's not known why some girls have more prostaglandins than others, but it seems that the level in Sharon's body has risen recently.

Prostaglandins accumulate in the uterine lining that eventually leaves the body as menstrual blood. While still in the blood of the lining, the prostaglandins are absorbed by the uterine muscles, released, then reabsorbed. The uterus contracts and cramps, which feels something like a charley horse in your abdomen. A girl can suffer real pain, which is clinically called **primary dysmenorrhea**. (Secondary dysmenorrhea involves pain brought on by a pelvic disorder such as infection or **endometriosis**, a condition described in the next question.)

It's only when the period starts and menstrual blood, which holds the cramp-causing prostaglandins, flows that a girl feels better. Relief can come sooner if she takes an antiprostaglandin medication. The classic antiprostaglandin medication—a drug that prevents the body from releasing the prostaglandins that cause cramps—is aspirin. Sharon might try two aspirins four times a day for two days *before* her period starts and during the first days of her flow. Timing is important. Aspirin or any other antiprostaglandin drug should be taken *before and during menstruation* to cut down on cramping.

As I've told many girls, the best anticramp medicine is the one that works for you. Aspirin, Midol, Advil (ibuprofen), and Nuprin (ibuprofen) are the antiprostaglandin medications sold over-the-counter. (They should be taken after meals, since they can affect the stomach's acidity.) Usually when a girl complains of menstrual cramps, my first response is to recommend aspirin. If aspirins don't stop Sharon's cramps, then she might try Midol, that time-honored, over-the-counter, aspirinlike drug. If neither aspirin, Midol, nor any other over-the-counter remedy helps, then she might need a stronger drug, prescribed by her doctor. The FDA-approved antiprostaglandin medications available, in stronger doses, by prescription are Motrin (ibuprofen), Anaprox (naproxen sodium), Ponstel (mefenamic acid), and Feldene (piroxicam).

As Sharon's body changes, her level of prostaglandins might drop and one day she may be free of cramps. During the teen years, a lot of hormonal changes are occurring, and she shouldn't think that the events of her current monthly cycle will repeat themselves from now on. She has more changes in store. It's a good time to be a young woman, though, because today menstrual cramps are medically treated. Twenty-five years ago doctors questioned whether menstrual cramps were "real," and many women heard physicians say, "It's all in your head." In today's pharmacies, a girl can find products clearly labeled "for menstrual cramps" lining the shelves.

CAN BAD CRAMPS BRING ON ENDOMETRIOSIS?
I've heard that your period can back up inside you and you can get a disease called endometriosis. I've also heard that bad cramps can make it happen. Since I get cramps, sometimes I wonder whether part of my period is staying inside, and I think about endometriosis. I want to know the absolute truth. Can bad cramps bring on endometriosis?

Jane W., age 15

Menstrual cramps usually begin a day before a girl's menstrual period appears, at a time when the level of prostaglandins is high. These cramps subside as the level of prostaglandins drops and the heaviest flow starts. If Jane is experiencing menstrual cramps that disappear with her flow, she is not likely to be suffering from endometriosis. With this disease, cramps worsen rather than subside as a girl bleeds. Endometriosis also brings on abdominal pain—not just a feeling, but a real soreness—before or after menstruation. It is often a difficult disease to diagnose and to cure, and it is seen more frequently among teenagers than it used to be. Here's what happens.

Every month the endometrium, the lining of the uterus,

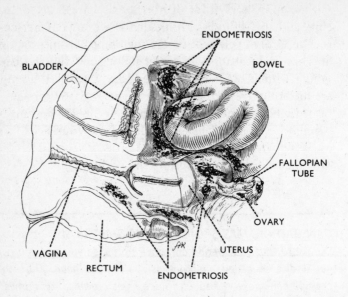

21. Endometriosis. Endometrial tissue can spread to other organs and cause such problems as discomfort, cramping, infertility, and severe abdominal pain. ILLUSTRATION BY LAUREL PURINTON RAND

grows rich in blood vessels as it prepares to welcome a fertilized egg. As I've mentioned before, when an egg is not fertilized the endometrium leaves a healthy girl's body as menstrual blood. When a girl has endometriosis, the menstrual blood does not escape completely. The blood-filled tissue that forms the endometrium may be found on the outside of the uterus, on the ovaries, and even on other organs, such as the bladder and kidneys. With each menstrual period, the tissue thickens and forms growths that can press on the organs and pull on nerve endings.

A girl who has endometriosis may feel a possible painful

ovulation two weeks before menstruation, severe cramps during menstruation, and a deep abdominal pain on one side or the other or an unspecific abdominal pain before or after menstruation. Also, women who want to start families often discover that their endometriosis makes them infertile, and causes them to have pain during sexual intercourse.

No one knows exactly what causes endometriosis, but one theory is that a uterus may be so narrow and tight that the lining is blocked, pushed backward through the Fallopian tubes, and sprayed out the tubes into the abdomen. I wrote *The Endometriosis Answer Book*[1] to help sufferers find relief, because once the disease takes hold, the tissue that is outside the uterus grows larger and more painful with every menstrual cycle.

If you experience abdominal pain, cramping, and bloating before and during your period, with no letup, you may be suffering from endometriosis. You should discuss the possibility of endometriosis with your mother, then consult a gynecologist who specializes in treating the disease. Endometriosis is best conquered if it's discovered in its early stages, before it spreads. If the disease is found, minor surgery called laser laparoscopy or drugs, such as Danocrine tablets, Lupron injections, and Syneral nasal spray, may be recommended.

This disease, unfortunately, is on the rise. *The Endometriosis Answer Book* is an excellent guide if you feel that you have symptoms of the disease. If you have questions that neither the book nor your doctor can answer, you can always write to me. (My address is listed at the end of Chapter 1.) I will do my best to help.

---

[1]Niels H. Lauersen, M.D., and Constance deSwaan, *The Endometriosis Answer Book* (New York: Fawcett Columbine/Ballantine Books, 1988).

CAN MY PERIOD BE GIVING ME A HEADACHE?

I always know when my period is a day or two away because I get a really bad headache, what I've started to call my "monthly signal." Sometimes it's right behind my eyes, which feel as if they're about to pop out. At first I thought I was getting migraines, but then I noticed that every time I got a bad headache, I got my period right after. I hope I'm right about this connection, because I don't like the idea of having migraines. Can my period be giving me a headache?

Kate C., age 15

Yes. In fact, it's quite common for girls to have headaches before their periods. Estrogen is the culprit. This female hormone starts to build right after menstruation and throughout the monthly cycle. As estrogen increases, it binds salt, which in turn binds water. Water retention leads to the swelling of body tissue, which is why you can feel puffy or bloated just before your period starts.

Sometimes the brain membrane is one of the body tissues that swell, but because the brain is encased in the skull, it swells within a confined area. The result is a headache that can rival a blinding migraine.

Kate should cut back on salt before her period and drink plenty of water to wash out her system. Many girls never experience headaches because they have a more balanced relationship between estrogen and progesterone. Girls who get headaches usually have slight hormonal imbalances, and sometimes daily vitamin B complex (100 milligrams [mg]) and vitamin B₆ (50–200 mg) can help. For some girls, these imbalances may also be corrected by a birth control pill, and if Kate ever chooses to be on the Pill, she may notice that her headaches disappear. For now, relief may come from cutting back on salt, drinking plenty of water, taking B vitamins, and exercising. Girls who stay in shape generally have fewer menstrual problems.

IT SEEMED AS IF MY PERIOD WAS NEVER GOING TO STOP.

Last month I had an incredibly heavy period. I had to wear a tampon and a pad, and keep changing them all the time. The first two days blood clots came out, which really got me worried. Usually I have a five-day period, but it kept on going for eight days. Thank God it ended. It seemed as if my period was never going to stop. Is there something wrong with me?

Maureen G., age 17

Maureen does not mention whether her period was late, but sometimes if a girl is under stress, if she's waiting to hear whether she won a role in the school play, or is anxious about a final exam, or is worried about a fight she had with her boyfriend, she can throw off her hormones and her period may be late. A late period then means that the endometrium has more time to thicken. When hormones finally do trigger the menstrual flow, it is heavier than ever because the endometrium—which is sloughed off as menstrual blood—is greater than ever.

As long as Maureen's heavy bleeding is not a regular pattern, she does not have to worry. An occasional heavy period, as well as an occasional light period, is normal at this time of life when hormonal balances are shifting.

If she notices that she is regularly using an unusual number of pads and tampons, and that her periods are consistently heavy with large clots in the flow, then Maureen should visit her doctor. A heavy flow can make a girl fatigued and anemic, and she may need iron and vitamin C to strengthen her blood count. Depending upon the cause of her bleeding, her doctor might prescribe a birth control pill to reduce the flow, the uterine-contracting drug Ergotrate, or a prostaglandin-blocking drug such as Motrin.

*I WONDER IF I'M EVER GOING TO HAVE A PERIOD
EVERY MONTH.*
*I got my first period one month after my thirteenth birthday,
which was a year and a half ago. I've only had about ten
periods since then, and I wonder if I'm ever going to have a
period every month. I've been taking ballet lessons since I was
seven, and many of the girls in my dance school say that danc-
ers don't get regular periods. Why is that?*
                                              Ariel J., age 14

For a year or two after a girl has her first menstrual
period her cycles are frequently irregular. In the beginning she does not ovulate every month, and by the time
most cycles include ovulation, her body is made up of
about 28 percent fat. So Ariel's haphazard cycles are quite
normal. The question is whether her periods will become
regular within the next year. Her dancing probably keeps
her thin as well as physically active, and a low body
weight can affect menstrual regularity.

When girls lose weight or have little body fat, the
pituitary gland in the brain prevents the hormones LH
and FSH from being released, and halts the menstrual
cycle. This menstrual arrest is nature's way of protecting
the body from the blood loss and added strain that a
period brings. When a girl who has been missing periods
changes her routine and gains a little weight, she usually
finds that her periods reappear month after month.
Sometimes, though, menstruation can be regulated
through good nutrition. A girl who is a dancer or competitive athlete might try eating small frequent meals of
fresh fruits and vegetables, keeping salt and sugar down,
and taking daily vitamins: B complex (400 mg), B_6 (100–
300 mg), E (100 IU), C (500 mg twice a day), and iron
(300 mg twice a day).

REASONS FOR UNPREDICTABLE PERIODS

Why You May Skip a Period	*Why You May Be "Irregular"**
Pregnancy	Stress
Stress	Hormonal imbalance
Weight gain or loss	Endometriosis**
Hormonal imbalance	Surgery (especially
Ovarian cyst	gynecological surgery)
Travel	Ovarian cyst
Emotional trauma	Stein-Leventhal syndrome***
(for example, a death	Breakthrough bleeding (due
in your family)	to the birth control pill)

*Instead of a typical twenty-eight-day menstrual cycle, you have a cycle that is longer or shorter, or you have spotting between periods.

**Explained in this chapter.

***Explained in Chapter 2.

TO THE OVERWEIGHT GIRL

There's a fine interaction between the brain and the ovaries that can be disturbed if a girl weighs either too little or too much. Like Ariel, an overweight girl may find that her menstrual flow skips months. Since fatty tissue can be converted into the hormone estrogen, when a period finally does arrive, it may be an especially heavy one. An overweight girl's added estrogen causes an extra buildup of the uterine lining that leaves her body as menstrual blood. She ought to try to heed her body's signals. If she's skipping her periods or is having heavy flows, she might try to exercise, eat low-fat foods, and take the daily vitamins listed above. A regular monthly period will tell her that she's getting in shape.

DOES SWIMMING AFFECT MY PERIOD?
Nothing could stop me from swimming. I've always loved the
water, and when I started high school this year I was deter-
mined to place on the swim team. I use tampons and I don't
let my period interfere with practice or meets, but I do some-
times wonder whether swimming affects my period.
                                              Melissa B., age 14

As long as you feel comfortable wearing a tampon, you should have no trouble swimming during the days of your period. Swimming has never been shown to affect the length of a cycle, or the length and intensity of menstruation. Melissa probably does not have a heavy flow since she is very active. It's known that exercise, which affects body weight and hormonal responses, usually results in light to medium periods. If you bleed heavily, you might need protection from a tampon and a pad during your heaviest days, and you obviously would want to wait until the flow lessens before you get back in the water.

PREMENSTRUAL SYNDROME

What It's Like to Have PMS

If you suffer from premenstrual syndrome (PMS) from two to fourteen days before your period, you may experience a number of conditions. (See table, PMS SYMPTOMS.) Tiredness, irritability, depression, tension, headache, backache, weight gain, nausea, heaviness in the abdomen and legs, asthma, and even acne have been brought on by PMS. (Note: Cramps, which usually occur at the start of menstrual bleeding, are *not* a symptom of PMS.)

PMS SYMPTOMS

Organs or Systems Affected	*Symptoms*
Neurological:	Headache
	Coordination
	Migraines
	Epilepsy
	Dizziness
	Fainting spells
Psychological:	Irritability
	Mood swings
	Crying periods
	Tension
	Frustration
	Panic
	Exhaustion
	Aggression
	Anger
	Tiredness
	Depression
	Attempted suicide
	Self-inflicted injury
	Alcoholic bouts
	Drug abuse
Respiratory:	Sniffles and runny nose
	Bronchitis
	Asthma
	Upper respiratory infections
Dermatological:	Skin rash
	Acne
	Boils
	Hives
	Herpes attacks

Orthopedic:	Backache
	Joint pains
	Stiffness
Muscular:	Muscle tension
	Water retention
	Abdominal pain
	Muscle cramps
Eye Symptoms	Pink eye
	Runny eyes
	Blackness around eyes
	Blurred vision
Ear, Nose, and Throat Symptoms	Hoarseness
	Sore throat
	Tonsillitis
Urological:	Urethritis
	Cystitis
	Frequent urination
	Water retention
	Bloatedness
Gastrointestinal:	Food cravings
	Hunger pangs
	Abdominal swelling
Breasts:	Breast tenderness
	Fibrocystic breast disease

About 40 percent of females between fourteen and fifty years old experience premenstrual syndrome to some degree, and 5 to 10 percent of these women may have symptoms severe enough to interfere with their daily activities. Once again, the symptoms of PMS begin anywhere from two to fourteen days before menstruation and last until the beginning of, or a couple of days into, the bleeding.

Scientists believe that the symptoms are caused by

A BRIEF HISTORY OF PMS

In 1980 the British murder trial of Sandie Smith, who stabbed a barmaid to death, brought international notoriety to premenstrual syndrome. Dr. Katharina Dalton, an English physician who had been researching PMS for years, testified that Ms. Smith was suffering from a severe case of the syndrome, that her hormonal imbalance was severe, and that she did not know what she was doing. Dr. Dalton went on to say that Ms. Smith's violent behavior could be controlled by the hormone progesterone. Sandie Smith was released on probation and ordered to receive daily injections of progesterone from the district nursing service.

The case of Sandie Smith brought PMS out of the laboratories and into the streets. Today everyone has heard of PMS. There's an awareness that did not exist when I conducted my studies and wrote the book *PMS: Premenstrual Syndrome and You.*[2] Back in the early eighties, most doctors refused to acknowledge that girls and women suffered before their periods due to hormonal imbalances. The idea that PMS might exist for real, physical reasons was considered "ridiculous." PMS was said to be "all in a woman's head," as if she were making up her symptoms, as if she didn't really feel irritable, clumsy, bloated, and achy.

Today no one questions whether PMS is real; instead, controversy rages over the most effective ways to find relief.

---

[2]Niels H. Lauersen, M.D., and Eileen Stukane, *PMS: Premenstrual Syndrome and You* (New York: Fireside/Simon & Schuster, 1983).

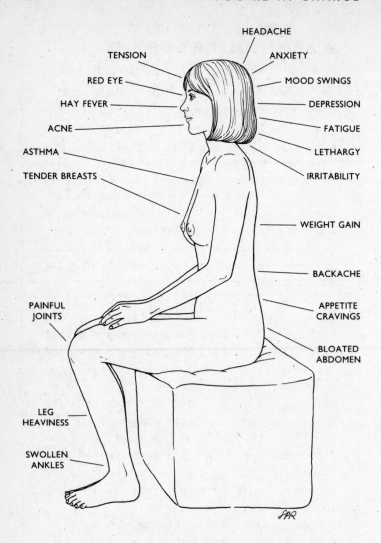

HEADACHE
TENSION   ANXIETY
RED EYE   MOOD SWINGS
HAY FEVER   DEPRESSION
ACNE   FATIGUE
ASTHMA   LETHARGY
TENDER BREASTS   IRRITABILITY
                                 WEIGHT GAIN
                                 BACKACHE
PAINFUL   APPETITE
JOINTS   CRAVINGS
                                 BLOATED
                                 ABDOMEN
LEG
HEAVINESS
SWOLLEN
ANKLES

22. Some of the Symptoms of Premenstrual Syndrome (PMS). The symptoms associated with PMS usually appear anywhere from two to fourteen days before a menstrual flow begins. You might suffer one or several of these symptoms at the same time. ILLUSTRATED BY LAUREL PURINTON RAND

hormonal changes, particularly the changing levels of estrogen and progesterone during the second half of the menstrual cycle. Yet when researchers have compared the amounts and types of hormones in women with severe PMS and in women with only mild symptoms, they have not been able to find significant differences. PMS continues to baffle doctors.

Most girls and women feel some physical and emotional changes before their periods. The only real way to know if you have an authentic case of PMS is to write down any physical and psychological feelings that you think may be related to premenstrual syndrome every day on a calendar. You should do this for two or three months, starting on the first day of your next period. Write an *M* on the date that you begin to bleed. From that day on, note your symptoms.

By keeping a menstrual calendar, you can see whether your symptoms—whatever they may be—become worse before your period and disappear after the bleeding begins. If you are a true PMS sufferer, you will notice that for a week or two you have no symptoms and feel fine. This period of good health proves that you have a cyclical problem rather than an ever-present condition.

Your ovaries take turns releasing an egg, or ovulating. This causes you to react to different hormonal levels, depending on which ovary is at work. During a month that the right ovary is responsible for ovulation, you may experience a different hormonal balance than you do when the left ovary is in charge. You may have a month when symptoms are hardly noticeable, and then a month of despair. Certain symptoms may get worse with stress. In the end it seems that symptoms change because of alternating ovaries, stress, or both.

You ought to keep a calendar to find out if you really have PMS. You shouldn't fall into the trap of saying, for example, that you just had a fight with your boyfriend

PMS patient

MENSTRUAL CALENDAR   Month **JANUARY**

WK	SUNDAY	MONDAY	TUESDAY	WEDNESDAY	THURSDAY	FRIDAY	SATURDAY
1							1
2	2	3	4	5	6	7	8
3	9	10	11	12 Restless Irritable	13 Insomnia Restless	14 Insomnia Restless	15 Depressed Irritable Insomnia
4	16 Depressed Irritable	17 Depressed Irritable	18 Irritable Depressed	19 ↑ Hunger Irritable Depressed	20 Bloated ↑ Hunger Migraine Headache	21 Bloated ↑ Hunger Headache Depressed	22 Bloated Irritable ↑ Restless Headache
5	23 ↓ Dep. ↓ Irrit.	24 Relief! M	25 Great M	26 Great M	27 Feel Good M	28 Good	29 Good
6	30 Energetic	31 Good					

Chart 2. The Menstrual Calendar of a PMS Sufferer. This calendar shows characteristic symptoms of a PMS sufferer. Notice how PMS-related symptoms worsen during the last few days before menstruation and disappear as a menstrual period begins. Menstruation for this girl is January 24.

because you have PMS if you don't know. PMS is not a joke or an excuse for mood changes; it is a condition that troubles a large number of females. We all—doctors and young women—have to band together to encourage research by taking premenstrual syndrome seriously.

How to Cope with PMS

PMS *can* be cured. The first step you can take to overcoming your premenstrual syndrome is to be aware of your particular symptoms and pattern. What do you feel and when do you feel it? The goal in coping with PMS is to try to keep hormones in a balance that will reduce symptoms.

Exercise affects the release of brain chemicals that influence the hormones estrogen and progesterone, which regulate the menstrual cycle. Regular exercise, therefore, can help.

A healthy diet also affects hormonal balance. The mood swings of PMS may be brought on by a high insulin/low blood sugar ratio intensified by those battling hormones. By eating frequent small meals, taking the "grazing" approach rather than the traditional three square meals a day, you can keep your blood sugar level steady and be less susceptible to sudden shifts of emotion. Of course, the food in your diet should be low-fat, with a special emphasis on complex carbohydrates—fresh fruits and vegetables, whole-grain cereals, breads, and pastas. (See Chapter 11 for more on diet.)

Either including or cutting back on particular foods may help. If you have bloating and headaches, you may find relief by eating less salt; if you get depressed, you may feel better if you eat sugars and starches. Normally, I would not recommend such nonnutritious foods. However, Dr. Richard J. Wurtman, a professor of neuroscience and a specialist in brain chemistry at the Massachusetts Institute of Technology, and his wife, Dr. Judith J. Wurtman, a cell biologist and nutritionist, studied PMS sufferers who ate a high amount of sweets, such as candy and cakes, and starches, such as potatoes and pasta, and found that the women became more emotionally stable. Sugars and starches increase the levels of a brain chemical called serotonin, which is a mood regulator, but serotonin can also make you sleepy.

From a nutritional standpoint, I prefer that you eat more of the complex carbohydrates in fresh fruits, vege-

tables, and whole grains, rather than the refined carbohydrates found in sweets. Some flexibility, of course, is
always allowed. If only a chocolate chip cookie will satisfy a craving, then a chocolate chip cookie it is!

Vitamins, especially B vitamins, every day help to
reduce tense, irritable feelings brought on by PMS. The
B vitamins have been shown to influence the transmission
of nerve signals that directly affect the release of female
hormones. To keep these neurotransmissions steady and
accurate, you might daily take 100 milligrams (mg) of
vitamin B complex with 50 to 200 mg of vitamin B_6.
Vitamin B_6 should only be taken in combination with
vitamin B complex to keep vitamin B intake properly
balanced. Since B_6 may cause stomach upset, it's a good
idea to eat before taking this vitamin. A study conducted
by Dr. Guy Abraham found that 500 mg a day, a high
dose of vitamin B_6, helped relieve premenstrual symptoms in twenty-one out of twenty-five women, and in
the past I have recommended that girls increase their
vitamin B_6 to 500 mg a day during the two weeks before
their menstrual period. Dr. Abraham's study, however,
has been hit with critical fire from other researchers. I
believe that because PMS is such a complicated syndrome, certain remedies will work for some women but
not for others. If you feel better when you're taking B
vitamins, you might try the higher dose in the last half
of your cycle.

There is no single cure for all of the many symptoms
of PMS. I recommend that you first try the above, natural
approach to coping with PMS. If the natural approach
doesn't help, then medications are available:

• **Diuretics,** which increase the flow of urine, can
help relieve weight gain and bloating.

• **Spironolactone** is a diuretic that might also be prescribed for water retention. Studies have linked PMS to an oversupply of hormones from the adrenal glands. Spironolactone seems to be able to counterbalance the effect of these hormones.

• Certain **birth control pills** may chase away PMS symptoms for some girls but not for others. Birth control pills contain a combination of estrogen and progesterone in amounts that vary from one brand of pill to another. If you begin to take the Pill, you may suddenly feel wonderful. On the other hand, if you start taking a birth control pill and feel worse than you did before, you should try another brand with a different hormonal balance. If your symptoms never go away, you may be highly sensitive to the hormones in all pills and should stop them altogether.

• The use of **natural progesterone suppositories** was pioneered by British researcher Dr. Katharina Dalton. (A suppository is a medication in solid form that is inserted into the vagina. It melts inside the body and releases the medicine.) She was against the use of synthetic progesterone, which she felt worsened PMS. Until recently, natural progesterone suppositories seemed to be one way to change the estrogen/progesterone balance and bring relief to girls with severe premenstrual syndrome. In 1990, however, researchers at the University of Pennsylvania questioned their effectiveness. For eight years they treated 168 PMS sufferers with progesterone suppositories and placebos, which were fake hormone-free suppositories, and found that the progesterone brought little relief.

I personally have seen natural progesterone suppositories, in combination with a well-balanced diet and exercise, transform the lives of women who have had such terrible PMS symptoms that they could not go to work or care for their families. What seems obvious is that some

cures for PMS help some girls, and some help others—
but all cures do not work for all girls!

• **Propanalol,** a drug often used to treat high blood
pressure, may bring relief to girls who suffer terrible migraine headaches brought on by PMS. This drug is taken
daily.

New work is also being done on **light therapy,** in
which PMS sufferers are exposed to bright light for certain periods of time. This is still experimental research.
Studies show that women who experience depression
from PMS release higher amounts of melatonin, a hormone from the brain. Melatonin levels, it seems, may be
lowered by bright light.

You ought to try different treatments to see what
works for you. There is no single cure for everyone, but
I don't see that as important. What's important, I believe,
is that when it comes to premenstrual syndrome, hope is
on the horizon.

The Best Approach

Most girls with mild to moderate PMS find that following the natural approach—daily exercise, a well-
balanced diet, and vitamins—makes a big difference. They
don't feel noticeably ill or upset as their periods near.

So if you're usually affected by PMS, first try the
natural approach. If that doesn't help, then you may
need prescription medication such as natural progesterone. A drug doesn't have to be taken forever—just until
you get your body under control. It's important to work
in partnership with your doctor, but he or she should
understand PMS. Trust your instincts. If you feel that
your doctor makes light of your PMS, then find a different physician.

THE MENSTRUAL CYCLE AS YOUR GUIDE

When you got your first period, how long you bleed, how many days fall in between periods, whether your periods are heavy or light, whether you get PMS, cramps, or just breeze along month after month—these are the signs of how your body works. Once you recognize your patterns, you can begin to notice when changes take place.

Perhaps you skip a month, or you're late, or you have a much shorter period than usual. This is the time for you to think about whether you're under too much pressure, are losing sleep or missing meals, or are simply exhausted from doing too much.

The menstrual cycle is your guide to good health. Staying fit through exercise, a well-balanced diet (minus junk food), and vitamins (particularly a balance of B complex and B_6) can help you have a regular monthly cycle. By understanding your body, you are learning all the ways you can control it.

CHAPTER SIX

Understanding Your Sexuality: What's Normal; What's Not

You are a sexual being from the day you are born. Your sexuality reveals itself to you through feelings, desires, sensations, and fantasies. You reveal your sexuality to others simply by being yourself. People feel your sexuality when they look at your eyes, hair, posture, gestures, and sense your emotional range and personal values. Sexual activity is only one aspect of the behavior of a sexual person. In fact, you can be quite sexual and choose to postpone sex indefinitely. Every girl has her particular timing. While you are considering what's right for you, think about whether you really know your sexual self.

Before becoming involved with someone else's sexuality, why not try to explore your own? The girl who knows herself intimately develops self-understanding and self-worth, two qualities that can help her refine her timing.

WHAT A DAY FOR A DAYDREAM

The teens are dreamy years. Even girls who are involved in time-consuming activities, such as after-school jobs, sports, and music, are not too busy to drift off on romantic fantasies. Sexual stirrings are so active right now that you may spend time thinking about guys you barely noticed before, or you may like a teacher so much that you have fantasies about marrying him. These are signs of good health. Sexual attractions and crushes are normal, and occasionally they are grounded in reality. You may want to be more than "just friends" with a guy in your school. Then one day, as the two of you are talking, your friendship may take a turn toward romance.

Most of the time, though, dreams should never leave dreamland. There's a great temptation to try to act out fanatasies exactly as you imagined them, but in real life they usually don't come out the same way, and when reality hits, it can hurt. Try to stay clear about what's fact and what's fancy. It's fine to let daydreams take you on a tour of your sexual feelings, as long as your heart and mind do return to planet Earth. Let your fantasies help rather than hurt you.

Sexual daydreams and fantasies are healthy outlets for girls who are not ready to be sexually active, as well as for girls who are already sexually involved. Fantasies are an outlet for emotions and urges. Unlike boys, when girls fantasize they often think of a romantic situation with someone they know or they relive a real experience, a first kiss, the touch of someone's hand on theirs. Although boys are fantasizing, too, they are more likely to be turned on visually, from pictures or photos in magazines and books, or by something sexy a girl is wearing.

You don't want to become a "space case"—a day-dreamer who never gets her schoolwork done, or can't find time to be with her friends because she's so wrapped up in her fantasies—but you ought not to feel so guilty about daydreams that you stop them from coming. Fantasies have their place; they give shape to your desires and help you define your sexual self.

YOUR EROGENOUS ZONES

Certain areas of your body are supersensitive to touch— your lips and mouth, fingertips, breasts and nipples, and all your external sexual organs (the vulva, as described in Chapter 3). These highly erogenous, sexually sensitive zones are filled with sensory nerve endings that respond to a kiss or a gentle stroke. It's the sensitivity of the fingers, for instance, that makes holding hands such a pleasure.

Both sexes have erogenous zones. (Sensitive areas for boys are described in Chapter 4.) The most sensitive area for a girl is her clitoris, while a boy's most highly charged erogenous zone is the glans, or head, of his penis. In a sexual situation where emotions are running high, the clitoris and glans change when they are touched. Blood travels to these areas and leads to swelling, pinkness, and heightened sensitivity. Then the whole body responds. Breathing, pulse, and blood pressure quicken.

The degree of your responsiveness is also influenced by your emotions. If a guy you like simply touches the back of your neck, you may feel sensations that a dozen kisses from another admirer could not activate. A strong emotional involvement can turn almost any area into an erogenous zone.

Aside from the highly sensitive zones, some girls may be particularly stimulated when their eyes and ears are kissed, while some may find their necks to be quite sensitive, and others may feel their pulse rate jump at a touch to their inner thighs. Everyone's sensitivity is different. The discovery of your own erogenous zones can be surprising.

MASTURBATION IS NORMAL

Masturbation is the sexual stimulation of yourself, by yourself. Girls are less likely to masturbate than boys, and a lot of girls choose not to masturbate. Many girls, though, are curious about what it feels like to touch the clitoris, which is a highly erogenous zone. Whatever you decide to do—experiment with masturbation or not—is normal. It's important to know, though, that many healthy people of all ages—single and married men, women, and teens—masturbate regularly.

If you choose to masturbate, you will gain immediate awareness about how you function sexually. Observations in sex therapy clinics have found that no two women masturbate in exactly the same way. Many women do not like to masturbate directly on the heads of their clitorises, because stroking the concentration of nerve endings there can be painful. Women are more likely to let their fingers slide around the labia and clitoris.

At a time when you feel relaxed and won't be disturbed, use your fingers to find out where and how your most pleasant sensations are produced. By using body oil or lotion on your fingertips, you will be less likely to irritate sensitive genital tissue. As you touch and stroke the labia and clitoris, you may feel the tissue swell and harden. The experience can give you a pleasurable rush.

This is your human sexual responsiveness. You may also notice a wetness coming from your vagina. Continued stroking of the area that gives you the greatest sensations may stimulate you to the point of orgasm, a series of electric pulsations throughout your body. (Orgasm is described in detail later on in this chapter.)

When you explore yourself through masturbation, you release sexual tension and experience a sense of relaxation. You also begin to understand your body more fully. For generations, the act of masturbation was looked upon in horror. People were told that if they "touched" or "played with" themselves, they would grow hair on the palms of their hands, go blind, become crippled, or go insane. By now, you know the truth, that masturbation is not harmful. Many healthy, normal people masturbate. (However, if you are uncomfortable about it or have religious beliefs that are in conflict with masturbation, don't do it.) If you choose to try it, masturbation offers a safe sexual experience and a sampling of sensations.

SEXUAL LEANINGS

European women often hold hands when they walk down the street, and Russian men greet each other with a kiss on the cheek. It's natural to show affection for someone who is the same sex that you are. This is a time in your life, though, when you are involved in defining sexual feelings, and you may be trying to sort out the meaning of your fondness for a girlfriend, or attraction to a certain boy.

You may be preoccupied with trying to figure out love and the girl/boy relationship, or you may have such strong bonds with a girlfriend that you cannot imagine the same kind of closeness with a boy. Sometimes a girl will tell me that her relationship with a girlfriend is so intense that she sometimes wonders whether she might be gay. Most often this is not the case. In their teens, girls are usually closer to their girlfriends than they are to boyfriends. You may notice that you can confide in a girlfriend more easily than you can a guy. Your friendship is based on communication, though, not sexual attraction.

Questioning your sexuality. A homosexual female is called "gay" or "lesbian." The word *lesbian* harks back to the Greek island of Lesbos. In the seventh century B.C., the unmarried lyric poet Sappho opened a school on Lesbos for young women. Sappho called her pupils her "companions." She taught them music, poetry, and dancing and fell in love with one after another of them. Many scholars regard the poems that Sappho wrote about her girls as expressions of sexual love between women.

The truth is that sometimes teens—both girls and boys—think about homosexual situations, or actually participate in sexual experiences with partners of the same sex, and most of the time they are not homosexual. Researchers consider this experimentation to be part of growing up. Many teens, of course, are completely uninterested in same-sex involvement, while others absolutely know they are homosexual, and still others cannot help questioning their sexual preferences.

If you are a questioning teen, remember that your sexuality—whether you think you are heterosexual, homosexual, or even bisexual (equally satisfied with a partner of either sex)—is still emerging. (Note: As a result of certain sexual practices, male homosexuals and bisexuals can be at high risk of catching and transmitting the deadly HIV/AIDS virus. See Chapter 8.)

As far as how many adults are gay, I do not have a definite answer. The most frequently mentioned figure is one in ten, but this is an estimated number taken from the sexuality studies done by the famous research team of Masters and Johnson decades ago. What I do know is that women and men in all walks of life, scientists, doctors, lawyers, clergy, artists, teachers, athletes, movie stars, even married people are homosexual. Some say that they knew they were strongly attracted to the same sex when they were very young; others encountered their homosexuality for the first time as adults, while others were married and parents before they realized that they were gay.

Still, the majority of the world's population is heterosexual. Most girls, even those who are confused, shy, and nervous around boys today, eventually are quite attracted to the opposite sex. The heterosexual mating instinct is strong; if it were not, there's a good chance that I would not be writing this book and you would not be reading it, because our parents might not have gotten together to have us. Test tube babies and artificial insemination still cannot compete with the primal pull that draws females to males with whom they can have sex and children.

IF IT ISN'T LOVE, WHY DO YOU FEEL THE WAY YOU DO?

You write his name in the margins of your notebook. You think he's the cutest guy you have ever seen. He makes you laugh. You can't wait to be alone with him, to touch him. You think you are in love. Why else would you feel this way? Well, you might be on a romantic high.

Physical attraction can be immediate. You can become excited about a guy right away. Rather than concentrate on your term paper, you daydream about him in his gym shorts. You may be completely swept away, but if you haven't known him very long, you are more likely to be infatuated—thunderstruck!—than in love. Time is the deciding factor.

True love takes time. That feeling of "love at first sight" is usually the thrill of an infatuation. You are involved in a mutual attraction and you are both a little in awe of each other.

Ask yourself if you really know this boy. Can you tell him about your family without worrying that he will judge them or you? Can you ask him for advice about a problem? Can you disagree with him and know that his feelings for you will remain strong? Can you trust him to consider your emotions and needs in different situations? And while you're thinking along these lines: Can he trust you? If you answer yes every time, and believe that you have a desire to support and nurture each other, you may truly love each other.

An infatuation may be the beginning of a love relationship, or a passing fancy. If you are moving into love, you will probably face a period when you get on each other's nerves and question your future together. Every relationship usually reaches a point where two people decide to understand each other more fully or to break up. If the two of you are not right for each other, you will lose interest and move on. You can only know whether an infatuation will turn into love by giving a relationship time to grow and change—not fast-moving television and movie time, where people meet, fall in love, and get married in minutes, but real-life time, which can mean months and months of being together.

You may enjoy numerous infatuations before you feel that one person really loves you, and you love him. When that happens, you won't just be excited by a guy and think you love him; you will also *like* him, and above all, you will trust him.

ARE *YOU* READY FOR SEX?

Your health teacher probably told you that

• half of all teenage girls are sexually active by the time they are eighteen.

• half of all teenage girls do not use birth control the first time they have sex.

• each year *one out of ten* girls between fifteen and nineteen years old gets pregnant.

• *one out of four* sexually active teenagers becomes infected with a sexually transmitted disease before graduating from high school.

Sex is passionate, playful, but at the same time, serious. When you think about having sex, you have to consider the very real possibility of becoming pregnant and/or catching AIDS or some other sexually transmitted disease, while you are evaluating your emotional maturity and the depth of feeling that you and your boyfriend share. You can be profoundly affected by sexual intimacy, and you should never feel rushed to begin a sexually intimate relationship.

No matter how old you are, if you are wondering whether you are ready to have sex, don't do it. When you are ready, you won't have any doubts. Sex is a powerful physical act that has responsibility and emotional strings attached to it. As psychotherapist and author Rollo May wrote in his book *Freedom and Destiny*:

Sex and the intimacy that goes with it are so basic a part of human existence that one cannot separate them from one's values. . . . Moral concern in sex hinges on the acceptance of one's responsibility for the other as well as for oneself. Other people *do* matter; and the celebration of this gives sexual intercourse its ecstasy, its meaning, and its capacity to shake us to our depths.[1]

No one can expect to become sexually intimate with another person without emotional stirrings. As much fun as you may have in bed, afterward either you or your boyfriend may feel possessive, jealous, angry, guilty, or embarrassed. You are only human, and you are involved in a merging of two bodies and two minds. Are you prepared for these emotions?

A lot of sexually active girls have told their gynecologists that they don't really enjoy sex, but they are doing it because their boyfriends want it. How tragic! They are not doing what *they* want to do.

No one can entirely escape the pressure to have sex. When students responded to my high school questionnaires, many boys said that they felt pressure from other guys, friends who teased and urged them to lose their virginity, while girls felt pressure from boyfriends. What seems to be happening is that guys are responding to male peer pressure more than they are acting on their own desires. Their lines certainly appear to be borrowed from one another:

"Everybody has to do it sometime, so let's do it now."

"You'll do it if you love me."

"If you don't do it, I'll die."

"If you do it standing up, you won't get pregnant."

Ideally, sex is a positive communication between two people who trust each other; at its best, it is joyful and, as I mentioned before, serious. Sex scenes on television, in movies, and in music videos often trivialize the sex act—do it; don't do it; it's your right to have fun. This

---

[1]Rollo May, *Freedom and Destiny* (New York: Norton, 1981).

pressure can rival any guy's come-on. What movies and TV shows don't show you is the thoughtfulness of two people who protect themselves against pregnancy and sexually transmitted disease because they are responsible lovers who care about each other. You also are not in on what happens afterwards—the pleasure experienced by the girl who is emotionally mature and using birth control, or the anxiety of the unprotected girl who has sex because she thinks she should and wants to be "spontaneous." You have the power to choose where, when, and with whom you will be sexually active. Sex is only one part of a much fuller relationship, one that takes time to understand and appreciate. Take all the time you need.

THE FIRST TIME

When you are in a loving, trusting relationship, whether you are dedicated to one boyfriend, engaged, or married when you have sex for the first time, open your mind to your body's sensations. You will feel the greatest freedom to enjoy yourself if you know that you are with a partner who shares your feelings, and that you are protected against pregnancy and sexually transmitted disease. Once you are sure that you are doing what's absolutely right for you, allow yourself to relax and enjoy this give-and-take experience.

You are going to need a little more time to be aroused than your partner. **Foreplay** between the two of you may take the form of kissing, hugging, and petting or stroking each other all over—face, breasts, thighs, sex organs. (Some couples also experiment with oral sex—**fellatio**, when a girl kisses, licks, or sucks a boy's penis, and **cunnilingus**, when a boy does the same to a girl's clitoris and vulva—

but although the risk is less than with vaginal or anal intercourse, oral sex may lead to exposure to the HIV/ AIDS virus. See question on page 183.)

While you are involved in foreplay, a guy can be so turned on that he has a hard time holding back his ejaculation. The male who can control his orgasm until his female partner is fully stimulated is usually older and more experienced. Girls who are disappointed after they have made love for the first time have often been with partners who ejaculated or, in the slang term, "came" too fast. A guy, though, does not always know when a girl is ready for him to penetrate her vagina with his penis; that's why it's so important to choose someone you can talk to openly when you select a sexual partner. During lovemaking, you want to be able to tell him that you are not ready, or to let him know that he is making you feel good. Ideally, two people who are lovers are able to sexually satisfy and please each other.

If you are truly ready to be sexually active, intercourse will not physically hurt. Your body will go through changes that will allow it to accommodate a penis comfortably. How will you feel during sex? Unlike anyone else does! You will have your own unique impressions of how sex feels, and they will definitely be different than your partner's. A female is sexually aroused, first throughout her pelvic region, where pulsations begin, and then throughout her entire body. A male's sexual sensations are more concentrated in his penis.

The best way to describe what happens when you are aroused during foreplay and sexual intercourse is to explain the four phases that you and your partner go through as you experience an orgasm. Our knowledge of the events that occur during orgasm comes largely from the research of William Masters and Virginia Johnson. These two pioneers investigated sexual responses of more than six hundred women and men from ages eighteen to ninety, and reported their findings in the groundbreaking book *Human Sexual Response*.[2] They concluded that the orgasmic response has four important phases: excitement, plateau, orgasm, and resolution.

The Excitement Phase

As you become sexually aroused and excited, many parts of your body respond. Your heart beats faster and your blood pressure rises. You breathe more heavily. As excitement grows, your skin, especially your face and lips, turns rosy. Your breasts swell and your nipples become erect, hard, and sensitive to touch. Within thirty seconds after you start to become aroused, your vagina begins to moisten as blood vessels there produce a natural lubricant. Blood pulses into the vessels in the vulva, and the vagina expands and lengthens. The inner walls of your vagina, which usually touch each other, open up and the outer labia part. The vagina and entire vaginal area become wider, softer, and wetter to accommodate an erect penis. Sometimes a girl's clitoris also hardens and becomes erect. (This particular response doesn't happen to everyone.) You may stay in the excitement phase for a few minutes or more than an hour. Meanwhile, the blood flowing to your vulva also affects your uterus, which begins to lift up from the pelvic floor muscles and tilt forward.

A boy responds to sexual arousal with an erection. Blood flows to his penis, is held there by a narrowing of the blood vessels, and his penis becomes erect. At the same time, his scrotum contracts and elevates. Other re-

---

[2]William H. Masters, M.D., and Virginia E. Johnson, *Human Sexual Response* (Boston: Little, Brown, 1966).

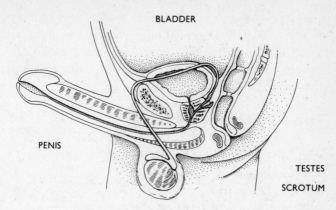

BLADDER

PENIS

TESTES

SCROTUM

23. Side View of Male Internal Organs During Erection.

sponses are just like yours: his heart beats faster, his blood pressure rises, and he breathes more rapidly and heavily. Although your breasts and nipples may become extremely sensitive, his do not. If you consciously rub or manipulate a boy's breast area, occasionally his nipples may harden, but most of the time they are not likely to change.

The Plateau Phase

These are the moments just before orgasm. Your breasts, nipples, and the surrounding areolae continue to swell from a rush of blood to the area. An areola can widen to the point of engulfing a nipple. You may feel hot and sweaty. Your heart beats even faster than it did in the excitement phase, and your blood pressure continues to rise. The upper two-thirds of your vagina balloons out and lengthens. The labia deepen in color as they become ever more engorged with blood. The vagina looks something like a balloon in the plateau phase, because while the upper two-thirds expand, the lower third narrows to form an entrance that can squeeze and excite a

UTERUS

SCROTUM

PENIS

VAGINA

BUTTOCK

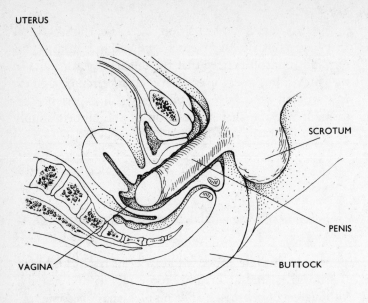

24. Side View of an Erect Penis in Relation to the Vagina, Uterus, and Other Female Organs. During intercourse the penis can thrust the uterus upward and cause pain if a girl is suffering abdominal problems, such as pelvic infection or endometriosis.

penis. The hood of the clitoris and the surrounding area swells, hiding the clitoris within. The uterus completely rises from its pelvic floor.

During the plateau phase a boy completes his erection and his penis extends to its full size. His testes become about 50 percent larger than they are when he is not sexually excited. A few drops of clear fluid, a lubricant, may leak from the head of his penis, which reddens like the labia. His pupils and yours dilate and nostrils may flare. You both feel lightheaded but are nonetheless aware that you are on the brink of orgasm.

Orgasm

When you surrender to your response, the sensations that have been escalating reach their highest point. Masters and Johnson believe that the female orgasm starts in the clitoris, but in cultures where female circumcision exists, women who have no clitorises still experience orgasm. It may be that stimulation of the clitoris simply creates a more powerful orgasm. The excited cluster of nerve endings in the clitoris links up with other organs and parts of your body, and your whole being responds to the sexual pleasure.

An orgasm, or climax, lasts ten or fifteen seconds. Your body stiffens and muscles contract all over. These squeezing contractions are quick and rhythmic, coming every eighth of a second, and in sync with the rhythm of a boy's ejaculation. You can feel the pulsation start at the base of your spine, go around your rectum, up inside your vagina, and deeper into the uterine muscles. Your uterus contracts rapidly, sending waves of pleasing sensation downward through your vagina. Your heartbeat, blood pressure, and breathing are at their highest point.

Meanwhile, a boy in orgasm ejaculates semen every eighth of a second. His contractions are so strong that he could project his semen several feet in this phase. His scrotum and testes are raised up in a contraction. His heartbeat, blood pressure, and breathing are elevated in the same way yours are. After his orgasm, he needs to rest for a bit before he can climax again. This rest period varies with age; a male needs less time between orgasms when he is young.

Unlike a male, a female can reach orgasm again and again if she continues to be stimulated. How an orgasm feels to you, whether you have none, one, or several orgasms during sexual intercourse, depends upon the

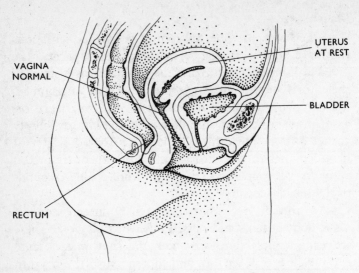

UTERUS
AT REST

VAGINA
NORMAL

BLADDER

RECTUM

25. Side View of Female Organs During Nonsexual Activity.
The uterus and the vagina are in their resting states.

amount of stimulation you receive and what's going on
in your mind at the time. Sexual intercourse and the
phases of orgasm are closely connected to your feelings.
Sexual satisfaction and pleasure are greatest with a partner
whom you know well and trust deeply.

The Resolution Phase

Your body takes about a half hour to return to normal. The uterine and vaginal contractions subside, and
your uterus goes back to its resting state. The clitoris also
returns to its usual position, and the blood that has been
coloring and swelling the vulva drains away from the area.
Heartbeat, blood pressure, and breathing drop back down,
and you may feel sleepy.

A boy's body goes through similar changes. His erection disappears, his testes relax, and his body rhythms

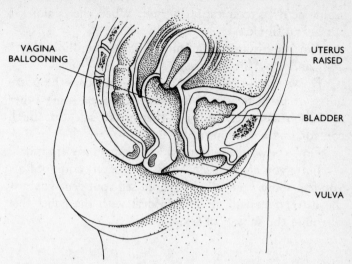

VAGINA
BALLOONING

UTERUS
RAISED

BLADDER

VULVA

*26. Side View of Female Organs During Orgasm. When
vaginal contractions are experienced, the vagina balloons out,
and during abdominal orgasmic contractions, the uterus
raises up. These changes can clearly be felt during orgasm.*

slow to their regular patterns. A boy also feels pleasantly
tired.

After orgasm, a couple shares a special closeness and
serenity. This is the time to be embracing someone you
love and trust, someone who understands that once you
are sexually involved, you are much more emotionally
vulnerable.

QUESTIONS ABOUT BOYS AND SEX

When it comes to sex, my teenage patients often are in
battle with their bodies, their brains, and the wishes of
their boyfriends. I advise each girl who is thinking about

sexual activity to question herself. When she is alone, I ask her to think:

Am I in a supportive, nurturing relationship?

Can I trust his judgment?

Do we both understand the consequences—the possibility of pregnancy and catching AIDS or some other sexually transmitted disease—that make safe sex, birth control, and a condom necessary?

Do I know what effect sex will have on my emotions?

How you handle sexual activity is a reflection of how you feel about yourself. The more self-confident you are, the better you will be able to deal with the issues that surround the subject of sex.

DOES A CONDOM MAKE SEX LESS FUN FOR A GUY?

My boyfriend doesn't want to wear a condom. He says that it cuts down on the feelings. Does a condom make sex less fun for a guy? What kind of feelings does he get, anyway? I don't want to make love without a condom because I'm afraid of getting pregnant or catching a disease. What should I do? I think I'm in love with him and I want to be with him, but the condom thing is a problem.

Eliza J., age 17

Eliza seems to understand that the use of condoms is highly recommended to prevent pregnancy and the possibility of catching AIDS or some other sexually transmitted disease (see Chapter 8, *The Scary World of Sexually Transmitted Diseases*). I have the feeling that she is contemplating sexual activity for the first time but that her boyfriend is already sexually experienced. How else would he know that wearing a condom reduces his feelings? And frankly, I don't agree with him.

Today's condoms are so thin and flexible that they really do not lessen the friction that leads to sexual pleasure. What Eliza's boyfriend is talking about, I believe, is a decrease in sexual pleasure because sex cannot be spontaneous. He cannot freely follow his sensations to the point of orgasm when he uses a condom. Instead, he must interrupt lovemaking to put the condom on, and then he risks losing his concentration on the sexual act because he is worried about the condom slipping off.

Eliza's boyfriend wants to be spontaneous, but his request is rather selfish. He seems to care only about uninterrupted pleasure and not about pregnancy, diseases, or Eliza's state of mind. Sexual intercourse is only one way for a girl and a guy to show that they love each other. In a good relationship, two people express their love by caring about each other in many ways. It should be important to Eliza's boyfriend to see her relaxed and happy in every situation; instead, he is making her anxious.

The two of them should talk openly and honestly with each other. If Eliza's boyfriend does not want to use protection, she might reconsider her relationship with him. He should be willing to be responsible toward her and enjoy being with her. Many boys accept the notion of using condoms. They say that they like participating in birth control. The protective value of condoms is so high that some states are now permitting high schools to distribute free condoms to students.

In the end, the issue of how much Eliza and her boyfriend share a mutual respect may be more important than their conflict over condoms. In general, if a girl does not sense that a guy carefully considers her opinions and wishes, she ought to be questioning why she wants to be sexually intimate with him. The sexual act is an experience to be shared by two people who understand, trust, and respect each other.

IS IT SAFE TO MAKE LOVE WHEN I HAVE MY PERIOD?
*I recently started having sex with my boyfriend. This month he
wanted to do it when I still had my period; it was at the end
when it wasn't too messy. Although I felt it was probably a
good time because I wouldn't get pregnant, I said no because
I thought that with the bleeding there might be more chance
of catching AIDS. I don't really think either one of us has AIDS,
though. Anyway, since I wasn't sure I didn't do it, but I want
to know from you. Is it safe to make love when I have my
period?*

Penny W., age 16

Many girls often feel sexually turned-on during the
last few days of their periods, after the fatigue and cramping are gone. Yet two conflicting myths exist in relation
to sex at this time:

1. that menstrual blood increases the possibility of
catching a sexually transmitted disease, so sex during menstruation is a bad idea, and

2. that a girl won't get pregnant if she has sex during
her period, so sex at that time is a good idea.

The facts are:

• Menstrual blood does not increase a girl's chances
of catching a sexually transmitted disease—the risk exists
all the time, which is why a condom must always be
used.

• A girl *can* get pregnant if she has sexual intercourse
during her period. Although a girl's peak time is in
the middle of her cycle when she is ovulating (see
Chapter 5, *Once a Month: What Really Happens!*), ir-

regular cycles and the unpredictable life span of sperm mean that any time she has sex without contraception, she can get pregnant.

• There are no absolutely "safe" days for sex as far as pregnancy is concerned.

HOW DO I KNOW IF I'M READY?

I've had the same boyfriend for over a year. There have been some rocky times, but we have a pretty good relationship. Now he thinks that it's time for us to be closer, to make love. In a way, he's right, but I'm still reluctant. How do I know if I'm ready? I want to be sure. I've lived through my parents' divorce and I don't want to make their mistakes. I want to know that I'm going to stay with the person I sleep with. What do I do?

Lola M., age 18

If a girl questions whether she is ready for sexual intimacy, she should wait. Lola is reluctant and it's clear that she wants her first sexual experience to be with a young man who sincerely cares for her. Many girls, whether their parents are divorced or happily married, feel the same way Lola does.

Lola's fears can lead her to learn more about her boyfriend. She should confide in him, tell him about her hesitation, and say that she would be more comfortable waiting. If he does care deeply for her, he will be patient. Sometimes a guy pushes for sex because he thinks that after going out for a while sex is the thing to do, but even he isn't ready. Lola's boyfriend may be grateful to her for wanting to wait. On the other hand, if he pushes even harder for sex, she should question whether she wants a relationship with someone who does not respect her wishes.

Sexual intercourse is only part of a relationship, but it is an intense part that touches many emotions. No one can tell a girl when she is "ready" for sex, and age does not make a difference. Half of the teenagers in this country are having sex, but that means that half of them are saying no. There is no one right time for intimacy. My hope is that the teenagers who are sexually active because they truly believe they are in important relationships are using birth control and condoms to protect themselves from pregnancy and diseases, and are able to handle the emotional side effects.

Only Lola herself can know when she has the maturity to make love with protection and to cope with the emotional ups and downs of a love/sex relationship. She may experience great ecstasy from sex, but on the other hand, she may feel possessive and vulnerable, which is normal. There's also the possibility that sometime after they have been sexually intimate, Lola and her boyfriend may break up. Is she strong enough to handle whatever fate has in store? Lola might find that by discussing her feelings with a best friend or an older sister, she can sharpen her sense of herself. When she is ready, she will be self-assured and not reluctant.

DOES YOUR VAGINA SHRINK UP IF YOU DON'T HAVE SEX?

I don't go out much and I don't have the problem of guys pressuring me to have sex. A girlfriend and I were talking and she said that when girls don't have sex, their vaginas shrink up when they're older. Then they can't have sex even if they want to. Is this true? Does your vagina shrink up if you don't have sex?

Miranda Z., age 15

The vagina is an elastic organ that can be so tight you cannot even fit a finger into the vaginal opening, or so expansive that a baby passes through. The vagina's ability to narrow and widen remains throughout your lifetime. Whenever you are sexually stimulated, the vagina moistens and opens up by itself.

MY BOYFRIEND WANTS TO HAVE ORAL SEX, BUT I DON'T. WHAT DO I DO?

My boyfriend isn't pushing me into intercourse. He says that oral sex will be enough for him, but I don't want to do it. I just don't like the idea of it. What do I do? Lately we can't talk without fighting.

Nora K., age 17

Oral sex, when partners use their mouths to stimulate their penis and vulva, often enhances foreplay and gives great pleasure to couples who have long-term, trusting relationships. Nora's boyfriend would like her to engage in fellatio, which means kissing, licking, or sucking his penis. (Cunnilingus is when a male stimulates the vulva and clitoris the same way.) For a girl and a guy to relax and enjoy the intimacy of oral sex, strong ties ought to exist between them—then oral sex pleases each of them equally. There is a risk, however.

Although a girl cannot become pregnant from oral sex, she could contract AIDS. If she has a tiny cut in or around her mouth, and an infected partner leaks semen during oral sex, the virus might enter her body through the cut. For this reason, doctors recommend that a male wear a condom, which might not be pleasing to either partner.

If Nora has tried telling her boyfriend that oral sex

doesn't turn her on and he continues to press her into performing this risky act, she ought to rethink her relationship. Why does he feel that oral sex is so necessary? Two people can express their love for each other by kissing, hugging, and touching in many ways. If he is pushing her to engage in a sexual activity that she does not want, it may be time for her to distance herself from him. In good relationships, a boy considers a girl's emotions and respects her wishes.

I REALLY LIKE THIS GUY, BUT HE SAYS HE'LL LEAVE ME IF I DON'T HAVE SEX WITH HIM SOON.

I could not believe my luck this year. The best-looking guy in the school started paying attention to me, and now we're constantly together. I really like this guy, but he says he'll leave me if I don't have sex with him soon. He's had a few girlfriends before me and he's experienced. I did have sex once before, so it wouldn't be the first time for me. After a while, I got bored with my last boyfriend, but this guy is really exciting. I don't want to lose him, but I'm worried because my friends say that sleeping with him is sleeping with all his girlfriends—you don't know what he's got! I'm torn.

Terri S., age 16

I understand how seductive this good-looking guy can be for Terri, especially since her last relationship seemed dull. If he is as experienced as she says he is, he probably uses the same strategy over and over. He seems to sweep a girl off her feet and then make sexual demands. Since she is hesitant about becoming more intimate, Terri ought to wait and find out whether he wants a full relationship or an isolated act of sexual intercourse. As I've mentioned throughout this chapter, if a girl feels that she isn't ready for sex, she should tell her partner. If Terri confides in her new boyfriend and he follows through on his threat to break up, then he probably was not looking for a dedicated relationship and would have broken up with her anyway. He might have waited until after Terri agreed to sleep with him to say good-bye, and then she would have felt worse.

There's some truth to what her friends are saying about "sleeping with all his girlfriends." If a guy does not always use a condom, he can pick up a sexually transmitted disease and pass it on. Of course, I would hope that Terri would only agree to intercourse with a condom, which would reduce her chances of being exposed to disease. A guy who has a reputation for sleeping around, though, is not a person a girl can bet on for either a lasting relationship or good health.

Terri ought to be strong and follow her instinct to postpone her boyfriend's request for sex. If he responds to her wishes with understanding, then he might truly care for her. As a rule, though, a boy does not make threats against a girl he likes.

MY GIRLFRIEND WAS RECENTLY DATE RAPED, AND I'M THINKING IF IT COULD HAPPEN TO HER, IT COULD HAPPEN TO ME. HOW CAN I MAKE MYSELF SMARTER?
My girlfriend was fixed up with a guy to go to a party. During the party, they went out for a walk and since he lived nearby, they stopped in at his house. His parents weren't home and they drank some of his father's vodka. When she wanted to go back to the party, he blocked the door and wouldn't let her leave. He pushed himself against her and forced her to have sex. I think that if it happened to her, maybe it could happen to me. She's not a wild person, but she was having a good time and she liked this guy. I might have done the same thing. How can I make myself smarter? How do you know when someone

is going to force himself on you later on, when he's being nice
when you first meet him?

Toni R., age 17

It's very hard to understand how someone you know,
whether he's a new date, a steady boyfriend, or a casual
acquaintance, can also be a rapist. Yet the statistics on
rape are astonishing. A woman is raped every three minutes in the United States, and more than four out of five
rape victims know their attackers. Your guard is down
when you're with someone familiar and you may not
realize the way events are unfolding around you, that a
"nice guy" is becoming a monster.

There is nothing that Toni's girlfriend did that gave
her date the right to rape her. In fact, nothing a girl does,
says, or wears ever gives anyone the *right* to assault her
sexually. In no way is a girl who has been raped at fault.
Yet having said that, there are a few things I can give
Toni and every girl to think about now, while there's
time to think ahead:

• There's a strong connection between the use of alcohol and drugs and sexual assaults, so you ought to be
extremely careful if you are in a place where people are
drinking or taking drugs. The safest thing to do, of course,
is not to take any yourself.

• If you feel slightly intoxicated or high, don't agree
to be alone with a guy. Alcohol and drugs weaken your
ability to make sensible decisions.

• Don't be afraid to speak out. You can send
mixed signals when you say no with a smile. A guy can
interpret an awkward smile or a quiet move as an act to
tease him. There's nothing like the spoken word from
you to let a guy know his limits—in other words, *your*
limits.

• Trust your instincts. If you're uncomfortable, then

something is probably not right. You can say what you're feeling and leave.

• Always be able to get home alone. It's also a good idea to have an arrangement with your parents so you can telephone them to pick you up at any time.

• On your first date with someone, plan to spend the evening at a public place, such as a movie, a concert, or a mall. You might even consider going out with a group of friends.

• There are many opinions about what you should do if you feel you are being overpowered by a much stronger male. Since each situation is different, there is no guaranteed course of action. Some women have told their attackers they have AIDS to try to stop them. Other women have made a lot of noise, or poked an attacker in the eye, or kicked him hard in the groin, or thrown up on him.

Giselle Harrington, who is the director of health promotion at Barnard College Student Health Services in New York, tells me, "There are some cases of date rape where it really is impulsive, but then there are guys who have told me that they have planned it out. They know, 'Tonight I'm going to have sex.' They don't say, 'I'm going to rape somebody.' They never say that. And if you ask, 'Did you rape her?' They say, 'No.' If you say, 'Did you force her to have sex?' they answer, 'Yes.' They don't see the two as the same thing."

A GUY I KNOW SAYS THAT HE IS SEXUALLY PRESSURED BY GIRLS. IS HE KIDDING?

I have a friend, a guy, and we talk about everything. He's not my boyfriend, just a good friend. Recently we got into a conversation about sex and he told me that he is sexually pressured by girls. He said that he did it with a girl who pressured him

IF IT HAPPENS TO YOU . . .

The single most important thing a rape victim can do is tell someone—parents, the police, a friend, a rape crisis center, a counselor. Don't isolate yourself, don't feel guilty, and don't just try to ignore it. Rape, whether by a stranger or someone you know, is a violation of your body and your trust.

• Do not shower, wash, douche, or change your clothes, even though that's your immediate reaction. If you choose to press charges, the rapist's semen, evidence of the rape, will be available.
• Seek medical attention. You can go to an emergency room of a hospital. Many hospitals have a rape crisis intervention team that can immediately take over.
• You may have internal injuries.
• You can have tests to see whether you have contracted a sexually transmitted disease.
• You may be given a morning-after pill if you want one. (See Chapter 7 for more about the morning-after pill.)
• Follow-up tests can be done for pregnancy.
• Seek counseling. All rape victims usually feel rage, guilt, anger, and helplessness. The best way to handle these emotions is to talk with sympathetic friends and family or counselors from a rape crisis center, mental health agency, or a women's clinic.

and then dropped him afterward. Is he kidding? This sounds like a girl's side of the story.

Gracellen P., age 14

He may not be kidding. In questionnaires that I've distributed in high schools, boys have frankly written that they have had sexual pressure from girls. I was surprised to learn this myself, but it seems that some girls may be more impatient to become sexually active than some boys.

A mature young man does not want to be treated like a sex object any more than a girl does. The girl who sexually pressures a boy because she is impatient to "get it over with" risks losing a relationship that involves friendship, understanding, trust, and respect—this kind of relationship is slower to build, but it endures. When speedy sex takes the lead, a relationship can become unhealthy.

MODERN ROMANCE

In the days before birth control pills, boys used to "court" girls by taking them out, buying them presents, and patiently waiting to get to "first base,' which usually meant a good-night kiss. Then came the Pill and the sexual freedoms of the sixties and seventies. Men and women who hardly knew each other's names went to bed together. By the early eighties, even before AIDS had become a well-known issue, many people felt that impersonal sex was unsatisfying. Couples sought emotional intimacy before sexual intimacy.

The desire to have a steady relationship with a partner and to understand his personality before you have sexual relations remains the way to fulfillment. The chance of catching the deadly AIDS virus and other diseases through sex gives this approach to relationships a "necessary" feel, but necessary or not, the slower, more romantic development of emotional intimacy is more rewarding. The longer you know someone, the more you can understand his feelings for you, and yours for him. In the long run, trust and affection still beat physical sex as the greatest turn-ons.

CHAPTER SEVEN

When You're Ready
for Sex,
What Birth Control Is Safe?

There is no deadline for "losing your virginity." Sexual activity will not make you a smarter or better person; it is simply the natural way two people deepen their already close relationship. Do you have such a relationship? Trust needs time to develop and until you are in a trusting, time-tested situation, there is no rush to become sexually active. Saying no is still the best way to keep your head clear, and it remains the world's most effective birth control. Of course, the pressure from your own hormones and the world around you can make you shrug and say, "Oh, what's the big deal? I might as well do it." Don't do anything you haven't carefully considered.

So often girls say that they have "unexpected sex," with no time to prepare, so they don't have a chance to use birth control. In a good relationship, you and your boyfriend respect each other and want to talk about sex and birth control beforehand, so that no one gets hurt later on. I know it's true that many of you are having "unexpected sex," but I also know that many of you are extremely anxious afterwards. I talk to girls who are counting the days to make sure their periods come on time, and hoping that they did not expose themselves to AIDS, which could kill them, or a sexually transmitted disease that could make them sterile and unable to have babies when they're older.

If you feel mature enough to handle sexual intimacy in a long-term relationship, you and your guy ought to talk about birth control *before* you become passionate. Should kissing and hugging shift into overdrive before your conversation about protection, then you must not be embarrassed to interrupt the "moment" to get a few things straight. If you feel embarrassed, you ought to ask yourself why. Are you with a guy who is not completely accepting of you? If so, why are you having sex with him?

WHO STARTS THE CONVERSATION ABOUT BIRTH CONTROL?

It doesn't matter who brings up the subject of birth control first, just as long as somebody does. Of course, you'd like a guy to make the first move. You probably have imagined the perfect boyfriend: he shows his concern by asking you if you are protected, and says that he has no problem using a condom. Unfortunately, the perfect boyfriend usually doesn't make the transition from imagination to real life.

Teenage girls are emotionally more mature than teenage boys, so your response to sexual intercourse is going to be more realistic than his. Also, you're the one whose body can conceive and give birth to a baby. As explained in Chapter 5, your body prepares itself for pregnancy every month. If you have sex without birth control, it's a surprise if you *don't* get pregnant. You can wait for him to mention birth control, but don't wait until you're both so excited that you lose your opportunity to have worry-free sex.

When sex is on the agenda—and you usually know when that is—confide in him. Briefly and directly tell him whether you're prepared with contraception. Perhaps you have to insert foam, a sponge, or a diaphragm. Let him know that that's what you're going to do. Ask him if he has a condom, which he must use for two reasons: to give you double protection against pregnancy, and to keep you both safe from exposure to AIDS and other sexually transmitted diseases (STDs). If you say you're on the Pill, he might think you have nothing to worry about and that you're both home free, but you're not. Only a condom can greatly reduce your risk of catching an STD, and you both must agree to use it in addition to your birth control.

YOU'RE ALREADY SMARTER ABOUT BIRTH CONTROL

Half of you are sexually active by the time you are eighteen years old, but when you become sexually active, half of you do not use birth control your "first time." That's what we doctors have heard for a long time, but now it seems that you're getting smarter about protecting yourselves. Researchers at the Alan Guttmacher Institute compared sexual behavior and contraceptive use in 1982 and 1988, in women fifteen to forty-four years old. After looking at the latest figures, they reported that in 1988 teenage girls were having sex more than ever, but they were being more careful than they were in 1982. Instead of half, nearly two-thirds of the teenage girls who were sexually active used birth control the first time they had intercourse. If other studies continue to report the same good news, then you're taking charge at last!

Still, over one million teenage girls in the United States become pregnant every year—that's one out of every ten girls—and half of them conceive within six months of their first sexual intercourse. So every year more than one million pregnant teenagers are faced with either a lifetime commitment to parenthood, giving up a baby for adoption, or an abortion. With birth control, you won't have to be in such an awful position. Birth control gives you some control over your destiny. Pregnancy wrecks your plans.

THE BEST BIRTH CONTROL FOR YOU

Although there are many types of birth control, when you are young and have never given birth, your choices are:

• the Pill, or
• barrier methods of contraception: the cervical cap or the diaphragm with spermicidal creams or jellies, the sponge, vaginal film, foams, foaming tablets, suppositories, and for your partner, condoms.

If used properly, the Pill offers 99.9 percent protection against pregnancy. That protection can drop to 94 percent, however, if pills are not taken on schedule. The Pill is the most effective contraceptive available, but girls who are sexually active only once in a while often shy away from a 'round-the-clock birth control method. Since many girls also feel that the Pill may give them acne, sore breasts, mood swings, or make them fat, they turn against it for those reasons. Since a lot of girls feel great on the Pill, you cannot know how you will respond. (The Pill and the other methods of birth control are described more fully later on in the chapter.)

The diaphragm and cervical cap are two contraceptives, which used with spermicidal creams or jellies, offer 82 to 94 percent protection, depending upon whether a girl is using them correctly. These are the second best methods of preventing pregnancy. Like the Pill, they require prescriptions, and it takes a little practice for a girl to be able to insert them into her vagina easily.

The sponge gives 76 to 92 percent protection against pregnancy, depending upon how properly a girl uses it, and it's somewhat easier to handle than a diaphragm or a cervical cap. The other barrier methods, such as film, foams, foaming tablets, and suppositories, are less effective alone (about 80 percent protection) than with condoms. Use any of these contraceptives with a condom, though, and your protection will equal the Pill's.

The condom, which can give up to 98 percent contraceptive protection (if you use a spermicide-containing brand perfectly), is a special case. It's not just a method of birth control, but a protection against exposure to sexually transmitted diseases. And if you become sexually active, no matter how old you are, you must use a condom. Do you have to use a condom until you're married and want to become pregnant? It's a question I have been asked.

If we lived in an ideal world in which everyone told the truth and you could be sure that someone with whom you wanted to become sexually intimate had never had sexual relations with anyone else, had never used drugs with needles, and you were absolutely certain of his personal history, then you still would have to wait before you could stop using a condom. At the beginning and end of a six-month interval, you would each have to have a blood test for AIDS which shows "negative" HIV re-sults. Finally, you would need your doctor's approval to have sex without a condom . . . but . . . *Your life is at risk and we do not live in an ideal world. You cannot know the truth about a person's health and sexual history or sexual future, so a condom is a must in sexual relationships.*

This means, though, that a condom is part of your love life for a long time. In fact, before you read further to find the right contraceptive for you, you should know everything about condoms.

THE CONDOM: TWO KINDS OF PROTECTION IN ONE WRAPPER

A condom is a sheath for an erect penis. Most condoms are made of thin latex rubber, although some of them are made from the intestinal tissue of sheep. The condom originally was used for prevention against venereal dis-ease. It gained notoriety as a contraceptive device only when a Dr. Condom supplied England's King Charles II with methods to prevent illegitimate children. Then the infamous lover Casanova made it essential equipment for a sexual rendezvous!

While the latex condom still traps sperm and prevents pregnancy, it has had a comeback as a protector against sexually transmitted diseases. Today there are about thirty STDs, with the fatal AIDS virus the most serious, and condoms keep them away from you.

The Best Kind of Condom to Use. When Georgia, an eighteen-year-old girl who was about to be-come sexually active, asked me which was the best con-dom to recommend to her boyfriend, I realized that even older teens just don't know the difference between brands. I feel that **the type of condom that offers the greatest**

BIRTH CONTROL: HOW WELL DOES IT WORK?*

Method	% Reliability (Used Perfectly)	% Reliability (Used Typically— Not Always Correctly)
The Pill	99.9	94
Condom	98	84
Diaphragm	94	82
Cervical Cap	94	82
Sponge	92	76
Spermicides	97	70
(including vaginal film, foams, creams, jellies, foaming tablets, vaginal suppositories)		

*Source: The Alan Guttmacher Institute

protection against pregnancy and exposure to a sexually transmitted disease is one made of thin latex, lubricated with the sperm-killer nonoxynol-9. Why? The
uniformly manufactured latex condoms block the smallest microbes, while the natural condoms made from a
sheep's intestinal tissue may have porous, weak spots. As
for nonoxynol-9, this spermicide increases the antipreg-
nancy factor of a condom, and also kills the bacteria that
cause gonorrhea, syphilis, and chlamydia. Condoms that
are lubricated with gels or silicone-based products do not
destroy living organisms.

A Note About Lubricating Condoms. Never
try to give more lubricating power to a condom with oils
or oil-based products. In less than a minute a lubricant
with oil, such as baby oil (like Johnson's), mineral oil,

THE WAY TO USE A CONDOM:

BEFORE SEXUAL INTERCOURSE

1. Always use a *new* condom when you are going to have sex, and think ahead. Make sure that the condom goes on *before a penis gets near your vagina or any other body opening*—this means that you must remember the condom *before* foreplay, before a boy might possibly leak fluid from his penis. Even a drop or two of semen leaking from a boy's penis can expose you to pregnancy and infection.

2. A condom can go on as soon as a boy's penis is erect and hard. One or the other of you should place the rolled-up ring of the condom over the head of his penis. The roll stays on the outside.

3. Leave room, about a half-inch or so, at the tip of the condom to collect the semen from his orgasm. The next step is to pinch the tip of the condom to release the air inside. One of you should then hold the tip while he is unrolling the condom down the shaft of the penis to the pubic hair. If the condom does not unroll easily, it's on wrong and ought to be thrown away. Unwrap a new condom and start over.

AFTER ORGASM

A boy should pull out while his penis is still erect and hard. While holding the condom in place on his penis, he should slowly withdraw. He should turn his body completely away from you before he loosens his grip on the condom. Then he can remove the condom and discard it. If the semen in the condom leaks on you at any point quickly wash it away with soap and water.

REMEMBER:

• A condom should not come in contact with oil of any kind—no Vaseline or other petroleum jelly, no baby oil, no mineral oil, no vegetable oil, not even talcum powder. Oil rots rubber condoms. (If you want lubrication, you can buy a water-based lubricant jelly in a drugstore.)
• A condom should be smooth and flexible. A condom that feels stiff or sticky, even if it's new, should be thrown away. Unwrap a fresh, undamaged condom.
• Unused condoms should be kept in a cool dry place, not in a wallet or warm pocket of a coat.

---

27. Proper Use of a Condom. The successful use of a condom depends upon how it is handled. Both a girl and a boy should know how to use a condom correctly. ILLUSTRATION
USED WITH PERMISSION OF PLANNED PARENTHOOD OF NEW YORK CITY, INC.

petroleum jelly (like Vaseline), cold cream, and hand or body lotions (like Nivea and Lubriderm), can make a condom leak. The safe lubricants are water-based: K-Y Lubricating Jelly, Today Personal Lubricant, Corn Huskers Lotion, and any spermicidal cream or jelly made for use with a diaphragm or a cervical cap.

A condom may have a plain or a reservoir tip, which is a nipple end that collects the semen and is a helpful design. Condoms may be contoured, ribbed, nubbed, or colored, but none of these features is as important as the two I mentioned earlier: (1) thin latex, (2) lubricated with nonoxynol-9.

If you are in a sexually intimate relationship and you feel more secure buying and keeping a condom with you, just in case your boyfriend forgets his, don't worry about whether you have to know his size. **Condoms only come in one size.** They stretch to fit.

How to Be Sure Your Boyfriend Is Using a Condom Correctly. Condoms are rolled up and sealed in individual wrappers. An unsealed packet can mean that a condom is damaged. If a condom is discolored, sticky, dry, or cracked, don't use it. A quality condom is soft and pliant. During sexual activity, after your boyfriend has an erection, he breaks open the wrapper, holds the tip of the condom, and unrolls the sheath to the base of his penis. He might fumble because he's inexperienced, but it's important that you support the responsible role he is taking in contraception. If the condom has a plain tip, he must leave about a half-inch free at the end to collect the semen. If the condom has a reservoir tip, he must press the tip to eliminate air bubbles.

Sometimes a well-placed condom can still fall off a penis during the thrusting action of intercourse. A boy should always use his fingers to hold the lower end of the condom at the base of his penis during intercourse, and especially during ejaculation. Then you both can have peace of mind because the sperm will definitely be contained. After he ejaculates, while continuing to hold the base of the condom, he must withdraw while he is still erect. If he lets his penis go limp before he withdraws, the condom might slip off and sperm might escape. Good timing is absolutely necessary for effective birth control with a condom. Since there is a fall-off factor and the possibility of leaks and tears with condoms, a girl should use additional birth control, whether it's the Pill or other barrier contraceptives, such as a diaphragm or cervical cap with spermicidal creams or jellies, a sponge, film, foams, tablets, or suppositories. When you use one of these contraceptives with a condom, you are about 98 percent protected against pregnancy. Remember: **For maximum protection, a condom should not be used alone!**

THE BIG QUESTION GIRLS ASK: WHAT DO I DO WHEN A GUY DOESN'T WANT TO USE A CONDOM?

So many girls want to know what to do if a guy simply refuses to wear a condom, or says that he will but then doesn't want to interrupt lovemaking to put one on. Since a condom is the only barrier between good health and the possibility of catching viruses that remain in your body for the rest of your life—such as AIDS, which can kill you, herpes, which can cause blindness in your babies during childbirth, and venereal warts, which can lead to cervical cancer—I am always shocked that teenagers think there is a choice here.

I tell every girl who asks that if a guy does not want to use a condom, she should not become sexually involved with him. To do so is to court catastrophe. When it comes to condoms, you have no choice. Your

se. It comes in various sizes and the
e version that's right for you. If you
not use a speculum at all but examine
he does use a speculum, it should be
y about asking him to take the chill

a speculum or a swab, a doctor takes
for a Pap test. (See Chapter 8 for a
n of the Pap test.) From that smear,
e to determine infections, sexually
precancerous conditions, and cervi-
ing the Pap smear, the doctor moves
internal organs.

dex and middle fingers of one of his
ina until he reaches the space behind
umb remains on the outside of the
nd rests on your abdomen. It's your
By moving his hands and gently press-
he can outline the shape and size of
ess its position. He can also examine
ubes and tell whether there are any
necologist is trained to conduct an
n with great sensitivity. At no time
y pain. Your internal examination
tly and slowly, and you should feel
ctor any questions about what he is

been examined and are dressed, your
with you about birth control. The
ap test will show whether you have
roblems. As long as you are healthy,
is a matter of your age, lifestyle, and
our doctor may suggest birth control
prescription, or birth control you can

these different types of birth control

choice is in the type of birth control you want to use
with a condom.

WHEN YOU CHOOSE
YOUR BIRTH CONTROL

The first few years after your period starts, you usually
have irregular cycles. At the same time, you are at the
peak of your fertility—you can easily become pregnant.
When you feel you are ready to become sexually active
and to decide upon a type of birth control, remember to
let your irregular cycles, high fertility, age, and personal
situation influence your choice.

For instance, I do not even suggest natural family
planning for birth control to my teenage patients, because
there are no "safe" days for sex when cycles are unpredictable. Your high fertility means that unless you want
to be pregnant, you must *always* use contraception, because you are more likely to conceive than an older
woman. At this time of your life, you want the most
effective contraception, but you can still choose the
method most appropriate to your personality and sexual
activity.

If you are a disciplined girl, familiar with your body
and comfortable touching yourself vaginally, the diaphragm, cervical cap, or sponge may be right for you.
Your age and the extent of your sexual activity are important to your choice. If you are a young teen who is
only going to be sexually active once in a while, you can
be protected on those occasions by contraceptive foam,
foaming tablets, or vaginal suppositories with a condom.
On the other hand, if you are older than sixteen and your
sexual activity is frequent, you might benefit from the
full-time protection of a low-dose birth control pill.

My best advice is to see a doctor when you start your

decision-making. If you have a close relationship with your mother, she might help you choose the birth control that suits you, but a gynecologist in private practice or in a family planning clinic can examine you, answer questions you may have about sexual activity, and suggest a contraceptive that is compatible with your feelings and lifestyle.

Of course, once you become sexually active you have an adult responsibility to take care of your health. Whatever your birth control, you should visit a doctor or a family planning clinic every six months for a contraception consultation, Pap test, and examination for sexually transmitted diseases.

VISITING A PRIVATE DOCTOR OR A FAMILY PLANNING CLINIC

A visit to a gynecologist is a normal first step in the process of choosing birth control. Your parents have always selected your doctor for you, and your mother may be the best person to talk to right now. She may know a physician who will care for you properly. I realize that some girls might be hesitant to bring up the subject of birth control with their mothers, but birth control is easier to understand if you discuss it with someone you trust, if not your mother, then an aunt, an older sister, or a close family friend.

Whether you decide to go to your mother's gynecologist or visit a doctor at a Planned Parenthood or other family planning clinic, a high school clinic, or a clinic run by a woman's health collective (listed under "clinics" in the yellow pages of your local telephone directory), ask your mother or a close friend to accompany you. It's more comfortable going to the doctor with moral support. By the way, the fee at a clinic is usually lower than

at a doctor
insurance t

Is this
you may n
gowned in
not nude.
tory either
office. Do
whether or
give you g
answers.

Before
bladder an
internal or
cup to be
indicate d
checks yo

The
neck to b
and that
checks yo
sually exa
of excessi
nal an ab
monal in
doing th
stand wh
exam.

You
your kn
feet in t
doctor si
on your
a small
inside th
uterus.

which open a
doctor can sel
are a virgin, he
you with a sw
warm. Don't
off if it's cold.)

Whether he
a cervical scrap
complete expla
a laboratory i
transmitted dise
cal cancer. Afte
on to examine

He inserts t
hands into your
your cervix. Hi
vulva. His othe
job to stay relaxe
ing on the orga
your uterus and
your ovaries an
abnormalities. A
internal examina
should you feel
should be done
free to ask your
doing.

After you ha
doctor can cons
examination plus
any gynecologica
your birth contr
personal situation
that is available b
buy in a drugstore

A description

immediately follows. You might want to read through these pages to be well informed during your visit to the gynecologist. Also, remember that if the birth control you choose causes difficulty—some boys, for example, are irritated by contraceptive foam—you can always switch to something else.

BIRTH CONTROL YOU CAN GET WITH A DOCTOR'S PRESCRIPTION: THE BIRTH CONTROL PILL

The Pill is the perfect birth control for a girl who is sexually active with her boyfriend on a regular basis. Yet time after time girls tell me that they do not want to take the Pill because they think it causes cancer, or they're afraid they will get fat. These are two big misconceptions held over from the days when birth control pills had very high levels of estrogen and progesterone.

The idea behind the first birth control pill was "once a woman is pregnant she cannot get pregnant again." The early Pill gave a woman the same hormonal levels of estrogen and progesterone that she would have if she were pregnant. Those high levels of estrogen and progesterone blocked the release of the brain hormones FSH and LH, and without them, there's no ovulation. Since a girl who does not ovulate does not become pregnant, the Pill seemed to be the perfect method of birth control. The high amounts of hormones in the early birth control pills, however, caused unhealthy side effects: high blood pressure, blood clots, and cancer.

Today's birth control pills are completely different. They stop ovulation with about one-fifth the estrogen and much less progesterone than the original Pill. Refinements of the low-dose pill have led to the "mini-pill," which uses only progestin (synthetic progesterone), and

28. Birth Control Pills. Each brand of birth control pill comes in its own special packet, which is designed to help you remember every pill scheduled for your monthly cycle. Be sure to know the brand name and type of pill you are taking, in case you are away from home and must ask a new doctor for a prescription. DIALPAK™, COURTESY OF ORTHO PHARMACEUTICAL CORPORATION.

"phasic" pills, manufactured in combinations that follow your monthly hormonal changes.

   • The **mini-pill** prevents pregnancy by thickening cervical mucus so that it acts like a diaphragm.
   • Of the phasics—**biphasic and triphasic pills**—the triphasics are considered the most advanced. The triphasic pills "phase in" a varying low dosage of hormones,

in pills that are color coded for the early, middle, and late phases of your cycle.

Since today's pills can lessen menstrual cramps, regulate the menstrual cycle, and make breasts less cystic, some girls go on the Pill strictly for these effects.

The Birth Control Pill Does Not Cause Cancer. The improved, low-dose pills do not cause cancer. On the contrary, today's pills have been found to protect against two kinds of reproductive cancer—endometrial (uterine lining) and ovarian. The many studies looking for a link between the Pill and breast cancer have not made a connection among women who waited until they were at least in their twenties before they started taking the Pill. What about the women who started taking the Pill during their teens and took it for years? To answer this question, researchers at Harvard University are currently involved in a major study with over 100,000 nurses between the ages of twenty-five and forty-five who began taking low-dose pills in their teens. So far, no link between the Pill and breast cancer has been made, and instead researchers have discovered that the Pill reduces the risk of benign breast tumors.

The question of a possible association between the Pill and cervical cancer continues to surface because more abnormal Pap smears can be found among women who take the Pill. Scientists usually agree that the Pill does not cause cervical cancer but that women who are on the Pill often have sex with many partners who do not wear condoms, and that they're more exposed to sexually transmitted diseases that can lead to cervical cancer.

The bottom line is that the Pill is a safe and effective contraceptive for most teenage girls to use for a few years, with the understanding that they will always have an annual Pap test.

High Blood Pressure, Blood Clots, and the Pill. Cardiovascular problems, such as high blood pressure, blood clots, and the heart attacks and strokes that can result from these two conditions, are virtually non-existent among teens. You should know, though, that studies suggest that 1 to 5 percent of older women who take the Pill may develop high blood pressure. Also, there is still some evidence that blood clots may occur. As I mentioned, high blood pressure and blood clotting are not considered the problems of teenage girls, so the Pill still remains a good choice for you. One point to remember is that since smoking can aggravate cardiovascular conditions, a girl who is on the Pill would be wise to stop smoking. If you are a smoker who cannot quit, at the least you should cut back. A teenager on the Pill is not at as great a risk for cardiovascular problems as an older woman.

Acne, Sore Breasts, Mood Swings, Weight Gain, and the Pill. Whether you experience one or some of the less serious side effects of the Pill, such as acne, sore breasts, mood swings, and weight gain, depends upon your own hormonal makeup and how it responds to the hormones in your pills. Some girls feel wonderful on the Pill, and some feel blue. Girls who never had a pimple suddenly have complexion problems, while those who have lived with blemishes wake up to clear skin on the Pill. (See Chapter 3 for more about acne and the Pill.) Breast tenderness, moods, weight gain—some or all of these conditions may be experienced, but not with every brand of pill. Since hormonal contents vary, different pills can affect you differently. Sometimes switching to a new brand brings you back to normal. As for getting fat, yes, you may put on a few pounds, but then again, you may not. It depends on how the Pill and you get along, and once again, a different brand can make a difference. What

I am sure of is that pregnancy will make you much fatter than the Pill!

QUESTIONS ABOUT TAKING THE PILL

WHAT HAPPENS IF I MISS A DAY?
I usually take my birth control pill every morning after I brush my teeth, but I was in such a rush this morning that I forgot. My boyfriend and I haven't had a chance to have sex lately, so I don't think I have anything to worry about right now, but will I be safe if we're together in a week or so? What happens if I miss a day?

Maggie B., age 16

A girl who forgets to take her pill for a day should gulp one down the moment she remembers. Maggie must take her missed pill right away, take the next pill on schedule, and use backup birth control such as a diaphragm with spermicide, foam, or the sponge for the rest of her cycle.

One missed pill can throw off a girl's hormonal balance and birth control. If a girl forgets to take her pills for a couple of days, she's likely to ovulate. Maggie doesn't mention whether she had any breakthrough bleeding, but spotting is also a possibility when a pill is overlooked. Like clockwork, birth control pills should be taken at the same time every day.

DO ANTIBIOTICS STOP THE PILL FROM WORKING?
I've been taking antibiotics for bad bronchitis this winter and I read in a magazine that they can stop the Pill from working.

Do they? When my boyfriend and I are together, he uses a
condom and I rely on the Pill. Do I need something else now?
Naomi G., age 15

It's true that some antibiotics make the Pill less effective and you should tell your doctor if you are taking antibiotic medication. Whether the hormones from the Pill are not completely absorbed from the intestines when a girl is on certain antibiotics, or some kind of interaction between the Pill and the antibiotics blocks the Pill's hormones, the result is that you may not be getting good birth control from the Pill.

Naomi says that her boyfriend uses a condom whenever they are together, so she still has protection against pregnancy and sexually transmitted diseases while she is on her medication. At age fifteen she is so very fertile, though, that until her antibiotic treatment is over, I would like her to be extra safe and also use contraceptive foam, foaming tablets, vaginal film, or the sponge during sexual intercourse.

IS IT SAFE TO TAKE MY GIRLFRIEND'S BIRTH CONTROL PILLS?

I forgot to pack my birth control pills when I went to my girl-
friend's for the weekend. She said I could take hers, but they
were a different brand than mine. I didn't take them, but I
wonder if I could have. Is it safe to take my girlfriend's birth
control pills?

Donna N., age 17

There are dozens of different birth control pills and the kind Donna's doctor prescribed for her is the only one she should be taking. A doctor usually considers a girl's age, weight, and hormonal makeup before he selects a pill for her. A different brand can have a different hormonal balance. If Donna had taken a pill that had more hormones than hers, she might have experienced tender breasts, cramping, or headaches. If she took a pill with a lower hormonal content, then she could have ovulated during her cycle.

Donna should take an extra pill every day for as many days as she missed while she's taking her scheduled pills on time. She must also use backup contraception, such as a diaphragm with spermicide, foam, or the sponge, for the rest of her cycle. (Her boyfriend should also use a condom.) She will not be fully protected by the Pill until her next menstrual cycle and round of pill taking begin. Any girl who finds herself away from home without her pills should call her doctor and ask him to phone in a prescription to a nearby pharmacy.

THE DIAPHRAGM WITH SPERMICIDE

The diaphragm is a soft, rubber, dome-shaped device that you fill with sperm-killing jelly or cream and insert into your vagina before intercourse. A diaphragm used with spermicidal creams or jellies offers 82 to 94 percent protection.

A diaphragm rests between the rear wall of the vagina and the upper edge of the pubic bone and covers your cervix. The diaphragm sets up a physical blockade against oncoming sperm, but the sperm can still get around the diaphragm's rim. That's why a **spermicide** (sperm-killing jelly or cream) is essential. A spermicide sets up a chemical barrier and kills the sperm that are not stopped by the diaphragm itself. **A diaphragm must be used with a spermicide for top protection.**

A diaphragm comes in various sizes, so you must be fitted for one by a doctor. After the doctor positions a diaphragm for you, he'll instruct you on how to remove and reinsert the device. (If you gain or lose weight, say about ten pounds, your diaphragm may not be the right size anymore, so ask your doctor to fit you again.)

Do's and Don'ts of the Diaphragm

• You can only count on a diaphragm for birth control if you use it according to instructions.

• Before you insert a diaphragm always squeeze about a teaspoonful of contraceptive jelly or cream into the inner dome. (A spermicide with nonoxynol-9 will help prevent certain STDs from taking hold.) A thin layer of spermicide can also be spread around the rim.

• Press the diaphragm between your fingers or have it attached to an introducer, a long-handled plastic hook for inserting the diaphragm, as you get ready to put it in.

• A diaphragm must be inserted into your vagina **from no more than two hours before up until the moment of intercourse. If you insert a diaphragm with spermicide more than two hours before engaging in sexual intercourse, the contraceptive may be ineffective.**

• Don't put a diaphragm into your vagina in the morning if you're going to have sex after dinner. It won't protect you.

• If you have intercourse more than once during lovemaking, before each exposure to sperm, place more contraceptive jelly inside your vagina. (Look for contraceptive jellies and creams sold with plungers for this purpose.)

• After intercourse, you must leave a diaphragm in your vagina for **at least six hours**, which is the life span of sperm in the vaginal environment. (This may seem confusing because you might have heard that sperm can live seventy-two hours, or up to three days. Those three days are in the uterus and the Fallopian tubes, which have the perfect environment for sperm survival. The vagina is so acidic that sperm live only six hours in there.)

• Never remove a diaphragm before the six hours are up!

Be honest with yourself and understand your personality. **Only a girl who knows she will be responsible about inserting her diaphragm ahead of time, a girl who is not afraid to touch herself, should consider the diaphragm to be the right birth control for her.** If you know you'll have problems thinking ahead, or you just can't stand the idea of the diaphragm inside you, then don't use it. You owe it to yourself to find the birth control that fits your personality and then, for maximum protection, use it with a condom.

THE CERVICAL CAP WITH SPERMICIDE

Like the diaphragm, the cervical cap sets up a physical barrier against fast-moving sperm and offers the same 82 to 94 percent protection. Since sperm can cross over the rim of the cervical cap, just the way they can get over the rim of the diaphragm, you must use the cap with a spermicide so you have a chemical blockade along with the physical one.

The cervical cap has been used by European women for more than a century. It looks like a rubber thimble, with a soft latex dome and a flexible rim. The cap is smaller, deeper, and, for many women, more comfortable than a diaphragm. A diaphragm is held in place by ten-

29. The Cervical Cap. Like the diaphragm, the cervical cap sets up a physical barrier that prevents sperm from entering your uterus. Unlike the diaphragm, which is held in place by tension, the cervical cap stays put through suction.

sion, while a cap slips directly onto your cervix, where the rim forms an airtight seal. Women who have used both a diaphragm and a cervical cap often find the cap more comfortable because it doesn't put pressure on the bladder.

Since caps come in different sizes, you must be fitted by a gynecologist. After he positions the cap within you, he will show you how to remove and reinsert it.

A convenience of the spermicide-filled cap is that it may be inserted into your vagina as long as six hours before sexual intercourse. However, the cap is most effective when it is used like a diaphragm and inserted no more than two hours before intercourse. If you have more than one exposure to sperm, extra spermicidal jelly should be injected into your vagina with a plastic plunger before each exposure.

Technically, a cervical cap can remain in your vagina for forty-eight hours, but my advice is to remove it six hours after your last intercourse, wash it in warm soapy water, then dry it and powder it with cornstarch to preserve the rubber. The latex rubber used to make the cervical caps can develop an unpleasant odor if the cap lingers in your vagina.

Do's and Don'ts of the Cervical Cap

• Always fill the dome of your cap about one-fourth of the way with contraceptive jelly or cream. A spermicide with nonoxynol-9 will help to destroy bacteria that can cause certain sexually transmitted diseases.

• Squeeze the rim closed and insert the cap into your vagina and onto your cervix, as the doctor who fitted you instructed. Expect a small amount of jelly to leak out.

• Insert your cervical cap from about two hours before up until the moment of intercourse for maximum protection.

• If you have intercourse more than once during lovemaking, before each exposure to sperm, place more contraceptive jelly inside your vagina. (Look for contraceptive jellies and creams sold with plungers for this purpose.)

• After a final intercourse, a cervical cap must remain in place for at least six hours, until any sperm left in your vagina have died. (Sperm can live up to three days, or seventy-two hours, in your uterus and Fallopian tubes, which have environments perfect for their survival. The vagina's acidic environment, however, causes sperm to die in six hours.)

• Never leave a cervical cap in your vagina over forty-eight hours or you will notice an unpleasant odor. Remove the cap six hours after your final intercourse and wash it in warm soapy water, dry it and powder it with cornstarch to preserve the latex rubber. If you think you will need it again soon, reinsert it.

The cervical cap requires the same kind of "thinking ahead" that a diaphragm does. If you feel that you have the discipline to insert the cervical cap ahead of time, and you are not afraid to touch yourself, the cervical cap may be right for you.

BIRTH CONTROL YOU CAN BUY IN A DRUGSTORE: THE SPONGE

The contraceptive sponge, which gives 76 to 92 percent protection, is a soft, cushiony circle of polyurethane foam that is treated with a high concentration of spermicide with nonoxynol-9. Sperm meet the physical blockade of the sponge itself and the chemical blockade set up by the spermicide.

Made by the VLI Corporation, the Today sponge comes in only one size. You don't need a doctor to fit you. You wet the sponge with water, squeeze it, and push it up into your vagina. It expands to cover your cervix and is held in position by the walls of your vagina.

The sponge protects you for twenty-four hours, after which you remove it by pulling on the loop that crosses its diameter and hangs down. After a sponge is removed, throw it away.

Do's and Don'ts of the Sponge

• Drench a sponge with water before insertion, to release the spermicide.

• A sponge can be inserted into your vagina up to twenty-four hours before intercourse. You are protected for every exposure to sperm you have within those twenty-four hours. You do not need extra spermicide during that period.

• After your final intercourse, the sponge must remain in your vagina for at least six hours before it can be removed. After six hours, any sperm that have lingered in your vagina will be dead.

• Removing the sponge can be tricky. The sponge becomes quite slippery in your vagina, and you may have trouble getting a grip on the loop. The easiest way to get a sponge out is to squat and bear down while you pull on the loop.

VAGINAL CONTRACEPTIVE FILM

Vaginal contraceptive film (VCF) is a small, thin, translucent square. Sold in packets of twelve as small as matchbooks, a supply of VCFs is easily tossed into a purse. It is an ideal contraceptive to use in combination with a condom.

VCF contains nonoxynol-9 spermicide, and studies show that spermicides offer 70 to 97 percent protection. One square of film must be used each time you have intercourse. You place the film high inside your vagina, where it dissolves into a gel that coats the vaginal canal and chemically kills any sperm in the area. Once you insert a square of film you have two hours of birth control. If you have intercourse more than two hours after inserting a square, you must insert another one.

Do's and Don'ts of Vaginal
Contraceptive Film

• At least five, but preferably fifteen, minutes before intercourse, fold the wafer over the tip of your middle finger and place it high in your vagina, near your cervix.

• After intercourse, the film washes away with natural body fluids. No douching is needed.

• If you do want to douche, you must wait at least six hours after intercourse, to make sure all the sperm have expired.

CONTRACEPTIVE FOAMS FROM
PRESSURIZED CONTAINERS

The four major brands of foam, which offer about 70 percent protection, are Delfen, Emko, Dalkon, and Conceptrol. Delfen, Emko, and Dalkon are sold in pressurized containers, and you must remember to buy a plastic plunger the first time you purchase any one of them. Conceptrol is sold in boxes of six individual packets with disposable applicators. Choose a foam that contains the nonoxynol-9 spermicide, which offers both sperm-killing and bacterial-killing protection.

When used with condoms, foams offer a higher degree of pregnancy prevention. Here's how they work: Shake the container, fit the plunger over the top of the can, and press down. The plunger fills with foam. Remove the foam-filled plunger from the container and gently glide the applicator into your vagina. You might want to lie down to get the best angle, because you want to aim up toward your cervix. Press down on the plunger, and foam covers your cervix and the walls of your vagina.

Do's and Don'ts Of Foam

• Foam is effective the moment it is released, so use it close to the time of intercourse. If you insert it more than fifteen minutes before sexual intercourse, it won't be effective. You can use foam from fifteen minutes before up to the moment of intercourse.

• If you have intercourse more than once during love-making, before each exposure to sperm, place more foam inside your vagina.

• The foam may seem messy, but you must wait at least six hours after intercourse, to make sure all the sperm have had time to die out, before douching.

FOAMING TABLETS AND VAGINAL SUPPOSITORIES

Contraceptive foaming tablets and vaginal suppositories, such as Semicid or Encare Oval, contain one of two sperm-killing chemicals—nonoxynol-9 or octoxynol. Once again, the nonoxynol-9 spermicide is the better deal, because it kills sperm as well as the bacteria that bring on certain STDs.

The tablets and suppositories need time to dissolve and coat your vagina, so you must place them within your vaginal canal at least fifteen minutes before intercourse. If you insert a tablet or suppository and have sex immediately after, you *will not* be protected. Also, if you want to douche after intercourse, you must wait at least six hours until sperm have died.

The foaming tablets and suppositories may not coat your vagina as evenly as foam, so I do not recommend them as readily as the pressurized foam or other types of birth control.

BIRTH CONTROL
YOU SHOULD NOT TRY:
THE INTRAUTERINE DEVICE (IUD)

Intrauterine devices (IUDs) are tiny plastic objects that come in all shapes and sizes. Some contain copper or synthetic progesterone. They all have string tails. A doctor fits an IUD into a woman's uterus. It is thought that the IUD prevents pregnancy by separating the inner walls of the uterus and making it impossible for a fertilized egg to implant itself in the uterine lining. Instead, the egg disintegrates.

Today two new copper-containing IUDs—the Copper T 380A and Paragard—are available. Although they give the same high protection that the Pill does, you should never use one. Major manufacturers removed IUDs from the market in 1986 because they were linked to pelvic inflammatory disease, an infection that can leave a girl's uterus and tubes so scarred that she can never become pregnant.

The new IUDs are said to be safer, but you should still stay away from them. The IUD is for women who are over twenty-five, married or in monogamous relationships, and already mothers.

IMPLANTED BIRTH CONTROL:
NORPLANT

The newest contraceptive in the United States is called Norplant. Some schools are offering it to teenage girls who have difficulty using other forms of birth control. With this method, six silicone capsules, each about the size of a matchstick, are surgically implanted inside a girl's upper arm. A doctor makes an incision about a tenth of an inch long and slides the capsules under the skin. The entire procedure takes about fifteen minutes, but it provides birth control protection for five years.

Once the six capsules are in place, they begin to release levonorgestrel, a synthetic progesterone (estrogen and progesterone are the female sex hormones). The synthetic progesterone changes cervical mucus, which helps sperm survive. Rather than help, the changed mucus hinders the sperm's trip to the uterus and the Fallopian tubes.

Women on Norplant have sometimes found that their menstrual periods are longer and that they have irregular bleeding between periods. At a time in your life when your periods are only starting to settle down, Norplant may cause a progesterone overload. There are some sexually active teens, however, who have difficulty following the procedures for other types of birth control, and for them, Norplant is a wise alternative. In fact, Baltimore public health officials have already decided to recommend Norplant through school clinics.

THE RHYTHM METHOD, OR NATURAL FAMILY PLANNING

Girls who do not like the idea of chemicals or devices often want to use the rhythm method. There are methods for finding out when you're ovulating and are most likely to become pregnant. These methods involve taking your temperature every morning with a basal thermometer, and checking your mucus every day for the changes described in Chapter 5. I try to discourage my patients from using these methods for birth control, because during the teen years menstrual cycles are often irregular and it's much more difficult to time ovulation. The tiniest miscalculation, and you can become pregnant. The risk is too great.

WITHDRAWAL IS A JOKE

Withdrawal, or coitus interruptus, when a guy who isn't wearing a condom withdraws his penis from a girl's vagina, is birth control for girls who want to get pregnant! Sometimes when a boy is pressuring you to have sex but doesn't have a condom with him he may brag that he can "take care of everything," but he can't. Withdrawal is one of the worst forms of contraception. Most guys don't really *want* to withdraw. They crave the full pleasure of intercourse and orgasm, and tell themselves: "Just a minute more and then I'll pull out." Well, the first few drops of sperm are the most potent, and even if your boyfriend thinks he's withdrawing "on time," he can still leak a little sperm.

DOUCHING DOESN'T WORK

Douching is good hygiene; it is not good birth control. Within ten minutes sperm can swim from the vagina, through the cervix, to the uterus and into the Fallopian tubes, where they can run smack into an egg. By the time you get up and get your douche equipment organized, you could already be pregnant!

BIRTH CONTROL AFTER THE FACT: THE MORNING-AFTER PILL

The morning-after pill is only given in emergency cases, and it should not be considered a form of birth control. If you have sexual intercourse when you know you are ovulating and the condom on which you are relying breaks, then your doctor may give you the morning-after pill. It is an emergency measure, however, which doctors rarely prescribe.

The medication is an estrogen-containing tablet. The pill must be taken within three days, or seventy-two hours, after sexual intercourse. The pill may be Premarin (1.25 milligrams [mg] administered in four tablets daily for four days) or DES (diethylstilbestrol; 25 mg twice a day for five days). The addition of estrogen prevents a fertilized egg from implanting itself in the uterus, but while it's doing that, it may cause cramping, nausea, vomiting, and water retention. The morning-after pill has far-reaching effects, and **it doesn't always work**.

Sometimes you can still be pregnant even after taking a morning-after pill, but because the medication makes the risk of birth defects to the fetus so high, your pregnancy must be terminated. The bottom line is that you should only seek a morning-after pill if you are willing to have an abortion if the pill does not work!

THE FRENCH PILL: RU-486

Some girls have asked me about the "French Pill," and I have explained that this may have possibilities as a birth control pill, but right now it is not even being tested in this country. A girl or a woman who takes RU-486, the official name of the French Pill, lowers the level of the hormone progesterone in her body. When progesterone drops, more prostaglandins, the hormonelike substances that cause contractions and cramping in the uterus, are released. The cramping contractions lead to miscarriage should a fertilized egg be in your body. Pregnancy ends during miscarriage when the product of conception, whatever stage it has reached, passes out your vagina and you begin to bleed. You can only turn to RU-486 within the first two months of conception, when the drug blocks progesterone, the hormone that nourishes a pregnancy.

The French Pill has been called an "abortion pill" because it operates on the principle of miscarriage. It angers those who are against a woman's right to have an abortion and receives praise from those who support that right. Scientists researching contraception hope that RU-486 can be removed from the field of controversy, because it holds the promise of birth control that is highly effective without interfering with hormones the way other contraceptives do. Researchers believe that if you took just two or three pills at the end of each month, you would bring progesterone to such a low level that you would never be pregnant. Although it has been available in France since 1988, RU-486 must go through years of research in this country before it can be accepted for use.

THERE ARE NO "SAFE" DAYS

Bonnie looked so sad. I had known her all her life. Her mother was my patient seventeen years ago, and I had been at her birth. Now I was watching her usually sparkling brown eyes fill with tears as we talked about her pregnancy. I knew that she was facing hard decisions that would age her before high school graduation.

"I thought I was 'safe,'" she told me. "It was only a few days after my period when Greg and I had sex. I was sure it was too soon for me to be ovulating."

I smiled when she used the word *ovulating*. She was aware of her body. She knew all the biological facts about her menstrual cycle, conception, and pregnancy. She was quite intelligent. I knew that she believed she was "safe," but when you're a teenager there are no "safe" days.

When you're under twenty-one your reproductive system is operating at peak performance—you're extremely fertile, and so are the boys your age. Their sperm are strong, healthy, and fast-swimming! So here you are with ripe eggs, hardy sperm, and guess what? Irregular periods. In the teen years, your menstrual cycles can be hard to predict.

Bonnie was relying on a regular cycle, but she was a track star and athletic girls are especially susceptible to hormonal ups and downs and changing menstrual patterns. She also told me that she wasn't taking her temperature or checking her cervical mucus; she was only counting days since her last period and calculating her ovulation. (See Chapter 5 for more information about ovulation.)

Now Bonnie was faced with tough decisions. Her boyfriend was away at college, and he didn't want her to have the baby. He was encouraging her to get an abortion. Bonnie was supposed to compete in a championship track meet, and college coaches were scheduled to watch her run. She was hoping to get scholarship offers after the meet. Yet she couldn't be pregnant and a track star! She didn't like the idea of an abortion, but she would be an unmarried teenage mother and probably lose her chance of going to college if she had the baby. As she talked about her options, she also worried about how she would handle giving the baby up for adoption. What was she going to do?

As I've mentioned before, pregnancy wrecks your plans. What Bonnie did doesn't matter as much as what you are going to do. I'm writing this book for you, the teenage girl who knows how her body works. You may be fourteen, fifteen, sixteen, seventeen, or eighteen, and, like Bonnie, you may have an awareness of your body that makes you feel confident about taking a few chances here and there.

Just remember the eggs, the sperm, and the unpredictable periods! You may become pregnant and you may catch a sexually transmitted disease. Please let your choices be ones you want to make, not ones you have to make.

CHAPTER EIGHT

The Scary World of Sexually Transmitted Diseases

The week after she graduated from high school, Kelly headed for a resort in Maine, where she lived and worked for the summer. At eighteen she was a virgin. A strong-willed girl, she did not see herself as the "swept away" type. Meeting Scott changed her mind. An experienced college guy, Scott took her for moonlit walks on the beach and chest-hugging trips on the back of his motorcycle. Still, she thought she knew what she was doing.

Kelly found a Planned Parenthood clinic in the area, made an appointment, and left with foam and condoms. She wanted a sexual relationship with Scott that was not going to include catching AIDS or some other sexually transmitted disease (STD), or getting pregnant. Then how

did she get a case of venereal warts so bad that I had to
tell her that she was on the verge of having cervical cancer
at age eighteen?

"We used a condom every time but once," she said.
"I know it was a stupid thing to do. I don't know why
I did it, but . . ."

Kelly was sitting across the desk from me and I
watched her mentally drift away. Whether she had sex
without a condom one time or many did not matter to
me. Any number over zero could mean exposure to an
STD and trouble. Her trouble was venereal warts, which
are closely linked to cervical cancer. The results of her
Pap test showed precancerous cells. Kelly was lucky
that her cells were still *pre*cancerous, and that she could
be treated by laser. If her precancerous cells had formed
carcinoma in situ, which is an early cancer, she might
have needed a procedure called a cone biopsy, which is
the surgical removal of a cone-shaped portion of the
cervix that contains the cancerous cells. A cone biopsy
is very effective in preventing the spread of cancer and
keeping a girl's reproductive organs in good health.
(The treatment for full-fledged cancer cells that travel
beyond the cervix into reproductive organs is a hyster-
ectomy, which means never being able to give birth to
a baby.)

I asked Kelly when she first noticed the warts and
she told me that it was shortly after she had moved
into her dorm. She felt two bumps on her labia when
she was removing a tampon. Then the bumps started
to hurt. She was going to see a doctor at the college
infirmary, but she kept putting it off. She did not
think that she had a serious problem. By the time she
came home for a visit and saw me, her condition was
far along.

Kelly was most concerned about AIDS and pregnancy when she became sexually active that summer.

Since she was using foam all the time, she didn't think she had to worry about getting pregnant. After knowing her college friend for two months, she felt sure he didn't have AIDS, so she let down her guard. She didn't consider how contagious other sexually transmitted diseases are!

Needless to say, Kelly should have never considered comdom-free sex. As I have mentioned before, *a condom is a must in sexual relationships.* Fortunately she was not exposed to HIV, the AIDS virus, but I told her that three million teenagers get an STD every year, so she had a good chance of catching something. Among my patients, I see more cases of sexually transmitted diseases today than ever before.

I was concerned about Kelly, and her situation made me realize that while many bright, aware girls are informed about AIDS and pregnancy, they often forget that other sexually transmitted infections can be quite harmful. Venereal warts, chlamydia, herpes, gonorrhea, syphilis, and trichomoniasis are among the diseases that can make a girl suffer.

I want you to know about *all* the different STDs. While I support romance, helping you stay healthy is my first priority.

THE STDS YOU HEAR LESS ABOUT, CAN STILL MAKE YOU SICK: VENEREAL OR GENITAL WARTS

You may hardly have heard about venereal, also called genital, warts, but they are speading like wildfire among teenagers. During sexual intercourse, you can catch the human papillomavirus (HPV), which causes the warts, from a boy who has been infected with the virus from someone else. He might not even know he is a carrier, because the warts may be inside his penis, in his urethra (urinary canal). If the warts are active in his urethra, the virus will be in his semen, so if he is not using a condom, you will be exposed. Also, if a boy has visible warts on his penis and does not use a condom, you can catch the virus from contact with his penis.

Venereal warts (*condylomata acuminata*) are not like the hard, crusty warts you may see on your hand. These are soft, uneven growths that can appear singly or in clusters. They can be round or long, small or large, pink, white, or gray. If you see any bumps that fit these descriptions on a boy's penis, do not have sex with him!

If you are exposed to the wart-causing virus, anywhere from six weeks to six months later, you may notice a small, painless bump on the vulva, the outer part of your vagina. If you don't make an appointment with a doctor right away for treatment, the virus may spread to internal areas—your cervix, vagina, and rectum. There are more than sixty different types of HPV, but five (HPV types 16, 18, 31, 33, and 35) may bring on cancers of the cervix, vagina, vulva, and anus. Since there is a cancer connection here, catching warts is serious business.

A New Test for Genital Warts. Sometimes warts are inside, on a girl's cervix, for example, and she doesn't know she has them. Since undetected warts can turn cells cancerous, girls who are sexually active, especially girls who have consented to sexual intercourse without a condom, must have a Pap test every six months.

Actually, today there are two tests for detecting warts:

- **ViraPap**, a new test, and
- the traditional **Pap test**.

ViraPap requires a swabbed sample from your cervix, just as a Pap test does, but while a Pap test can detect a variety of problems (see How a Pap Test Works in the following section), ViraPap is only designed to detect HPV.

The wart virus can change the structure of your cervical cells very quickly and make them precancerous. Warts that are visible, however, can be treated right away, before they start altering cells and causing cancer.

How Warts Are Treated. As soon as you notice a bump that could be a wart, go to a doctor. Warts must be removed immediately by your physician. He should do a ViraPap or a Pap test and examine you internally to see if warts are visible in your vagina or on your cervix. A colposcopy, which is the technique of looking at the cervix through a colposcope, a telescopelike instrument that magnifies the vagina and cervix, offers him a good look.

If your warts are the visible kind and your test is normal, treatment with either podofilox (Condylox) or podophyllin, which are wart-killing medications, may quickly clear up the problem.

• **Condylox** is a liquid that you can get by prescription and use at home. Your doctor should instruct you on how to apply Condylox.

• **Podophyllin** is a medication the doctor applies during your appointment. You remain on the examining table ten to fifteen minutes after a podophyllin application to give the medication time to penetrate and destroy the warts. You may need several treatments before all the warts are gone. (If Kelly had seen a doctor right away and been treated with Condylox or podophyllin, her warts would have been a minor annoyance rather than a big problem.)

Instead of medication, a doctor may choose to

• **electrocauterize**, or burn off, the warts with an electric needle, or
• destroy the warts through **cryosurgery**—freezing off the warts with liquid nitrogen.

When a ViraPap or Pap test is abnormal, the warts have had a chance to spread. A doctor will do a **cervical biopsy**, and take cell samples from different sections of the cervix. Depending on the results of the biopsy, he may suggest treatment with:

• a laser, or
• with the anticancer drug interferon.

Sometimes a physician will choose to perform a **cone biopsy**, a surgical procedure through the vagina that enables him to remove an outer, cone-shaped portion of the cervix. (The removed cervical cells grow back in ninety days.) The cone biopsy eliminates cancerous cells that may have traveled farther into the cervix.

Note: The HPV, or wart virus, remains in your body even after the warts are removed. The virus may stay inactive and you may never see another wart, never have an abnormal Pap test, but on the other hand, you may have a flare-up. A cream called fluorouracil (Efudex), which is used to treat certain types of skin cancer, is being prescribed by some physicians as a vaginal medication for killing the wart virus. Numerous studies support Efudex as a wart killer, but the drug is not yet approved by the Food and Drug Administration for this use.

Sometimes warts become large enough to obstruct the birth canal, and a pregnant woman cannot deliver her baby vaginally. She must have a cesarean section, surgery in which the baby is removed from the abdomen. Even if the warts are small, a C-section is usually recommended because a baby can take in the virus while passing through the birth canal and the warts can spread on his or her vocal chords. All of these problems can be avoided, though, if a condom is used during intercourse.

If you discover that you have warts, you must stay healthy, eat nutritiously, and get plenty of sleep to keep your immune system strong. You must also ask your boyfriend to be checked for warts or you risk becoming reinfected.

HOW A PAP TEST WORKS

The Pap test, which was named after Dr. George N. Papanicolaou, was created by the doctor in the 1920s to identify cervical cancer. Today the test helps a doctor know if you have an STD such as venereal warts, gonorrhea, or trichomoniasis, besides giving him an idea of whether you're at risk for cervical cancer. Although the American College of Obstetricians and Gynecologists (ACOG) recommends a Pap test only once a year, I believe that you should get a Pap test every six months if you are sexually active. A Pap test is a good way to find an infection early on.

During a Pap test, a gynecologist opens your vagina with a speculum, the instrument that looks like a pair of narrow duck bills and that allows him to look at your cervix. **This is a gentle procedure. A Pap test does not hurt.**

Your doctor then inserts a cotton swab into the cervical canal, and rotates the swab. Cells from inside the cervix stick to the swab, and he applies them to a glass plate, which he sends to a lab for analysis.

The Results of a Pap Test. A laboratory classifies your pap smear according to the degree of cell abnor-

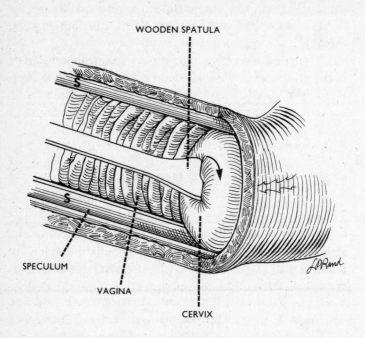

30. The Pap Test. During a Pap test, aside from the swabbed sample taken from inside the cervix, a physician also obtains a cell sample from the surface of the cervix. A doctor gently presses a wooden spatula against the cervix, rotates it, and a few cervical cells adhere. He removes the spatula from the vagina and smears the cells onto a glass slide, which he sends to a lab. A lab analysis of the cervical cells can not only tell whether a girl has a precancerous condition, but also whether infection or venereal/genital warts exist. ILLUSTRATION BY LAUREL PURINTON RAND

mality the technicians find. The Pap test is invaluable to your good health because it detects inflammations, infections, certain STDs, and cervical cancer.

Often a doctor will only contact you if your Pap test shows a problem.

The results of a Pap test are classified from Class I through Class V. The higher the class, the more abnormal the cells are. If you have a Class I result, which is an entirely normal smear, you may not hear from your doctor. He may only call you if your test results are out of the ordinary.

He may say, for example, that you have a Class II Pap test and that your cervix has an inflammation caused by a yeast infection, which is described in the section A Yeast Infection Called Monilia, Candida Albicans, and Candidiasis later on in this chapter. Many laboratories analyzing Pap tests are now explaining inflammations, infections, and cell changes on their reports, in addition to the "classes":

Class I is a normal smear.

Class II is a smear with slightly abnormal cells, and the lab report will usually describe a cause of the abnormality. You may have a yeast infection (see A Yeast Infection etc. later on in this chapter) or venereal warts, for example.

Class III usually means that you have mild, moderate, or severe cell changes associated with cervical dysplasia, which is not cancer. Dysplasia means that cells are not perfectly normal. Often an STD is the source of the dysplasia.

Class IV or V indicates a serious situation. You have either precancer or cancer. You must immediately undergo a cervical biopsy, a technique that allows your doctor to take cell samples from your cervix to identify your condition.

CHLAMYDIA

I can't tell you the number of times I have seen a shocked expression on the face of a teenage girl who has just learned that she has chlamydia, a sexually transmitted infection caused by the bacterium *Chlamydia trachomatis*. "I feel fine. I have no symptoms. Are you sure you haven't made a mistake?" are the questions I hear over and over.

The Symptoms Are "No Symptoms." Chlamydia is called a "silent infection," because you can have no symptoms and still be sick. It is the most common sexually transmitted disease in this country! A guy is more likely to have symptoms, such as a burning urination, a cloudy or clear discharge from his penis, but most girls do not notice any signs of the disease. I tell all my teenage patients that any type of vaginal discharge, or sensation during urination, or vague abdominal ache should send them to me immediately. These can be symptoms of chlamydia.

This STD usually starts within three weeks after a girl has been exposed through contact with sperm. As chlamydia travels, it can spread beyond the cervix into the Fallopian tubes and ovaries, then throughout the abdomen.

The Chlamydia/PID Link. Chlamydia is the leading cause of pelvic inflammatory disease (PID), an infection in the abdominal area that can spread to the Fallopian tubes and ovaries. PID is especially dangerous in the Fallopian tubes because the scar tissue it forms can either prevent conception or cause an ectopic pregnancy, in which the fetus grows in a Fallopian tube instead of the uterus. This is a life-threatening condition, and the fetus must be removed. (When an ectopic pregnancy is removed early on, a doctor may be able to save the Fallopian tube. The longer an ectopic pregnancy grows before it's removed, the greater the chance that you will lose the use of your tube along with the pregnancy.) The chlamydia/PID link is known to be a cause of infertility. If you have undetected chlamydia, by the time you have the abdominal pain of PID, your reproductive organs may already be damaged.

Also, if a girl whose cervix is infected becomes pregnant, her baby may be in danger at delivery time. Contact with chlamydia during a vaginal delivery could cause a newborn to suffer eye infections or even pneumonia.

Testing for Chlamydia. The good news is that there are laboratory tests that can detect chlamydia in a cervical sample. A girl who has sex without a condom should ask her doctor to check her for chlamydia at the same time she has her Pap test. As I mentioned before, if you are sexually active, especially if you are active with more than one partner, or you have had intercourse without a condom, you should have a Pap test every six months. A test for chlamydia should go along with the Pap test, because when you are in your teens, your cervix is more open to infection and chlamydia is much more common.

How Chlamydia Is Cured. Once it is found, chlamydia can be cured. The usual treatment is ten to twenty days of the antibiotic tetracycline. A girl who is allergic to tetracycline can take erythromycin. Her boyfriend must take antiobiotics at the same time, or they will continue to pass the bug back and forth if they continue to have unprotected sex.

GENITAL HERPES

Herpes is the shortened name of the herpes simplex virus (HSV), which causes highly contagious, painful, itching, burning, blister-type sores on your genital area—on your vulva, vagina, cervix, perineum (the area between the vulva and anus), and/or anus. There are two types of herpes simplex viruses:

• HSV-1 causes cold sores (also called fever blisters) around the mouth.
• The second type, HSV-2, accounts for most of the herpes that attacks the sex organs of both girls and boys.

Oral sex, however, can transmit both viral types from the mouth to the genitals and back again, and fingers that touch the sores can spread the virus to different parts of the body.

If you are sexually active, you should always look at a boy's penis before intercourse. If he has a bump of any kind, he could be carrying an STD such as warts, herpes, or syphilis. Herpes is so contagious that a sore on a boy's penis need only touch your genital area to pass on the virus. Also, a person with herpes may be contagious twenty-four hours *before* the sores erupt, which means that even if you don't see a bump, a boy might still be able to infect you. Here's another reason why a condom, which covers the penis, is so important.

If you are exposed to herpes, you are likely to come down with the disease from two to twenty days later, although sometimes an outbreak does not occur for months or years. A first-time herpes outbreak usually starts with a general achiness, run-down feeling, and sometimes, a slight fever. You may think you have the flu at first, but then you notice a tingling or itching in the genital area and tiny, red blistery bumps appear. Very quickly, the bumps grow into ugly, painful, fluid-filled blisters that may burst and ooze. If the sores are near your urethra (urinary opening), you may have burning urination. On the other hand, if a herpes sore is located on your cervix, you may have no symptoms at all, but the sores will spread just the same.

The herpes sores usually run their course in about two weeks and after they heal, they may never return. After an outbreak, the virus retreats to nerves clustered near the spinal column or finds a home in the ganglia, which are nerve cells throughout the body. **Once you have the herpes virus in your body, it remains with you for the rest of your life.** The virus stays dormant, but if something happens to lower your immune response, sores may emerge. A stressful situation, an emotional crisis, a poor diet, insomnia, anything that disrupts your body's balance can cause herpes to recur. About half the people who get HSV-2 have a recurrence within six months. Some girls live the rest of their lives without outbreaks, while others have unexpected attacks years later.

More Dangerous for Girls. The herpes virus is more dangerous for girls than it is for boys because HSV-2 has been linked to cervical cancer. A girl who has had a herpes outbreak must have a Pap test every six months to be assured that she has no abnormal cervical cells. (See How a Pap Test Works in this chapter.) When a girl reaches the time in her life when she decides to become pregnant, she should be frank with her obstetrician about her history of herpes. An unborn baby can be infected by the virus during childbirth and suffer blindness, birth defects, or death. Cesarean section is recommended for women who have active herpes at the time they are ready to give birth.

Testing for Herpes. Your doctor will be able to test you for herpes by requesting a tissue culture test from a laboratory or getting a laboratory analysis of a scraping from a sore. There is also a blood test that tells you if the antibodies to HSV-1 and -2 are in your system. A positive blood test means that the viruses entered your body sometime in the past. To test specific sores, you need a tissue culture or a scraping.

How Herpes Is Treated. Since the herpes simplex virus never leaves your body, you can never be completely cured. An outbreak of herpes sores can be shortened by a drug called acyclovir (Zovirax) in cream or pills. Zovirax shortens an outbreak by blocking the spread of the herpes virus. The cream works better for boys, who can apply it directly on genital sores. It's a lot harder to put cream on internal vaginal herpes. The Zovirax pills are more effective for girls. (If you suffer from regular outbreaks of herpes, your doctor may suggest a daily dose of Zovirax for several months, to prevent recurrence.) You can also help lessen the severity of a herpes outbreak by cleansing your vulva, keeping the area dry, and using the Zovirax cream wherever possible.

GONORRHEA

Girls fifteen to nineteen years old have the highest rates of gonorrhea ("clap" in slang terms) among women. You can get the *Neisseria gonorrhoeae* bacteria, which causes gonorrhea, when the mucus membrane, the thin, sensitive tissue near the opening of an infected boy's penis, makes contact with the mucus membrane of your vagina, mouth, throat, or anus. Unprotected sexual intercourse and oral or anal sex are the main means of transmitting gonorrhea, but once again, a condom can protect you.

Signs of Gonorrhea. A boy usually knows when he has gonorrhea because he experiences an obvious discharge from his penis and painful urination. Most girls usually have no signs, although two days to three weeks after exposure some girls occasionally notice a slight vaginal discharge or some pain during urination. (If a gonorrheal infection is in the throat, you will only feel a slight soreness.) I always hope that the teenage girls in my care will choose boyfriends with integrity, young men who will tell them whether they have exposed them to this STD.

Gonorrhea and PID. If a boy does not admit that he has exposed you to gonorrhea, during your menstrual period uterine contractions may pull the bacteria into your uterus and Fallopian tubes. Then once inside your reproductive organs, gonorrhea can spread quickly and cause pelvic inflammatory disease (PID), an infection of the uterus, Fallopian tubes, and ovaries. You can suffer severe abdominal pain. As I mentioned in the section on chlamydia, PID can damage the Fallopian tubes so badly that you cannot conceive a baby. The potent bacteria, even if they showed no signs of existing at the beginning, are behind many tragic cases of PID and infertility.

Testing for Gonorrhea. If you tell your doctor that you have been exposed to gonorrhea, expect him to take a swabbed sample from your cervix, urethra, throat, or anus for a culture test. The culture is then grown in a special medium in a laboratory, and within two or three days the disease can be identified. Since this test is only 82 percent reliable, however, if you get a negative result you must take another culture test a week later. **You need two negative cultures to be certain that you do not have gonorrhea.**

How Gonorrhea Is Cured. Gonorrhea has been quickly cured with penicillin injections, oral tetracycline, or cephalexin (Keflex) tablets. Lately, though, new strains of the *N. gonorrhoeae* bacteria have been appearing that are resistant to these drugs. The old reliable medicines are not destroying the disease. As a result, a number of new antibiotics, such as spectinomycin by injection, are being introduced to fight this STD.

SYPHILIS

Although syphilis is not as common as gonorrhea, it is at its highest level in forty years. You can get syphilis if you have condom-free sexual intercourse with someone who is infected with *Treponema pallidum*, a spiral-shaped bacterium that penetrates the sensitive mucus membrane of your vagina. (During anal and oral sex *T. pallidum* may invade the anal tissue or the tissue in the mouth or on the lips.) When you have syphilis, a hard, painless sore called a chancre appears at the site of your infection. A chancre doesn't hurt the way a herpes blister does, but it is extremely contagious and the slightest contact with the smallest chancre can make you sick. That's why it is so important to look at a boy's penis to make sure it has no signs of bumps. If something seems "strange" to you, avoid sexual intercourse.

The Four Stages of Syphilis. Within ten to ninety days after you have unprotected sex with a partner who has syphilis, you have a 30 percent chance of catching the disease yourself. Syphilis has four stages: primary, secondary, latent, and tertiary.

It is a nasty disease because it *seems* to disappear after the primary and secondary stages, even without treatment. Yet there is a 33 percent chance that the disease has not gone away. Syphilis can be undetected for years, but decades later it can come alive with devastating consequences such as blindness, deafness, paralysis, insanity, and, ultimately, death.

If you contract syphilis, ten to ninety days later you enter the **primary stage**. A small bump appears at the site of your sexual contact. The bump becomes a hard, painless chancre. A girl who notices a hard sore should make an appointment with her doctor right away. In public health clinics or hospital labs, a physician squeezes or scrapes the sore to get a sample of its contents, which he places on a slide and views under a dark-field microscope, an instrument designed for diagnosing syphilis. Most doctors in private practice take a blood sample and send it to a lab for a venereal disease research laboratories (VDRL) blood test.

Note: Since a VDRL can have a false positive—it says you have syphilis when you don't—if you get a positive result it must be verified with a fluorescent treponema antibodies (FTA) absorption test.

Sometimes a chancre hides in the folds of your vagina and you don't notice it. If you never spot this sign of primary syphilis, the sore may heal and disappear in one to five weeks. The *T. pallidum* bacteria does not leave your body, however. It remains in your bloodstream and about six weeks after the first appearance of the sore you move into the **secondary stage**. You may develop a skin rash, possibly accompanied by enlarged lymph nodes, a fever, or hair loss. Sores may show up on the palms of your hands and the soles of your feet, and flat, wartlike growths may surface on your genital area. This stage lasts two to six weeks, as long as the rash does. The lingering rash is another cue to visit your doctor for a VDRL blood test. If syphilis is not controlled in this stage, it becomes quite dangerous.

When you seem perfectly healthy for decades syphilis is in its **latent stage**. Then suddenly one day you begin to show signs of paralysis. This is the last, **tertiary stage**, when syphilis can cause brain damage, mental problems, and eventually death. It should never be allowed to advance so far. When syphilis is diagnosed early on, it is easily cured with antibiotics.

How Syphilis Is Cured. When diagnosed at the start, syphilis can often be cured with two injections of penicillin, one shot in each buttock, as a one-time therapy, but some people need additional, prolonged treatment. Girls who are allergic to penicillin are treated with other types of antibiotics.

Note: A woman who is pregnant should have a blood test for syphilis during her first visit to an obstetrician. After the first three months of pregnancy, a woman who has syphilis can pass the disease to her unborn baby, who may die from it. If the baby lives, it may be born with defects of the skin, bone, liver, and nose. Early detection and prompt treatment of syphilis can protect a developing fetus from harm.

VAGINITIS

Rachel called me up between classes one day to ask for an emergency appointment. She said she had an itch that was "driving her crazy" and she was "going out of her mind." I guessed that she had vaginitis and told her to come to my office as soon as she could. She had never heard the word *vaginitis*, which is a simple term to describe a variety of vaginal infections that you can get for any number of reasons, sexual intercourse among them.

One of the signs of vaginitis is an abundant vaginal

discharge. Some discharge is normal, since hormonal changes during the menstrual cycle cause increased wetness from time to time. You do not have to worry about having vaginitis unless you notice **an excessive discharge with accompanying pain, itching, and/or odor.** Then your vaginal environment may have been invaded by microorganisms that are irritating or inflaming the sensitive walls of your vagina. The two most common types of vaginitis, which may be sexually transmitted, are a yeast infection that goes by the names *monilia, candida albicans*, and *candidiasis*, which is caused by a fungus, and trichomoniasis, which is from the single-celled parasite *Trichomonas vaginalis*.

A YEAST INFECTION CALLED MONILIA, CANDIDA ALBICANS, AND CANDIDIASIS

Monilia/candida albicans/candidiasis is a yeastlike fungus that lives in your vagina, mouth, and gastrointestinal tract all the time. It only works against you when it multiplies too much, and that happens when there's a change in the acid content of the vaginal area. Some of the things that can cause that change are:

- antibiotics
- a weight gain
- a change in blood sugar levels (girls who are prediabetic or diabetic have high rates of vaginitis)
- the birth control pill
- douching
- stress
- airtight pantyhose, leggings, or tight pants
- sexual intercourse with an infected partner

What Happens. Monilia makes the vaginal canal and outer lips of your vagina bright red and swollen. You also experience a frothy white vaginal discharge, which looks like cottage cheese. The vaginal walls become more inflamed and itchy as the fungus itself, the *C. albicans*, spreads. Along with the redness, swelling, discharge, and itch, an unpleasant odor can start to come from your vagina.

The itch is usually the symptom that sends you to a doctor. Most gynecologists are so familiar with yeast infections that they can spot one during an examination, but to confirm a diagnosis, a doctor will also take a vaginal smear for a slide test.

How a Yeast Infection Is Cured. Doctors in the past prescribed antiyeast vaginal suppositories or creams, but today more products to fight yeast infections are sold over the counter. Monistat, which used to be available only by prescription, can now be purchased in pharmacies. Other medications are Mycostatin, Vanobid, Gyne-Lotrimin, Myocel-G, and Terazol. Suppositories or creams must be inserted deep into the vagina once or twice a day to stop the spread of *C. albicans*. Mycolog, a cream that combines antiyeast and cortisone medications, makes the outer lips of the vulva less sore.

You want to restore your vagina to its natural environment, first with antiyeast medication, and then by taking healthful measures such as only wearing cotton underwear and avoiding tight pantyhose, leggings, and jeans. A douche of warm water and betadine, a medicated iodine solution, or a water and vinegar douche, can also be healing.

You also ought to be aware of what you eat:

• Yogurt is a good idea since it contains lacto bacillus, a healthy bacteria that helps maintain the acidic balance in the vagina.

• Sugary sweets are a bad idea because they elevate the blood sugar level and upset vaginal acidity.

TRICHOMONIASIS

"I smelled something awful, sourlike, when I was sitting in a movie with my friends," explained my seventeen-year-old patient, Annie. "I looked to see if someone had left food rotting under my seat. Then, as I moved my legs, I realized it was me. I was so embarrassed."

I told Annie that she should be grateful that she noticed a sign of trichomoniasis, before this form of vaginitis became more severe. Trichomoniasis, which many girls refer to as "trick," is an infection caused by *Trichomoniasis vaginalis*, a microscopic parasite that a boy (who may not know he is carrying the disease) can pass along to you in his semen if you have sexual intercourse without a condom. You can also get it by using an infected person's moist towel or by sitting on an infected toilet seat, but most often the disease is sexually transmitted. Some girls have had "trick" without sexual activity, however.

What You'll Notice. Like Annie, you'll notice a foul smell. This is often accompanied by a greenish-white or yellowish discharge. A boy may not have a discharge or any other sign to warn him of trichomoniasis. Once you get it, though, a few weeks later you have the odor, the discharge, and also the itching. Your vagina can become red and sore, and the itching can drive you crazy if it's not treated.

Testing for Trichomoniasis. A doctor can tell if you have "trick" by taking a sample of your vaginal discharge, placing it on a slide with a saline solution, and examining it under a microscope. Under the microscope the *T. vaginalis* protozoa are unmistakable. They are pear-shaped microorganisms with tails that rapidly flick back and forth to propel them all over the place. They are easy to spot on a slide and on a Pap test.

How Trichomoniasis Is Cured. The medication that kills the *T. vaginalis* and cures trichomoniasis is metronidazole (Flagyl). Flagyl must not be taken during pregnancy, however. It has been found to cause birth defects in animals, and it might harm a developing fetus. Flagyl has also been suspected of causing cancer in laboratory rats and mice, but it is still the only cure for trichomoniasis. All alcoholic beverages must be avoided if you are taking Flagyl. The two do not mix, and you could become quite ill.

CREEPY CRAWLIES: CRABS, OR PUBIC LICE

It's like being invaded by microscopic aliens! Tiny blood-sucking lice that look like mini-crabs are responsible for a sexually transmitted condition known as pediculosis, phthirius pubis, or "crabs." These parasites (*Phthirius pubis*) resemble black dots about the size of a period made with a ballpoint pen. They live on human blood and breed in pubic hair, but they can also live in underarm hair, eyelashes, moustaches, and chest hair. Usually they bury their mouth parts into skin and hold onto pubic hair with their hind legs. The movement and heat of love-making disturbs them, and they lose their grip and travel from one partner to another.

A condom won't stop you from getting crabs. If you

are sexually active with a boy who has them, then you can get them. They cannot survive more than twenty-four hours without feeding on a human, but they can infest clothing, towels, bedding, and even toilet seats. Crabs lay their eggs at the base of your pubic hairs, and two weeks later those eggs are grown adults causing a tremendous itch. You can look down and see them moving. You may even notice a few strays on your underpants. Since lice can carry disease, you should get rid of crabs right away.

How Crabs Are Cured. There are a number of over-the-counter crab-killing solutions you can buy, among them A-200 Pyrinate, RID, Triple X, and Vonce, but Kwell lotion, by prescription, seems to be the most effective. Make sure your boyfriend works on his crabs, too! If you see a doctor, he will prescribe Kwell lotion or shampoo, which you rub into the infested area and wash off twelve to twenty-four hours later. Most girls leave it on overnight. Make a point of picking the crabs off your body as you wash away a medicated solution. Then all clothing, towels, and bedding should be washed in very hot or boiling water. In two weeks you must repeat the treatment. After you rinse off the solution again, examine yourself with a mirror to be sure that every crab is gone.

SCABIES

This is another sexually transmitted disease from a microscopic creature. A tiny mite (*Sarcoptes scabiei*), which may have been feeding on your boyfriend, burrows under your skin and lays eggs. The mite could have also been in bedding, towels, or clothing with which you made contact. Sexual contact is just one way to get scabies.

When the eggs mature into adults in ten days, the scabies mites are barely visible. If you become itchy and examine the place where you want to scratch, you may notice a small red opening in your skin and raised red or gray wavy lines where the mites have burrowed. A doctor can diagnose scabies from the burrows. The mites invade skin folds in the vulva, and go between fingers and toes, inside wrists or elbows, around the waistline, nipples, navel, and in creases of the buttocks, but they never travel above your neck.

How Scabies Are Cured. A doctor can prescribe Kwell lotion or shampoo. You (and everyone who lives with you) should cover yourself from the neck down. Your boyfriend should do the same! Keep the Kwell on your body for twenty-four hours, then wash it off. Since scabies are highly contagious, you must launder all your clothing, towels, and bedding in very hot water to prevent reinfection. A second application of Kwell is usually not necessary, but if you feel you would like double protection, a week after your first treatment you may reapply the lotion.

THE SEXUALLY TRANSMITTED DISEASE THAT CAN KILL YOU: ACQUIRED IMMUNE DEFICIENCY SYNDROME (AIDS)

So many people have talked about AIDS to you, that you probably do not want to read or hear another word about this sexually transmitted disease. You know you can catch it through sexual intercourse, but you may feel that you'd never go out with anyone who has AIDS. How can you know? The disease is spreading alarmingly among teen-agers, and girls and guys who are infected may be un-aware themselves. Among adults, many more men than women have AIDS, but among teenagers, the sexes share the disease equally. You ought to find out everything you can about AIDS. You are living in its shadow, and you must protect yourself. By making protection a priority, you show that you care about yourself and your partner.

What AIDS Is. AIDS is caused by the human im-munodeficiency virus (HIV), which can settle in your body and live for years without your knowledge. HIV infects and slowly destroys your body's disease fighters, the white blood cells of your immune system. While some infected people don't seem sick, all males and females with HIV eventually show signs of illness. The virus can live in your body for ten years or more before it develops into AIDS, and all the while, even if you're not ill, you can be passing the virus to someone else.

About AIDS-Related Complex (ARC). Some people who have the HIV/AIDS virus have illnesses that come and go over a long period of time. They are said to have AIDS-related complex, or ARC.

If you have ARC, you are tired a lot and may lose weight. You may also be sick fairly often with fever, swollen lymph nodes, and infections in your mouth. Peo-ple who have ARC can

- live in an unchanging weakened state, or
- get sick, then better, on and on, or
- develop full-blown AIDS.

What Happens When AIDS Develops. You can come down with a tiring illness accompanied by swollen glands, or the flu during the first few weeks that you are exposed to HIV, but the tiredness and flu-like symptoms will disappear. Then months or even years later, you find that you are constantly tired and cannot fight off infection. This is the beginning of AIDS.

Some early signs of AIDS are extreme fatigue, a huge weight loss, a lingering fever that brings on night sweats, chronic diarrhea, and/or an infection you cannot shake. You may have swollen lymph nodes around your neck, armpits, or groin. A girl or a woman may develop a vaginal infection that doesn't go away.

With AIDS, your immune system becomes so weakened that even a cold can kill you. People with HIV/AIDS often wind up getting an unusual pneumonia, a rare form of cancer, a rare type of meningitis (infection in the brain), or a tuberculosis that usually ends their lives.

How You Get AIDS. You can get HIV, the AIDS virus, through an exchange of body fluids, usually semen and blood. It can also be passed through vaginal secretions. The HIV/AIDS virus has also been found in tiny amounts in urine, feces, tears, and saliva, but there are no known cases of anyone transmitting AIDS through these fluids. French kissing, or deep kissing, is only considered risky because there could be an exchange of blood, if either of you has a cut in or around your mouth.

Most of the time HIV/AIDS is sexually transmitted to a girl during unprotected intercourse because the virus is in semen. A boy who has HIV/AIDS can pass the virus to you when he ejaculates semen into your vagina, anus, or, during oral sex, into your throat. Since the virus is in vaginal moisture and menstrual blood, an infected girl can give a boy HIV/AIDS during intercourse if he has a cut on his penis. Also, there are a few things that make you more vulnerable to HIV/AIDS during unprotected sexual intercourse:

• Unprotected sex with an uncircumcised male. AIDS cases are usually lower among circumcised males.
• Having another type of sexually transmitted disease, such as venereal warts, chlamydia, trichomoniasis, or gonorrhea.
• Cervical ectopy, a condition in which abnormal tissue covers part of the vagina, is more common in girls in their teens and twenties than among older women. This condition makes you more vulnerable to AIDS.
• If you touch an infected boy's penis when you have a cut on your hand and his semen penetrates the cut, you could catch HIV/AIDS.

Besides unprotected sexual intercourse, you can get the HIV/AIDS virus by being pricked with a needle that was just used by an infected person and is still tainted with blood. In fact, one of the most common ways of spreading AIDS is through infected needles. You also may be exposed to infected blood from shared toothbrushes, razors, and needles used for ear piercing. Any instrument that has been stained with blood can be dangerous.

Before scientists discovered how to test donated blood for HIV, blood transfusions used to infect people. With the screening of blood supplies, transfusions are now unlikely sources of infection.

A pregnant woman who has HIV/AIDS can also pass the virus to her unborn baby in the uterus and during breast-feeding.

You cannot catch HIV/AIDS from touching or getting near someone who has the disease. You cannot get it from a toilet seat or a public swimming pool.

If you think you might have been exposed to

HIV/AIDS, you can have a blood test for the presence of HIV antibodies, which is the only way to test for AIDS. The antibodies can take up to six months or longer to show up, though, so if you get a negative test result within six months of your suspected exposure, then you should go for a second test.

How AIDS Is Treated. There is no cure for AIDS. At the time this book went to press, however, three drugs had been FDA-approved for AIDS sufferers: azidothymidine or AZT (Retrovir); didanosine or ddI (Videx); dideoxycytidine or ddC (Hivid). These drugs slow but do not stop the progress of the disease.

Someday though, a cure for AIDS may come in a vaccine or a drug. Molecular biologists are researching the life cycle of the HIV/AIDS virus so that drugs may be created to interrupt its survival pattern. These drugs may not exist for another ten to twenty years. The most you can do for yourself right now is be careful.

How to Protect Yourself from HIV/AIDS. The absolutely surest way to protect yourself from HIV/AIDS is to not have sexual intercourse and to never use needles, whether for drugs or ear piercing, that have been used by anyone else. If you are sexually active, then you ought to follow these guidelines:

• Every time you have sex, use a spermicide-containing condom.

• Don't believe, like Kelly in the beginning of this chapter, that you can know a young man's sexual history well enough to judge whether he is carrying the HIV/AIDS virus. You are at risk of catching a disease that could kill you. Even if your partner has never been an intravenous (IV) drug user, and has never had sex with an IV drug user, and has never had sex with a man, he may have picked up the HIV/AIDS virus by having sex with someone who had sex with someone who has AIDS. Your partner might also have had sex with someone who caught HIV/AIDS years ago from a blood transfusion, or had sex with someone who had sex with someone who had an infected blood transfusion. The possibilities are endless and tragic.

• You are more protected if you are having sex with only one person.

• If you have any questions about AIDS, you can call the National AIDS Hotline at 1-800-342-AIDS or the National AIDS Information Clearinghouse at 1-800-458-5231.

THE TWO MOST ASKED QUESTIONS ABOUT STDS:
1. HOW DO I BRING UP THE SUBJECT OF A CONDOM?
2. HOW CAN I ASK HIM TO HAVE AN AIDS TEST?

In some ways talking about sex, sexually transmitted diseases, pregnancy, and protection can be more intimate than the actual act of sexual intercourse. Some girls are more nervous about asking a guy to use a condom or to be tested for HIV/AIDS than about having sex. They worry that guys will be offended and break up with them.

As I mentioned in Chapter 7, teenage girls are emotionally more mature than teenage boys. You may not want to be the one who starts a conversation about condoms, or who suggests an AIDS test, but you may be the more sensible one. If you have never been sexually active and are embarking on your first experience, you know you are "safe." It's your body that can become pregnant and catch an STD. It's your body that needs protection with a condom.

YOU MAY WANT TO TRY

The first Condom for Girls. In 1993, you probably will be able to buy a female condom, called a vaginal pouch, for about $2. Manufactured by Wisconsin Pharmaceutical Company of Chicago, the pouch has been going through the FDA-approval process. It is a sheath of polyurethane that goes from your cervix to the outside of your vagina, and completely lines your vagina. Two flexible plastic rings, one at the cervix and one outside your vagina, hold it in place. Overall, the vaginal pouch is about six and a half inches long. As of this writing, the condom for girls is not considered a birth control device; it is meant to be used only as protection against exposure to STDs.

All the facts about male condoms are in Chapter 7. Learn them. You might even lend this book to your boyfriend to read about condoms. Then let him in on your feelings *before* you have sexual intercourse. You may want to use something from the book to open the conversation. In a world filled with sexually transmitted diseases, you and your partner must agree on a safe approach to having sex.

Some girls tell me that there's so much to worry about, they are just hoping for the best when it comes to sex. Realize that a partner who tries to pressure you into having sex without a condom is jeopardizing your life.

Sex is a beautiful, wordless communication between two people who respect, love, and trust each other. Yet in this age when a sexually transmitted disease can seriously harm or kill you, reality must come before romance. I believe that when you express affection in ways other than intercourse and postpone sex, you form a bond that allows you to open up completely about your feelings. Your relationship is based on understanding. Only then, when you and your boyfriend have a strong tie with each other, does it make sense to consider having intercourse. There's no rush. Remember, the longer you postpone sex, the longer you are fully protected against STDs.

CHAPTER NINE

What It Means to Be Pregnant and Have a Baby

Courtney was fifteen years old and four months pregnant. She had been hoping something would happen to make the pregnancy go away. She had prayed that her period would come, but instead, the baby just kept growing inside her. She said that she hadn't decided whether to have the baby or not, that her boyfriend was seeing someone else, and that she had not wanted to marry him anyway. I told her that she was too far along to have an abortion, that she had already decided to have the baby. She had confided in her best girlfriend, and now she had to tell her parents. Soon her loose clothes would not hide her secret.

As an obstetrician, I have delivered the babies of many teenagers who never intended to get pregnant. I have cared for girls during their pregnancies and child-births, and examined them afterward—some with their babies and some without, because their babies had been adopted.

In the course of their pregnancies I have watched girls discover the shocking ways in which their bodies change and behave, and I have seen them adjust to life as expectant mothers. They must be careful of what they eat, drink, smoke, and breathe, since they are no longer living for themselves alone. They are faced with the enormous responsibility of a baby's survival. Often the teenage expectant fathers are emotionally unable to be supportive.

All the girls who have said "I didn't know it was going to be this way" to me during their pregnancies have inspired this chapter. Even girls who wanted to become pregnant have found themselves overwhelmed by the creation of a new life within their bodies. I would like you to know the true story about what happens during a pregnancy.

I am writing for girls who are at least fourteen and already in high school, girls who have had health or sex education classes, girls who have an awareness of their bodies. If you become pregnant unintentionally, you have the choice of ending your pregnancy through an abortion (discussed in Chapter 10), having the baby and raising it yourself, or allowing your baby to be adopted. (There is also the option of permitting your child to go into foster care, which is temporary care with a family chosen by the state until you are able to care for the child yourself. This should only be an emergency measure, however, since switching families can be emotionally difficult for a child.) You are not alone if you choose to have your baby. Every year one million teenage girls become pregnant, and about half a million of them give birth.

Allowing your baby to be adopted is an emotionally

wrenching decision, but so is the decision to raise your child. You can still fulfill your dreams if you have a baby, but you will have to work much harder for every goal you set. Your child will be totally dependent upon you for its life. You must be mature enough to decide what is best for your child, and you must have the money to feed, clothe, and shelter him or her. You may be a married teen with a husband who is working to support you, or you may have relatives who will financially and emotionally help you bring up your baby, but no matter what your situation is, it's never easy to be a teenage mother.

WONDERING WHETHER YOU ARE PREGNANT

Any time you have unprotected sexual intercourse, you may become pregnant. You may even become pregnant if you are doing everything *but* having sexual intercourse. If while "making out" you take your clothes off, a small amount of sperm may leak from a boy's penis into the warm, moist area of your vagina. Sperm can survive in the moisture, travel up into your vaginal canal, and once in your body, easily swim toward an egg.

You may have a "feeling" that you're pregnant before your period is late, but **the only concrete sign of pregnancy is a missed period.** Once you skip a period, you may notice other signs:

- unusually tender or heavy breasts
- a sense of being bloated, stuffy, and headachy
- the need to urinate more than usual
- a slightly queasy feeling, with a heightened sensitivity to smells

SPERM   EGG CELL   FERTILIZATION

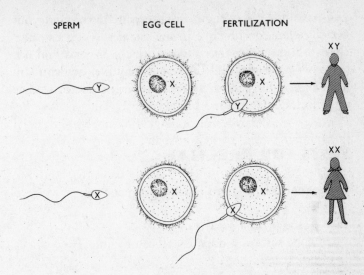

31. Conception. A boy's sperm cells contain either a Y (male) chromosome or an X (female) chromosome. A girl's eggs contain only X chromosomes. If a "male" sperm fertilizes an egg, a boy (XY chromosomes) will result. If a "female" sperm enters an egg, the fertilized embryo will be a girl (XX chromosomes).

• greater body heat, with a 1° rise in temperature
• the severe nausea and vomiting of "morning sickness," which can occur any time of the day (Note: Morning sickness is talked about so much that you might think it happens to everyone. The fact is that many pregnant girls *never* experience morning sickness.)
• an unbelievable feeling of tiredness

Of course, sometimes the stress of thinking that you might be pregnant can make your period late. Then you can imagine all sorts of signs. You feel nauseous, but your nausea may only be from nervousness. If you know you have had sex without using birth control, and your period is late, do not live in high anxiety. You can purchase a home pregnancy test at a drugstore and find out the news right away. If the test is negative, but you still do not get your period, you should visit a doctor's office or a clinic for a urine or blood test.

TESTS FOR PREGNANCY

There are three ways to test for pregnancy:

- home pregnancy tests
- urine tests at a doctor's office or clinic
- blood tests

Home Pregnancy Tests. A few days after your period was due to arrive, you can test for pregnancy yourself with a home kit. First Response, Q Test, EPT, and Clear Blue are among the home pregnancy test kits that are widely sold in drugstores. With one or two tests to a package, kits cost from $9 to $20. **You must read the instructions carefully and follow them exactly.** No matter what brand you buy, the testing method is basically the same. You add a few drops of your "first morning" urine to other chemicals, allow the mixture to sit in a holder for a specified time, then read the results. Human chorionic gonadotropin (HCG) is a hormone that rises during pregnancy. The chemicals in a home pregnancy test kit will react to the HCG in your urine. Some kits use a stick that changes color for testing, some use small test tubes in which the solution changes color, and some have specially designed containers with color-changing indicators. Newer tests can even give results with "any time of the day" urine.

If you test positive, you are pregnant. A positive test is accurate, but a negative result may mean that the HCG in your system was not high enough to show up when you did the test. You may still be pregnant. If your test is negative but you still do not get your period, go for a urine or blood test at a doctor's office or clinic.

Urine Tests at a Doctor's Office or Clinic.

Urine tests are available in private doctor's offices and health clinics. Depending upon where you go, a test may be free or cost up to $30. It's best to ask about the price of a pregnancy test before visiting a doctor or clinic. If you do not want to visit a private gynecologist, the yellow pages of your local telephone directory should have listings under "health services," "family planning clinics," "medical clinics," "pregnancy," or "abortion." (Free pregnancy testing is often available at abortion clinics. You can go for a test even if you do not want to consider having an abortion.) You can also call your local Planned Parenthood for a pregnancy test. Here's how the tests work.

The latest urine tests can tell you whether you are pregnant *just after* your period was due to start. One highly sensitive test is called TestPack. A doctor adds a few drops of your urine on a button-size disk, and within three minutes either a plus or minus sign appears on the disk. A plus means you're pregnant; a minus, you're not.

When more time has gone by and it's *two weeks* after your period was due, another type of urine test can be performed. A physician or technician puts a drop of your urine on a slide, then adds a test solution and HCG antibodies. If you are pregnant, in two minutes the mixture on the slide turns milky white and smooth. If you are not pregnant, the mixture looks clear and lumpy.

There is also a "morning urine" test you can take two weeks after you miss your period. You bring in a sample from your first urination of the day, and a doctor or a technician mixes it with a test solution and HCG antibodies in a test tube. If you are pregnant, about one hour later a whitish ring appears in the bottom of the test tube.

Blood Tests. Available through a doctor or at a clinic, blood tests can tell whether you are pregnant within two weeks after you conceive, *even before* you miss your period. One test, the **radioimmunoassay (RIA) blood test**, detects the beta-subunit of HCG, the placenta-producing hormone that rises during pregnancy. If you give blood in the morning, a lab should be able to report the results later that day. Another blood test is the **radio-receptor assay (RRA)**, which is used less often but is just as sensitive as the RIA. These blood tests may cost anywhere from $25 to $70, so ask the price before you ask for the test.

YOU'RE PREGNANT: WHAT HAPPENS NEXT?

While some teenage girls do plan their pregnancies, I am writing for the girl who unintentionally gets pregnant. My advice, as soon as you learn that you are a teenage expectant mother, is to tell your parents, or at least, one parent, a relative, or a family friend to whom you feel close. Although the choice is ultimately yours, you should not try to decide "What happens next?" by yourself. Those who love you will want to help you. Pregnancy requires mature decision-making; ready or not, it swiftly transports you into adulthood.

Among your options are to follow through on your pregnancy and childbirth and either raise your baby, allow your child to be adopted, or permit your child to be put into foster care, which is a temporary situation until you are able to care for him or her yourself. You and the father may consider getting married and raising your child together. On the other hand, you may decide to end your pregnancy. (This option is discussed at length in Chapter 10, *When a Pregnancy Ends Before Childbirth.*)

Of course, the final decision is yours. If you choose to give birth, will you be able to be a full-time mother, or would you rather see your baby adopted by a happily married couple? You must ask yourself honestly: "Am I able to, and do I want to, raise a child?" Here are two different decisions from two girls who chose to give birth to their babies.

One girl chose to become a teenage mother:

Erica, age seventeen, became pregnant when she was fifteen, the first time she ever had sex with her boyfriend. They did not use a condom or any other form of birth control. Erica's mother had died when she was seven years old, and she lived with her father, stepmother, and two half-brothers. Her father, stepmother, and boyfriend wanted Erica to end her pregnancy by having an abortion, but she was strongly against that. "This baby was going to be a part of me, something that belonged to me," she says. Erica went to a city health clinic for care during her pregnancy. She also dropped out of high school. "I'd fall asleep in class or get sick. I had morning sickness all day long," she recalls.

After three days in labor, she gave birth to her son, Adam, by cesarean section (see If You Need a Cesarean Section later on in this chapter). When she left the hospital, she moved in with her twenty-four-year-old sister. Between the money her sister earned as a word processor and Erica's part-time job as a supermarket cashier they managed to raise Adam for two years. Today Erica receives public assistance and is enrolled in a YWCA Teen Parent Program, for the education of teenage mothers.

Adam is in the program's day care while Erica is in class, studying for her high school diploma.

"I don't live anymore for myself; I live for Adam," says Erica. "I don't know what would have happened to me if I didn't have him. When you get pregnant it's a big step. I couldn't go through an abortion, and if you live those nine months pregnant, why should you give the child to someone else, for adoption?" Erica feels that her son "keeps her going" and, although she would have preferred waiting until she was a little older to become a mother, she's glad she has him. Her advice: "If you don't use some kind of birth control, you will have a very good chance of coming up pregnant, and if you are not willing to take care of that child, I don't think you should be having sex without protection."

One girl chose to offer her child for adoption:

Mandy, age eighteen, believed her boyfriend Jon when he said that he would not get her pregnant, that he knew what to do. She was sixteen at the time, and her only sexual experiences had been with him. When they had had intercourse before, everything had worked out all right, so she was not worried. She went to a doctor because she was feeling so sick—nauseous, weak, tired—and she wasn't getting better. The doctor asked Mandy if there was any possibility that she could be pregnant, and she said no. He tested her urine anyway. At first, when Mandy learned that the test was positive, she walked around as if someone had cast a spell on her. Jon apologized and asked whether she would get an abortion; if not, maybe they could get married.

To Mandy, the thought of an abortion was as unreal as the thought of becoming a wife and mother at age sixteen. She felt that if she knew the baby would have a good home, she could allow the infant to be adopted. She told her parents, who already suspected that her nausea was a sign of pregnancy, and they agreed to support whatever decision she made.

"My mother especially helped me," says Mandy. "She found out that there are basically two ways to offer a baby for adoption. One is to work out a private adoption through a lawyer, and the other way is to go through an agency. We decided to use an adoption agency. I learned all about my rights and I felt sure that adoption was the way for me to go. Why should a baby have to suffer because I made a mistake? I wanted the baby to have a good home with someone who knew how to raise it. I wasn't ready to become a mother, and it wouldn't have been fair to make my mother take care of it."

Mandy was able to go to school through most of her pregnancy. She succeeded in camouflaging her expanding body underneath oversized clothes, but she didn't really get big until the end of the school year anyway. She gave birth in the summer, when school was out.

"I had ten hours of labor and I held my baby girl for a few minutes after I gave birth," says Mandy. "I didn't want to hold her too long, because I thought I would get too attached. I want to have a baby someday when I'm older and married, but right now I'm still going to school and learning who I am."

To give teenagers an idea of what it is like to take care of a baby, a teacher in a New York City high school offers a course in which students are required to carry around a five-pound bag of flour, which actually weighs less than most newborns, all the time. If a student wants to go somewhere or do something without the flour, he or she must find someone who will take care of it. If the bag of flour gets ripped or messed up in any way, the "parent" is brought up on charges of child abuse in a law class. Once you decide to be a mother, your baby comes first!

YOU ARE GOING TO HAVE A BABY: IT'S TIME TO SEE A DOCTOR

When you know you're pregnant and are going to have a baby, you must make an appointment to visit an obstetrician, a baby doctor. This is the beginning of your commitment to have a healthy baby. You need an obstetrician to advise you on prenatal (which means "before birth") care during the next nine months, and to be there when you give birth.

Your First Visit to the Doctor is the longest one because he takes your health history, examines you internally (as explained in Chapter 7), and performs a number of tests. The usual tests for an expectant mother are a complete blood count, blood type and antibodies, a VD (venereal disease) blood test, and a rubella (measles) test. Other blood tests may include tests for toxoplasmosis, sickle cell anemia, Tay-Sachs disease, or other conditions. The doctor also takes a Pap smear, and many now perform an AIDS blood test as well.

After the physical examination, you and your doctor consult and you have a chance to ask him questions. You might want to know, for example, how active you can be during your pregnancy, whether you can travel, how long you can stay in school. The doctor will outline a general health plan for you, with diet and exercise, information on weight gain, and vitamin recommendations. He may also mention skin care, because young women have a tendency to develop stretch marks, white squiggly lines that look like mapped-out rivers, on the skin that pregnancy stretches. Many of my pregnant patients tell me that constant moisturizing with cocoa butter lotion or cream helps reduce stretch marks.

Sometimes a doctor wants you to come back two weeks after the first visit to discuss the results of blood

WHY YOU NEED A DOCTOR

Teenage expectant mothers have more problems during pregnancy than women who are in their twenties and thirties. Although women rarely die during childbirth, statistics show that a girl of fourteen is 60 percent more likely to have fatal pregnancy-related complications than a woman in her twenties. Problems come from smoking, poor nutrition during pregnancy, a lack of vitamins, and too much physical stress. Pregnant teens are known to suffer toxemia, pregnancy-related diabetes, and premature labor more routinely than women who are older.

• **Toxemia** is a condition that can kill both mother and baby. When you are not eating a well-balanced diet, symptoms of toxemia may appear: high blood pressure and water retention, which leads to bloating, kidney damage, and a buildup of protein in your urine. All this cuts down the blood supply to the unborn baby. When you have toxemia, which can change into an internal blood poisoning, your baby may either die or grow at a much slower rate and be seriously damaged. You, too, can die if your blood pressure stays high. An obstetrician can spot early signs of toxemia and work to keep you and your baby healthy. He can help you follow a nutritiously well-balanced diet to lower your blood pressure.

• Teens can also have **pregnancy-related diabetes** from eating too many cookies, cakes, pastries, and other sugary sweets. This condition can lead to miscarriage or stillbirth (the baby is not alive at birth). An obstetrician conducts routine urine tests during pregnancy, and a rise in blood sugar will show up in your urine to warn him of a diabetic condition. Like toxemia, diabetes in its early stages can often be corrected through changes in diet.

• Girls can also go into **premature labor**, which is labor before the baby's due date, or estimated day of birth, more often than older women because their bodies are stressed from lack of rest, a poor diet, and from being weakened by conditions like the two mentioned above, toxemia and pregnancy-related diabetes. An obstetrician can advise rest and, if necessary, medication to slow or stop premature labor. A baby that is born prematurely might not survive at all, or may live with a weakened body that makes him or her susceptible to illnesses throughout life.

tests and laboratory analyses and to check the progress of your pregnancy. Then he sets a schedule of revisits. You must see your obstetrician regularly for a trouble-free pregnancy.

Your doctor will check your urine, blood pressure, and weight gain at each visit. He is on the alert for anything that may go wrong, such as pregnancy-related diabetes, kidney problems, and any early signs of toxemia. He wants to monitor your weight gain because a steady rise is good for the fetus, but a slow gain with a sudden jump in poundage can be unsafe. Anything out of the ordinary may be a sign of trouble.

VISITING THE OBSTETRICIAN

During the nine months you are pregnant, your appointments will fall this way:

from the first visit to 28 weeks	every 3 or 4 weeks
from 28 to 32 weeks	every 3 weeks
from 32 to 36 weeks	every 2 weeks
from 36 weeks to delivery	once a week

Regular visits are important because an easy pregnancy can take a sudden turn and become complicated. If you are in good hands, trouble can be spotted right away and overcome. Should high blood pressure, pre-eclampsia (a mild form of toxemia), or full-fledged toxemia occur, your doctor will recognize the situation during a visit and bring you back to good health. Sometimes a doctor can reverse a premature labor and prevent a premature childbirth, but you have to be in the office for him to know what's happening. Although babies are born every day, nothing in pregnancy is routine. Having a healthy baby means being alert, smart, and careful. For instance, do you know that when you are pregnant

• **You cannot smoke.** The nicotine, carbon monoxide, methyl alcohol, arsenic and tars that enter the bloodstream when you smoke cigarettes affect the baby. Smoking increases the risk of miscarriage, premature birth, and stillbirth, and is linked to low-birth-weight babies, who can have developmental problems throughout their lives.

• **You cannot drink alcoholic beverages.** The alcohol that enters an expectant mother's bloodstream and reaches a fetus may lead to fetal alcohol syndrome (FAS). Babies affected by FAS may have low birth weight, facial defects, heart and kidney damage, or may be mentally retarded. While it's possible that babies of expectant mothers who drink may not be born with FAS, they may display fetal alcohol effects, such as hyperactivity, low IQ, and learning disabilities.

• **You cannot take hard drugs.** If you are in a situation in which recreational drugs such as marijuana or cocaine, hallucinogens such as LSD (lysergic acid diethylamide) and PCP (phencyclidine hydrochloride), amphetamines, barbiturates, or narcotics of any kind are offered, decline. Scientists do not know every drug and chemical that might be harmful to an unborn baby, but LSD and a number of narcotics have been linked to serious problems in fetuses.

• **You ought to stay away from caffeine.** Caffeine is a drug. Coffee, tea, cola and other soft drinks, chocolate, cocoa, and a number of nonprescription drugs contain caffeine, which easily passes into the bloodstream. Since 1980 the Food and Drug Administration has been warning pregnant women to limit caffeine consumption because birth defects were discovered in the offspring of mice that were given twelve to twenty-four cups of coffee a day. A study conducted in 1982 at Brigham and Women's Hospital in Boston showed that women who drank more than four cups of coffee a day were more likely to go into premature labor or deliver a baby in the breech (with the buttocks where the head should be) position.

You are going to experience dramatic, new sensations and have many questions during these nine months. My books *Childbirth With Love*, published by Berkley Books, and *It's Your Pregnancy*, published by Fireside/Simon &

Schuster, offer answers and lots of advice about how to handle pregnancy and childbirth.

WHAT'S GOING ON INSIDE YOUR BODY

When a doctor calculates your due date, the day when your baby is most likely to be born, he counts from the first day of your last menstrual period, when you weren't even pregnant! You became pregnant when you ovulated, about two weeks later. Nevertheless, he sets your due date forty weeks after the first day of your last menstrual period.

To have the healthiest baby, you ought to gain twenty-five to thirty pounds during those forty weeks. You might put on an average twenty-five pounds like this:

At ten weeks, one to two pounds
At twenty weeks, approximately eight pounds
At thirty weeks, approximately fifteen pounds
At forty weeks, which is full term, a total of twenty-five pounds

The weight you gain in the early part of pregnancy goes toward building an internal support system for the fetus. Your uterus expands, the placenta (the blood-rich uterine lining that is nourishing the fetus) grows, and your fat and blood volume increase. Toward the end of pregnancy, your weight gain goes to the baby, who puts on most of its weight in the last trimester, the final three months of pregnancy.

Here's how the baby develops.

Weeks 1 to 12. In the first four weeks the embryo looks more like a seahorse than a baby, yet a brain and nervous system are forming. By the fifth week, a primitive heart begins to beat and a circulatory system starts. The heartbeat can be heard by the end of the sixth week. The head is forming.

EGG CELL SURROUNDED BY GIRL AND BOY SPERM

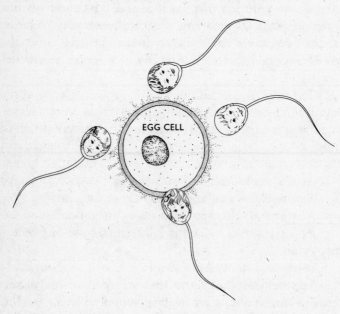

32. Will a Girl or a Boy Be Born? A baby's sex is determined by the male's sperm, which can carry either a "female" or a "male" chromosome. If a "female" sperm enters an egg first, a baby will be a girl. If a "male" sperm enters first, a boy will be born. As soon as one sperm enters an egg, the surface of the egg changes and no other sperm can enter.

In the seventh week the chest and abdomen take shape and other important organs, such as the liver and kidneys, appear. The embryo is about a half inch long and weighs approximately one-thousandth of an ounce. Features on the head, such as depressions for eyes, openings of nostrils, the shape of ears, the jaw and mouth, are apparent. The embryo is becoming human at this point, and by the eighth week, limb buds are obviously hands and feet. The spine can now make tiny movements.

The embryo is about one and a half inches long and weighs about one-fifteenth of an ounce by the end of the ninth week. The eyes are fully developed, and by the tenth week the fetus can move them, although they remain closed. **The embryo becomes a fetus at around Weeks 10 to 12.** At ten weeks, it is large enough to be seen on a sonogram, and by the eleventh week, the sex of the baby may be discovered if it's facing the camera during an ultrasound screening. The tiny fetus is complete by the end of twelve weeks. It has fingers and toes, ears and eyes, a circulatory system, internal organs, and recognizable male or female sex organs. It is about three and a half inches long and weighs about two ounces.

Weeks 12 to 24. The fetus looks almost "normal" at this point. During these weeks the head, arms, and legs become fully developed; the fingers and toes separate, and fingernails and toenails appear. Between Weeks 20 and 24, your pregnancy becomes obvious and you begin to "show." At this time you also experience "quickening," which means that you can feel the fetus move because its muscles are getting stronger. By the end of the twenty-fourth week the fetus is almost twelve inches long, and about one pound five ounces in weight.

Weeks 24 to 40. The fetus grows rapidly and becomes quite active during these weeks. Between Weeks 24 and 28, hair appears on the head, and eyebrows and eyelashes sprout. The testes of a male descend by Week 32. By the end of thirty-six weeks the fetus measures about eighteen inches and weighs about five pounds. Your uterus rises up out of your pelvis and into your abdomen during pregnancy, so that by about Week 36, the fundus, or top of your uterus, is right up under your ribs. Until the baby descends into your pelvis and is "engaged," it moves around quite a bit. You may feel swinging and turning and shifting until the baby is in its lowered, vertex (head down) position. Then the movements may become more subtle as the baby flexes and extends within its limited space. By forty weeks movement is slight. The baby is fully mature and at its birth weight, which is about two pounds heavier than it was at the end of thirty-six weeks. Now you have only to wait until labor begins.

HOW THE BABY IS BORN

The first step toward childbirth starts at the end of pregnancy when the fetus slips inside the pelvis and begins to maneuver its head into the birth canal. Ninety-five percent of the time, the baby is in the **vertex** (head-down) position in your pelvis, but 4 percent of babies may be in a **breech** position, which usually means that the buttocks are where the head should be. Sometimes a doctor may try to turn the baby, but a breech frequently calls for a cesarean section. (See If You Need a Cesarean Section below.) In 1 percent of all births the baby is in a **transverse lie**—positioned from side to side with neither head nor buttocks in the birth canal. The contractions of

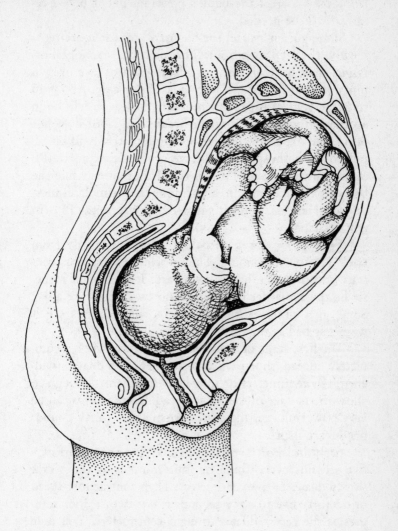

33. *Fetus in the Uterus. A full-term, or nine-month, pregnancy is pictured. The fetus is in the vertex (head-down) position for a normal, easy birth.*

labor may correct the baby's position, but if not, a cesarean will be needed.

Some girls may feel the bag of water (or more technically, the fetal membranes) break at the start of labor. A girl may have an uncontrollable gush of one or two pints of fluid or just feel a long-lasting trickle. About 10 to 20 percent of expectant mothers, however, will be in a situation where their water breaks and labor does not begin. An expectant mother in this situation will be admitted to the hospital to receive synthetic oxytocin (Pitocin) intravenously. Pitocin is a drug that acts like the body's natural oxytocin, a hormone that stimulates uterine contractions. Once it's in a girl's system, the Pitocin triggers labor.

True labor for a first-time mother can last from twelve to fourteen hours. The muscles of the uterus contract and push the baby downward. It is difficult to describe the actual feeling because no two labors are alike. Some girls suffer excruciating pain, while others say it wasn't as bad as they thought it would be.

The **first stage of labor** lasts until the cervix has completely effaced (shortened and softened) and dilated (widened) ten centimeters or four inches, which is enough to allow the passage of the baby's head. Contractions can be very powerful, exerting a pressure of about thirty pounds per square inch.

Early in labor, contractions may last thirty to forty-five seconds every three or four minutes as the cervix slowly dilates to five centimeters. Then contractions speed up to forty-five to sixty seconds every two to four minutes as the cervix dilates to eight centimeters. You may feel as if you have to urinate constantly due to pressure on your bladder. The most active phase of labor starts after the cervix is opened up eight centimeters. Contractions hit their full intensity, lingering for sixty to ninety seconds every thirty to ninety seconds. The cervix opens wider and wider, and when it stretches to ten centimeters, you are at your greatest period of discomfort, but this is the shortest phase.

The **second, or "pushing" stage of labor** comes after your cervix is fully dilated and the baby has moved into the birth canal. Then you have to push, as you learned to do in childbirth classes, to bring your baby into the world. (During your pregnancy, the private doctor or clinic overseeing your care will recommend a childbirth educator to you.) You are completely in charge of the amount of force you put into your pushing, but fierce contractions are going on at the same time to help you along. Usually you have someone with you, the baby's father or a close relative or friend, to be your labor coach and help you through the "pushing" phase. Sometimes you see your baby after only two or three pushes. The baby's head "crowns" and slips out. Then the baby turns to come into line with its shoulders, which are still inside. Usually the shoulder nearest the mother's abdomen appears first, and then the other shoulder. Then the rest of the body slides out. Actual childbirth can be less taxing than the earlier contractions.

In the **third stage of labor** the baby is a live, breathing human being, but a mother is not through with labor until she delivers the placenta, the uterine lining that has nourished the baby during pregnancy. The placenta may come out by itself a few minutes after the baby is born, or it may take up to a half hour to coax it out. The umbilical cord, which is attached from what will become the baby's navel to the placenta, can be clamped and cut immediately after birth or a few minutes later, after it stops throbbing. A doctor may have to tug gently on the umbilical cord to pull out the placenta. Once the placenta leaves your body, labor is over. Doctors and nurses may want to observe you for a time to be sure you have no postpartum (after-birth) problems.

IF YOU NEED A CESAREAN SECTION

Sometimes an emergency arises during childbirth: the placenta may block the birth canal or separate from the wall of the uterus; the baby may be in a breech position with its head not in the birth canal; the baby's heartbeat may drop or the pattern might change to signal trouble. These are a few of the situations that can mean that the baby will have to be born by cesarean (C-section). Erica, who is mentioned earlier in this chapter, had a C-section because her small pelvis at age fifteen could not accommodate the vaginal birth of her baby.

When a C-section is needed, you may be given an epidural or general anesthesia. An epidural is an injection into your lower back in a space between your vertebrae. An epidural "takes" in ten to thirty minutes and deadens all feeling from the waist down, which means you are awake during the C-section. Sometimes in an emergency there is not enough time to wait for the numbing power of an epidural, however, and you must be given general anesthesia, which puts you to sleep during the surgery.

Then the doctor makes an incision in your abdomen. Most of the time, he performs a bikini cut below the pubic hairline, but in an emergency, when the baby is in distress, he may do a vertical incision. He follows the abdominal cut with a transverse (horizontal) incision of the uterus and lifts the baby out of the womb. Then he closes the incisions he has made, and the operation is over. The entire procedure takes five to ten minutes.

TEENAGE GIRLS USUALLY DO NOT HAVE TWINS

Twins are usually conceived by people who have twins in their family histories. They are carrying on an inherited tendency.

Identical twins spring from a single egg fertilized by a single sperm. No one really knows how it happens, but the egg divides in two soon after conception. The two babies that are born are identical in every way: same sex, height, appearance, blood type—even their personalities are often the same.

Fraternal twins are created when two different eggs are fertilized by two different sperm. Either one egg bursts from each ovary or two from one ovary during ovulation. Fraternal babies may be the same sex, or different, and have similarities more like siblings than identical twins.

Teenage girls rarely become pregnant with more than one baby at a time. The number of women having twins, triplets, or more, increases after age twenty, and hits its peak between ages thirty-five and forty, when twins are born to one out of every sixty women. After age forty, the likelihood of having twins decreases again.

During pregnancy, each twin is smaller than a baby that has been growing by itself. If twins have grown to term without complications, are both the same size, and are in the vertex (head-down) position, an expectant mother should be able to have a trouble-free vaginal childbirth. Since the positioning of more than one baby in the uterus can be awkward, however, the chance of a cesarean section is greater for a woman carrying twins.

PREGNANCY MAKES YOU
GROW UP QUICKLY

When you are a pregnant teen, you have a decision-making responsibility that requires great maturity. As you weigh your options, it's a good idea to seek the advice of school and family planning counselors, or a family doctor, or a close relative, or better yet, your parents. While counselors, doctors, and relatives might respect your confidentiality, your choices can be easier to make if you have the full support of your parents.

Whether you decide to have an abortion, carry your baby to term and offer it for adoption, raise the child yourself either with or without the father, your parents can help every step of the way. Some girls have told me that their parents would disown them if they revealed their pregnancies, but when those girls finally did confide in their parents, their mothers and fathers surprised them. While parents may make threats, when faced with a pregnant daughter's plight they are usually ready to help. Most parents come through for their children.

• If you are considering an abortion, which is discussed in the next chapter, you will need advice about the laws in your state, and how to choose the most qualified doctor or clinic.

• If you choose to have the baby, you will need immediate prenatal care from an obstetrician in private practice or at a clinic. To have a healthy baby, you must follow a special diet, exercise program, and rest schedule, which an obstetrician provides. You will also face a decision about whether you are going to remain in school until you give birth, hire a private tutor, or enroll in a special program for pregnant teens.

Of course, if you decide to continue your pregnancy, your most important decision is whether to offer your baby for adoption or to raise the child yourself. These are difficult choices. You can experience bonds with the baby during pregnancy that can influence the adoption option. On the other hand, even under the best circumstances, with financial support from your family and the chance to complete your education, you are accepting an enormous responsibility when you become a parent. Doing what's best for the baby during pregnancy takes its place as only one small step in learning how to care for someone else. Once you become a mother, your childhood gives way to your child.

CHAPTER TEN

When a Pregnancy Ends
Before Childbirth

Not every pregnancy ends in childbirth. One of three things can happen: (1) a miscarriage, which is also called a spontaneous abortion because your body naturally ends your pregnancy; (2) an ectopic pregnancy, when an embryo settles outside your uterus—in a Fallopian tube, on an ovary, or in your abdomen—and has to be surgically removed (this rarely happens to teens); (3) a voluntary interruption of pregnancy, which is another way of saying that you may choose to have an abortion.

Of the three, having an abortion is most controversial and the laws regarding abortion are changing all the time, yet it's an experience that affects hundreds of thousands of teenagers—many more than will ever have a miscarriage or an ectopic pregnancy. In the pages of this health book, abortion is neither condemned nor condoned, but medically explained.

Over a million teenagers in this country become pregnant every year, and more than 400,000 of them have abortions. Most of these girls are between fifteen and nineteen years old, unmarried, and unintentionally pregnant. They made a difficult decision, but if you become pregnant when you do not want to be, you have the right to give birth to your baby as well as the right to end your pregnancy early with a safe, legal abortion.

Since the Supreme Court has upheld an executive order forbidding health clinics receiving federal funds from voluntarily offering information about legal abortion, you may have to visit more than one clinic to get complete medical advice. Many clinics, such as those affiliated with Planned Parenthood, have chosen to refuse federal funds in order to give a pregnant girl information about all her rights. (Call your local Planned Parenthood or the National Abortion Federation at 1-800-772-9100 in the United States, 1-800-424-2280 in Canada to locate clinics that offer information about abortion.)

As I mentioned in Chapter 9, while you ultimately make your own life choices, the people who love you can help you sort out your conflicts. I counsel the pregnant teens in my care to confide in their parents and to be open to others, such as school and family planning counselors, a family doctor, a close relative, or a friend. These people often offer valuable advice.

THINGS TO THINK ABOUT: LEGAL ISSUES

Over thirty states now have laws that require you either to notify your parents or to have their consent before you have an abortion. In each state, the particulars of the law for girls under eighteen vary. Sometimes both parents are needed, sometimes one, and sometimes a judge can take the place of a parent. You can go to juvenile court, plead your case in front of a judge, and receive judicial instead of parental consent. This is called the judicial bypass procedure, and you will need guidance from a counselor at a health clinic to help you set a court date.

A counselor can tell you what to expect. Sometimes girls appear in court alone; sometimes they have court-appointed attorneys or, if they can afford them, their own attorneys. Some clinics have volunteer attorneys, or just volunteers, who will stand by you. It's a good idea to have a "bypass buddy." A court appearance, whether it be in front of a judge who is a stranger, or worse, in front of a judge you may know, can be emotionally stressful. If you are considering an abortion, however, you have to abide by the laws in your state or travel to a state with different laws.

Whatever you do, make every effort to think ahead. The safest abortion is one performed during the first eight weeks of pregnancy—the earlier, the better—for less chance of complication. The longer a pregnancy continues, the more costly and difficult an abortion becomes. If you wait until you are more than twelve weeks pregnant to consult a doctor or to visit a clinic for an abortion, you are putting yourself at risk. With a late abortion, you face the possibility of seriously damaging your cervix and impairing your ability to conceive. Also, doctors and clinics are generally reluctant to perform abortions for anyone who is more than twelve weeks pregnant, and in some states twelve weeks is the legal cutoff point for the procedure.

A legal hassle can add days or weeks to your pregnancy, and can bring you closer to a more complicated abortion. So while you're working out feelings, visit a clinic for counseling and learn the legal requirements in your state. Timing is crucial. You can always change your mind once you have legal permission, but if you wait weeks before starting to work your way through the system, you will be placing yourself at a health disadvantage.

COST

The average cost of an abortion is $200 to $300. Since insurance coverage is uncertain, you will usually be responsible for paying the fee yourself. Ask about discount plans, however. Health facilities sometimes offer discounts for students or people with low incomes.

YOUR EMOTIONAL STATE

The question of whether an abortion will cause emotional problems has been studied and analyzed extensively, and experts tell us that the greatest period of stress is actually *before* an abortion, when you are deciding what to do about an unwanted pregnancy. Most women, once they reach a decision, have feelings of relief after an abortion is performed in the first trimester. One study reports that women who have late abortions, after the first trimester, suffer distress because in the second trimester a fetus is much more developed.

It's understood that no one really wants an abortion, and that you may have anxiety about whether an abortion will damage your body in a way that will prevent you from having babies in the future. There is *very little* health risk in an early abortion performed by a competent doctor in an office, in a hospital, or at an established clinic or health center.

Yet once you unintentionally become pregnant, you are faced with choosing between two things you do not want: a baby or an abortion. Which path do you take to feel best about yourself? Here's what three girls decided.

Dawn, age sixteen, thought about her options when she discovered she was pregnant. She was against abortion, but she could not imagine losing her freedom and becoming a mother so young. Also, her occasional boyfriend, Clark, did not want to be a father. Dawn went to a clinic to find out about an abortion. There she learned that she had to notify her parents or get the approval of a judge. She did not think her parents would agree, so after a counselor at a health clinic helped her petition the court, she went before a judge and was granted permission. With the signed judicial bypass consent in her hand, she returned to the clinic and then something happened. Dawn changed her mind. In the waiting room of the clinic she decided to keep her baby. When her parents learned about Dawn's pregnancy, they offered to support her in every way possible. Today Dawn is living at home, and while her son, Patrick, is in day care, she is finishing high school.

Sharon, age fifteen, always seemed older because she was so level-headed. When she became sexually active with her fifteen-year-old boyfriend, she thought she was in love. Pregnancy was not in this cheerleader's plans when the condom she and her boyfriend were using slipped off inside her vagina. She did not have backup protection, and she knew she was pregnant with her first round of nausea. Sharon could not picture herself, someone just beginning to feel independent, caring for an infant, yet she knew she could not emotionally handle having a baby and giving it up for adoption. She decided on an abortion, but her state's law required that both parents be told. Her parents were divorced and she had no relationship with her father, so Sharon and her mother went to court to get permission, which a judge granted. Sharon had an abortion at a reputable clinic and has not regretted her decision. She is continuing her plans for college, a career in journalism, and someday, marriage and a family.

Merry, age seventeen, became pregnant when she missed a couple of days of birth control pills. Her friend Danielle had had a baby the year before, and Danielle had gone back to school. Having the baby didn't seem difficult. Danielle's parents helped her take care of her son, Ethan. The baby seemed like a good thing. Merry thought Danielle appeared more grounded than she used to be, so she was surprised when Danielle suggested she have an abortion. "Having a baby is a bigger thing than it seems. I love Ethan, but I don't know what my life might have been. Also, I hurt people and changed their lives by having a baby." Merry considered Danielle's advice and thought about her own dreams. She wanted to learn languages, travel, and perhaps, after college, become a foreign diplomat. Merry lived in a state that allowed an abortion without parental consent. She underwent the procedure at a doctor's office and quickly put the experience behind her.

THE QUESTIONS GIRLS ASK ABOUT ABORTION

Every girl who is contemplating an abortion wants to know the answers to three crucial questions.

DOES AN ABORTION HURT?

The earlier in pregnancy that an abortion is performed, the less risk there is of complication and pain.

So if you are thinking about ending your pregnancy, if possible, consider having an abortion early in pregnancy, preferably within eight weeks of your last menstrual period, when a doctor can perform the easiest, safest procedure.

An abortion within six weeks of your last menstrual period is called a **menstrual extraction, or miniabortion**. With this procedure, you are given a painkiller, such as Motrin. Then Novocain is injected around your cervix to numb the area. If you are very sensitive to pain, a doctor may give you an intravenous injection of a stronger painkiller, such as Demerol or Nubain, mixed with a tranquilizer, such as Valium. You are awake during the menstrual extraction if you do not have an injection of stronger painkiller, but if you choose to have the injection, you will be out of it for a few minutes. You might feel cramping and a little pain during the procedure. If you experience anything greater than "a little" pain, a doctor can increase the amount of painkilling medication he is giving you. Plan to rest a short time after the abortion until you feel strong enough to go home. Someone should accompany you to a clinic or doctor's office, so they can be there to take you home afterward. You may feel weak or faint for a few hours, and you will need rest throughout the day and night.

An abortion between six and twelve weeks of your last menstrual period is called a **suction curettage**. You may receive either painkilling medication, as described above, or a general anesthetic. A "general" puts you to sleep and you are unaware of what's happening until the abortion is over. With this procedure, as explained in the section The Safest Abortion Methods, an abortion is performed by creating a vacuum action through a catheter, a narrow tube that is inserted through the cervix into the uterus. After the suction, a doctor performs a curettage, which is a gentle scraping of the walls of the uterus with a spoonlike instrument called a curette. He makes sure that the uterus is free of all tissue.

For a few days after an abortion, you can expect to bleed—occasionally quite heavily—as your uterus cleanses itself. (If your bleeding seems unusually heavy, however, call your doctor right away.) What you bleed and expel is the uterine lining, tissue that represents a portion of the placenta that has grown into the wall of your uterus and cannot be removed during the abortion. At childbirth this lining is fully formed and completely separates by itself.

Your doctor may suggest that you take antibiotics for a week to prevent any chance of infection, but you should not feel any significant pain. If you do have mild cramping or pain a few days after an abortion, an over-the-counter medication such as Nuprin or Advil should bring relief.

You must keep your reproductive organs as germ free as possible during this time, which means staying away from sexual activity, baths, and tampons for at least a month. Following a properly performed abortion in sterile conditions, however, your body will heal itself within about a month's time. Your doctor should schedule a follow-up visit one to two weeks after the abortion to make sure you are healing well and to give you a sense of when you may resume all activities.

A reminder: If you experience extremely heavy bleeding, severe pain, or fever after an abortion, immediately call your doctor or health clinic, or go to the nearest hospital emergency room to be examined.

CAN I BE PUT TO SLEEP?

Before an early abortion, if you are especially concerned about pain, a physician can give you an intravenous injection of a strong painkiller, such as Demerol, combined with a tranquilizer, such as Valium (as explained in the previous section), and sometimes a local anesthetic. You may choose to have general anesthesia, but most doctors try to avoid giving a "general," which in a small percentage of people has been associated with complications. A less risky "local" is preferred.

WILL I STILL BE ABLE TO HAVE CHILDREN?

After experiencing one abortion performed by a competent physician under safe, sterile conditions, you can expect to return to your formerly good physical condition. You can feel secure about becoming pregnant when you are older and ready to start a family, because your fertility has been proven; you now know that you have the ability to conceive a child.

Future problems with childbearing occur when a girl has more than one unwanted pregnancy and more than one abortion. Once you have undergone an abortion, you should be very strict with yourself about using birth control. While one abortion usually does not physically affect a girl, more than one abortion can wear on the reproductive organs and may alter your ability to carry a baby when you are older. Of course, it is best never to become unintentionally pregnant and never to have an abortion, but if you do undergo an abortion, try to make it your last.

THE SAFEST ABORTION METHODS

The safest abortion is performed within six weeks of your last menstrual period, when you can have a menstrual extraction, also called a miniabortion. Between six and twelve weeks, a suction curettage is performed. I feel that it is important to repeat that if you decide you must end your pregnancy, do it within eight weeks of your last menstrual period to have the option of choosing the safest procedure.

A menstrual extraction, also called a miniabortion, is a method that can be used within six weeks after your last menstruation.

In his office or at a clinic or health center, a doctor will give you a painkiller about half an hour before he begins. You are on your back on the examining table with your feet in the stirrups. As you begin to feel the effects of the painkiller, the doctor will inject numbing Novocain around your cervical area, which is high inside the vaginal canal. (If you are concerned about pain, he can give you an intravenous injection of Demerol or another strong painkiller, in combination with a tranquilizer, such as Valium, before he numbs your cervix with Novocain.)

The doctor will steady your cervix with an instrument called a tenaculum and slip a very narrow tube through the numbed cervix into your uterus. He then places suction on the tube and gently moves it around. This action removes the product of conception. The whole procedure takes only a few minutes. (The earlier the pregnancy, the quicker and easier the procedure.)

You may have some pain during the procedure, and you may feel weak and crampy for a few hours afterwards. A friend should come with you, and you should rest for an hour or so before leaving the doctor's office or clinic. Following a menstrual extraction you may bleed for three to six days, as if you had your period, and you may feel some pain now and then. If any of your symptoms are more severe, call your doctor immediately.

Suction curettage method is safely used from six to twelve weeks after your last menstrual period.

For the suction curettage you may be given either a painkiller, such as Demerol, with a tranquilizer, such as Valium, or general anesthesia, which completely puts you to sleep.

The procedure is usually not performed in a doctor's office, but in a clinic or a hospital. The doctor will advise you not to eat or drink for two hours before an intravenous injection, or eight hours before general anesthesia.

Usually the doctor gently opens your cervix with dilators, smooth steel rods of increasing diameter. If your pregnancy is farther along and the doctor has difficulty opening your cervix, he might place **laminaria digitala** (dried seaweed stem) into your cervix for twenty-four hours before your abortion is scheduled. The laminaria will dilate (open) your cervix and make the abortion safer.

Once the cervix is open, the doctor extends a tube through the cervix and into the uterus. The tube is attached to a suction machine with vacuum action that gently removes the tissue that is a product of conception. The procedure is over in ten to thirty minutes. Afterward, as your body cleanses itself, you may experience bleeding for five or six days and slight cramping, which can be controlled by Motrin or Anaprox, two drugs that fight inflammation and reduce swelling.

If you do not want to continue your pregnancy, you should make your decision as early as possible after your last menstrual period, when the safest methods of abortion are available to you. The safest methods, once more, are menstrual extraction and suction curettage.

AFTER TWELVE WEEKS OF PREGNANCY

Since a woman who has an amniocentesis (a procedure that tests the fluid surrounding the fetus for certain birth defects) might only learn in her fourth month (the earliest that she can get the results of this test) that her baby has Down's syndrome or another type of birth defect, many states still allow a pregnancy to be ended up to twenty weeks. An abortion after twelve weeks is much more difficult, however, and only a skillful physician is able to perform it.

The two most frequently used techniques for abortions past twelve weeks are:

• D&E (dilation and evacuation). In order to perform a D&E, a doctor places laminaria digitala (dried seaweed stem) into the cervix to expand it sufficiently. He then carries out the D&E using suction and forceps to remove the placenta.

• Injections of drugs that can start an abortion. A doctor injects into the amniotic sac (the fluid surrounding the fetus) prostaglandins or a solution called hypertonic saline, either of which will start the contractions of labor. Your body will then expel the pregnancy as if you were experiencing a mini-birth.

Warning: If after a late abortion, you have bleeding, a high fever, or cramping, immediately call your doctor. Any complication after a late abortion could damage your reproductive organs and make it more difficult for you to conceive in the future.

RU-486, THE FRENCH PILL. Since 1988 French women who have wanted to end their pregnancies have been able to take RU-486, the "French Pill." This "abortion pill" was developed in France during the eighties and has been found to be 95 percent effective for women who take it within forty-nine days after their last menstrual period. The French Pill is not approved yet in this country, and no doctor practicing in the United States can prescribe it.

RU-486 is taken in combination with prostaglandins, which bring on laborlike contractions and loosen the uterine lining that nourishes a pregnancy. When three pills are taken on three consecutive days, cramping begins, followed by the bleeding that signals a miscarriage. Over 60,000 women have safely used RU-486 in Europe, but recently a thirty-one-year-old woman, a heavy smoker who was experiencing her thirteenth pregnancy, died after using the French Pill. RU-486 obviously needs further investigation, but it is a step on the road to finding a safer means of interrupting pregnancy.

AFTER AN ABORTION

With safe, legal abortions being performed in sterile conditions today, there is much less risk of infection than there used to be in the days when illegal abortions were done in unclean environments. Still, no medical procedure can be guaranteed to be infection-free. Even in hospital surroundings with the latest equipment and the best doctors, complications may occur. The later a pregnancy, for example, the greater the risk of internal bleeding during an abortion.

Whenever you seek an abortion, you should know that there is always a risk of infection afterward. Your uterus or cervix may be cut or torn, and you may have more than the normal amount of blood loss, especially if the abortion is "incomplete," which means that a doctor missed some of the tissue that was part of the pregnancy. A doctor often prescribes antibiotics for a week as a precaution against infections. A fever, bleeding, or cramping ought to send you to your doctor right away. Any delay could mean damage to your reproductive organs and your ability to have a baby in the future.

As I mentioned earlier, for three to four weeks after an abortion, you must be careful to protect yourself from infection. You will probably bleed for five or six days following the procedure. Some girls are slightly queasy for a day or two, but others say they feel fine. Sexual activity, tampons, baths, and douches should be avoided for three to four weeks (even longer if your abortion occurred after twelve weeks of pregnancy) because they may contribute to infection.

After an abortion, since you have just been pregnant, you are much more fertile and much more likely to become pregnant again. So it is important to be aware of this and to use birth control.

WHERE TO GET A SAFE ABORTION

Although it is safest to have an abortion as early as possible, an abortion undertaken within twelve weeks is still considered an early abortion. An early abortion can be performed by a doctor in his office, or at a reputable health clinic, or in a hospital. A family physician would be a good person to consult about your options when you are pregnant. If you decide to have an abortion, he ought to be able to help you find a doctor to perform the procedure, if he does not feel qualified himself. Your local Planned Parenthood office, listed in your local telephone directory, and the National Abortion Federation (1-800-772-9100) also recommend health clinics that perform safe, sterile abortions.

You are not alone in your pregnancy. Doctors and counselors are available to help you, and as I have mentioned before, the people who love you—your parents, relatives, friends—are sources of support for you, too. Surveys have shown that most pregnant girls confide in one or both of their parents, and more times than not, their parents come through for them.

WHAT HAPPENS IF YOU HAVE A MISCARRIAGE

At least one out of three pregnancies ends in a miscarriage, usually during the early months of pregnancy, and a teenager is just as likely to have a miscarriage as an older woman. For some reason, sperm and egg do not develop properly and the body rids itself of an abnormal conception. This is the natural law of selection at work. A miscarriage usually prevents the birth of a malformed child.

Bleeding or spotting during pregnancy may be a sign of miscarriage, so you should always consult your doctor if you find that you are bleeding or staining. Sometimes spotting occurs when the embryo is implanting itself in the uterus, sometimes progesterone, the hormone that supports pregnancy, has not increased enough, but sometimes a miscarriage may be about to occur. It can take anywhere from a few hours to several weeks from the time you notice staining to the moment of miscarriage.

If you have spotting, you should go to bed, avoid physical activity, and call your doctor. Sometimes bed rest stops the bleeding, and a miscarriage not caused by an abnormal conception can be prevented. (A hormonal imbalance or an internal problem, such as a damaged Fallopian tube, may bring on a miscarriage.) On the other hand, if you go to bed and feel increasing pain in your abdomen along with the bleeding, a miscarriage may be inevitable.

You are having a threatened miscarriage if you experience vaginal bleeding and abdominal pain at the same time. During a miscarriage, your uterus begins a steady cramping, your cervix stretches open causing great pain, and bright red or brown blood flows from your vagina. Call your doctor at the first sign of spotting and keep him informed of your condition. If you miscarry, you may be treated in a doctor's office or admitted to a hospital, where you would have a D&C (dilation and curettage) to stop the bleeding. (A D&C involves the slow widening of the cervix with dilators, steel rods of increasing diameter, and the scraping of the uterine wall with curettes, small spoonlike instruments that gently clean the uterus.)

In the hospital you would receive intravenous fluids and medication to help control the bleeding. A dramatic blood loss happens only occasionally, but it is very serious because it means that blood is being shed from outside the reproductive organs. In extreme cases, you may need a blood transfusion. Most of the time this is not the situation.

During a complete miscarriage, you bleed (often in clots) and have cramping pain. As soon as the bleeding is over, though, you feel fine. This is often a sign that all the tissue has left your body, but you should see a doctor to be absolutely sure you are not still pregnant. A doctor must always examine you after a miscarriage to determine whether you need a D&C.

ECTOPIC PREGNANCY: RARE AMONG TEENS

In an ectopic pregnancy, a sperm and egg unite perfectly, but the embryo never finds its way to the womb, where it is supposed to make its home. Instead, an embryo attaches itself within a Fallopian tube, on an ovary, or in a girl's abdomen. A pregnancy outside the womb is called ectopic, and the most common ectopic pregnancy is in the Fallopian tube, which is where the name **tubal pregnancy** comes from.

Teenage girls rarely have ectopic pregnancies, but

you should know the signs. (Note: As sexually transmitted diseases, especially chlamydia, spreads among
teens, there is more likelihood of scarring in a tube, and
that scarring can increase the chance of ectopic pregnancy occurring.) If an embryo stations itself in your
tube, between the sixth and eighth weeks of pregnancy
you begin to feel abdominal pain. The pain, which usually comes in waves, may be hard to pinpoint, or you
may know right away that it is on the right or left side.
Usually this rhythmic pain means that an embryo is expanding a tube.

If you are pregnant and experiencing this kind of pain,
tell your doctor immediately. He will perform a blood
test to find out how long you have been pregnant, and
he will locate the site of the embryo through ultrasound.
Sometimes an ectopic pregnancy brings on pain without
bleeding, but other times it causes pain with bleeding.
The difference between blood that signals a miscarriage
and bleeding from an ectopic pregnancy is that with a
miscarriage the pain is over as soon as the bloody tissue
leaves your body; with an ectopic pregnancy, no amount
of bleeding seems to end the pain.

After the pain and possible bleeding begin, your Fallopian tube is close to bursting. You may have only a
day or two before it ruptures, or breaks open, so it is
crucial that you tell your doctor what's happening right
away. A skilled surgeon may be able to remove the embryo and save your tube before it bursts, but if a doctor
performs a **culdecentesis** (which means that he inserts a
needle through your vagina into your abdomen and ex-
tracts blood), then the tube has already ruptured. A burst
tube can start internal bleeding, which can lead to shock
and death, so a doctor has to operate immediately to
remove the damaged portion of the tube and stop the
bleeding.

THE GOOD NEWS IS YOUR FERTILITY

This chapter focuses on the different ways that a pregnancy may come to an end. Whether you became pregnant unintentionally or you planned your pregnancy, do not be discouraged by the fact that you were unable to experience childbirth. You were able to conceive a child. Your reproductive organs are working well, and you can be assured that you are capable of becoming pregnant again. Let your experience give you one more reminder that birth control is essential until the time is right to start a family. You will become an expectant mother if you have unprotected sexual intercourse. You have been given another chance to be smart about your choices!

CHAPTER ELEVEN

How You Eat Reveals How You Feel About Yourself

"If you could, what would you like to change about your looks?" is the question I asked sophomore girls in New York City high schools, and they gave me their honest answers:

"I'd like to be taller, more in shape, flatter stomach, less skinny ankles."

"Stronger teeth, flatter stomach, bigger chest."

"I'd *get rid* of my freckles! Make myself taller! Make my chest bigger."

"I would like to lose a lot of weight. I would like to look thinner and be more muscled. I wish I didn't have a bump on my nose."

"I would like to lose weight, get taller, and have a more shapely body."

"I'd like to have long, flowing hair and to be two inches taller."

"I would get a nose job and lose weight."

"I'd like to be thinner."

Do you notice that more than anything else, girls wanted to be thin? More often than not, they also wished for bigger breasts, flatter stomachs, and greater height. Not a single girl in my survey was happy with the way she looked.

The responses to my question suggest high schools are full of plump, short, flat-chested teenage girls, and I know this is not the case. You know it, too. There is a lot of distortion in girls' body images because the pencil-thin, perfectly proportioned fashion model—often with breast implants and "silicone" lips—has been held up as an ideal. If you don't fit exactly into this mold, you may feel that changes are needed. How do you see yourself? Have you bought into the idea that the fashion model image is "perfect"? I hope not, because beauty lies in diversity, and striving for a body type that is not your own can negatively affect you and your eating habits. It's a vicious cycle: your body image influences the way you eat, and the way you eat influences your body.

Good food can give you high energy and make you feel and look terrific. Once you follow the basics of healthy eating, you can exercise or play sports or just think better. Your eyes, hair, and skin will radiate from a balanced diet.

"AVERAGE" HEIGHTS AND WEIGHTS INDICATE THE STATURE OF MANY— BUT NOT ALL—GIRLS

There is no "ideal" body type. There are beautiful girls who are short and curvy, tall and wiry, with many dif-

AVERAGE HEIGHTS AND WEIGHTS FOR GIRLS
12 TO 19 YEARS OLD

Age	Height in Inches	Weight in Pounds*
12 years	60.8	102.4
13 years	62.5	112.3
14 years	63.3	120.8
15 years	64.3	121.5
16 years	64.1	128.0
17 years	64.4	131.4
18 years	64.0	130.0
19 years	64.4	132.6

Source: The National Center for Health Statistics, Data from the National Health Survey, Series 11, No. 238.
*Includes clothing

ferent skin tones and hairstyles. Years ago, from 1976 to 1980, the government surveyed the population to learn the height and weight, in general, of Americans. The statistics for young women are still the only ones available, and I present them in the above table, as indicators of what the average is for height and weight in this country, but not as ideals. A look at the numbers can give you an idea of whether you are running short or tall, under- or overweight.

As you can see, although height changes little between the ages of fifteen and nineteen, the "average" girl gains more than ten pounds over those years. Any weight you gain should be from good, nutritious food and the toning of your muscles through exercise.

HAVE YOU SLIPPED OFF THE "HEALTHY EATING" TRACK?

When you were between eleven and fifteen years old your body added extra fat in preparation for your menstrual period. Your breasts grew, your hips widened, and then your menstrual cycle began. During these years, girls sometimes wonder whether they are ever going to see an end to their weight gain. Of course, once menstruation starts, a girl's body reshapes and slims, but the transition time can be confusing. Many girls suddenly begin to think of dieting, or feel so stressed by their changes that they eat more than usual.

You may have gone off the "healthy eating" track in your early teens when you gained weight, and be dieting to lose pounds that have been already shed. Or, you may be so worried about not having the kind of figure you want that you are gorging on ice cream and sweets to comfort yourself. No matter what your eating habits, you ought to understand good nutrition—there is a connection between what you eat and how you look. **Food is fuel for building a strong, healthy body!** A diet shaped by a balance of healthful foods can energize and beautify you. By eating well, you can show everyone how much you care about yourself—you will look that good.

UNDERSTANDING FOOD

The National Academy of Sciences tells us that moderately active women from ages eleven to fifty need about 2,200 calories a day from food. A **calorie** is a measure of energy, and the major nutrients in food—carbohydrates, fat, and protein—have different calorie contents. One gram of carbohydrates or protein contains about four calories, but one gram of fat has nine calories. Also, researchers have found that a calorie from a fatty food may add body weight more readily than a calorie from a low-fat food. You don't have to be a fanatical calorie counter to remember that fatty foods add calories, fat, and increase the artery-clogging cholesterol in your body that can bring on heart disease.

If you stop for a fast lunch at McDonald's, you have a heavy helping of calories mainly from fat: a quarter pounder has 427 calories; a serving of fries, 220; a chocolate shake, 383.[1] That's 1,030, or almost half of your daily calories, on a lunch that offers more fat than vitamins and minerals! (A slice of cheese pizza, by the way, is 290 calories.)

No one wants to be a prude about fast food, but if you choose to feast at McDonald's one day, you might try less fatty foods the next. Have a tuna sandwich on whole-grain bread, a glass of low-fat milk, and an apple for lunch. That way you can get more fiber, less fat, and a wider variety of vitamins and minerals.

Nutrition experts have been trying to encourage all Americans to eat more of the less fatty foods like grains, vegetables, and fruit. In fact, the U.S. Department of Agriculture created a "Food Guide Pyramid" for healthy eating, and the federal government suggests that we follow it: choose more of the foods at the bottom of the pyramid and less of the foods near the pyramid's peak.

Although you may think so at times, **you cannot become physically addicted to fat or sugar**. A craving for ice cream, potato chips, cake, or cookies is different from a chemical dependency, which can be created by

---

[1]All calorie counts are from Jean A. T. Pennington, *Food Values of Portions Commonly Used*, 15th ed. (New York: Harper & Row, 1989).

USE SPARINGLY
FATS, OILS,
AND SWEETS

2–3 SERVINGS
MILK, YOGURT,
AND CHEESE

2–3 SERVINGS
MEAT, POULTRY,
FISH, DRY BEANS,
EGGS, AND NUTS

3–5 SERVINGS
VEGETABLES

2–4 SERVINGS
FRUIT

6–11 SERVINGS
BREADS, CEREAL, RICE, AND PASTA

34. The Food Guide Pyramid. Here's an excellent guide to good nutrition from the federal government. Every day, by eating more of the foods at the bottom of the pyramid, and less of the foods at the top, you will have a diet that is less fatty and most healthful. ILLUSTRATION BY TONY KRAMER

alcohol, caffeine, tobacco, and other drugs. Your body becomes addicted to substances that stimulate the release of certain body chemicals, and you go through withdrawal without these substances. You would not show signs of withdrawal if fat or sugar were taken away from you. You may be conditioned to the taste and feel of a food high in fat or sugar. You may like fudge brownies, for instance, because your personal history is somehow bound up with this food. Maybe your mother or father makes them. Or perhaps you receive them as treats on special occasions. If you can withstand longings for fats or sweets from time to time, you can change your conditioning. You may start to crave strawberries instead of strawberry ice cream!

IN PRAISE OF BREAKFAST

At the University of California in Los Angeles, a ten-year study of 7,000 adults found that men and women who regularly ate breakfast lived longer. If you remember one thing from this chapter, I hope it is to eat a nutritious breakfast. Many teens are on the run in the morning, grabbing high-fat, high-calorie foods, and all those muffins and doughnuts can drag you down. When your first nourishment after eight hours of sleep contains mostly fat and refined carbohydrates (from sugars and white flour), you are not getting the nutrients you need to increase your stamina and keep your mind and body at peak performance. Eating sugary food may zap you with a quick burst of energy, but by midmorning you'll be out of it.

The best breakfast foods are low in sugar and fat and contain energy-sustaining protein and complex carbohydrates. A whole-grain cereal with fresh fruit and low-fat or skim milk, a fresh fruit yogurt shake, a wedge of cantaloupe with cottage cheese, and a slice of whole-grain toast are among many excellent selections. Even a peanut butter and banana sandwich with a glass of low-fat milk is a healthy breakfast special. In making these choices you are getting a good amount of calcium, iron, and vitamins C and D at breakfast.

If your parents tend to stock up on English muffins rather than fruit and yogurt for breakfast, perhaps you could suggest that they buy whole-grain cereals and fruit for you. They may be on the run themselves and eating easy-to-grab foods. You can set the example at your house, and you will be a family leader with a new energy level, because you know the most healthful way to start your day.

HOW TO QUENCH YOUR THIRST

Many teens reach for a can of soda rather than a glass of water when they're thirsty, but soda with its preservatives, artificial color and flavoring, sugar, corn syrup, or sugar substitutes, and occasionally, caffeine, will not add a glow to your skin and hair the way water will. Also, water is calorie-free, and a twelve-ounce can of soda contains from 120 to 140 calories. (Although diet sodas can contain only one or two calories, there is some controversy over whether their sugar substitutes increase your appetite for other foods.)

Water used to be the number one thirst quencher in the United States, but soft drinks have taken over that position. According to the latest figures from the National Soft Drink Association, every adult in this country is swallowing approximately forty-five gallons of soft drinks every year. If you automatically down a cola or other type of soft drink when you're thirsty, then you're probably not drinking water or even milk with any regularity. Remember, water is nature's own moisturizer for the skin and cleansing agent for the body. Try to drink up to eight 8-ounce glasses of water a day.

Also, think twice about milk. During your teen years (ages eleven through eighteen), the Recommended Dietary Allowance (RDA) for calcium jumps from 800 milligrams (mg) a day to 1,200. This rise occurs because right now your bones are growing to their full thickness, so the more calcium you can take in, the denser and stronger your bones will be. This is your last major opportunity for bone strengthening! And for girls, thick bones are essential because the stronger your bones, the less likely you will develop a bone-thinning disease called **osteopo-**

rosis, which strikes when you are older. Women who have thin, delicate bones are often frail looking and can easily fall and break their arms, legs, and hips. I know that you are more interested in what calcium can do for you right now, though, so, most immediately, the calcium in milk can boost your physical power. You develop a sturdy frame today, which is as crucial as avoiding osteoporosis tomorrow. Regular exercise goes hand in hand with healthy eating, and bones strengthened by calcium and made even more powerful through exercise can give you good posture, athletic prowess, and a commanding presence.

A glass of low-fat milk provides about 300 mg of calcium, so four glasses of milk would meet the 1,200 mg RDA. You do not have to get all of your calcium from low-fat milk, however. Yogurt, cheese, ice cream, and ice milk all contain calcium. Eight ounces (one cup) of plain, low-fat yogurt contains 415 mg of calcium, one ounce of Swiss cheese has 205 mg, and a half cup of vanilla ice cream or ice milk offers about 90 mg. The low-fat choices, of course, are the most healthful. (Some other sources of calcium are sardines, salmon, tofu, broccoli, and artichokes.)

In addition to water and milk, you might try other natural, chemical-free thirst quenchers whenever you have a choice: fruit juice or "natural" sodas sweetened with fruit juice; plain or naturally flavored seltzers; mineral or spring water.

EATING TO FEEL AND LOOK GOOD

Researchers have become fascinated with how we can eat to strengthen our immune systems and stay healthy. Today a lot of new information about food exists because there is a trend to using food's natural power for preventing illness. It seems that good nutrition will not only make you taller than your grandparents but also help you look and feel better today, and live a longer, healthier life in the years ahead. Here are some of the best eating bets.

Vitamin A and the Carotenoids. Yellow-orange fruits and vegetables and dark green leafy vegetables, such as carrots, squash, pumpkin, sweet potato, cantaloupe, papaya, spinach, watermelon, kale, collard, mustard, and turnip greens, contain a compound called beta carotene, which converts into vitamin A in your body. Of the more than 500 compounds called carotenoids in food, 50 are forms of vitamin A, and beta carotene is the best known. Although you can get vitamin A (in the form of retinol) from liver, cheese, eggs, butter, chicken, and whole and fortified milk, nutritionists like us to get this vitamin from carotenoids because more and more research shows that these compounds can help protect against certain cancers. Carotenoids are weapons in the fight against stomach, lung, esophageal, colon, rectal, and bladder cancer.

Vitamin A is also an antioxidant, which means that it neutralizes "free radical" cells, troublemakers that can damage internal cells, age your skin, and bring on cancer. These free radicals may be created by pollution, smoking, or radiation in the environment. Vitamin A and other antioxidants, such as vitamins C and E, fight free radicals. Overall, vitamin A boosts your body's natural immunity, helps fight infection, strengthens your eyesight, and, as mentioned in Chapter 3, contributes to smooth, healthy-looking skin.

Folic Acid, or Folate. The B vitamin folic acid, also called folate, is found in such vegetables as brussels sprouts, broccoli, spinach, beets, collard greens, romaine lettuce, parsley, soybeans, black-eyed peas, and beans. Yet whole grains, especially wheat germ, and liver also are good sources of this important vitamin. Folic acid is essential for healthy blood and for helping your body use protein from food, but women especially need folic acid for healthy pregnancies. This vitamin can so greatly reduce the risk of serious birth defects that the U.S. Public Health Service wants young women to have added folic acid during their childbearing years—yours now, and your unborn baby's when you want to start a family. Researchers also believe that folic acid may fight precancerous conditions in the cervix. Note: Folic acid can be drained from vegetables that are cooked to softness in water. The best way to keep folic acid in food is to microwave or steam vegetables, or whenever possible, to eat them raw.

Vitamin C. This important vitamin is in many fruits and vegetables. It's high in citrus fruits such as oranges, grapefruit, lemons, and limes, but it's also in berries, melons, papaya, cantaloupe, cherries, tomatoes, green peppers, cabbage, spinach, broccoli, brussels sprouts, turnip greens, and cauliflower. Vitamin C may be one of your immune system's strongest players. Like vitamin A, it helps to fight cells that can age you prematurely. Vitamin C counteracts the effects of stress and environmental pollution on your body; it helps wounds heal, strengthens your eyes, helps your body absorb iron from food, and helps you overcome colds and that run-down feeling.

Vitamin E. Look for vitamin E in wheat germ, seeds, nuts (which means it's in peanut butter), vegetable oils, lobster, and salmon. Like vitamins A and C, it attacks the cells that can trigger cancerous tumors in your body. Vitamin E also keeps your blood flowing smoothly, helps your eyes stay in good health, and prevents scarring when you have a wound.

Iron. There are two kinds of iron in food. Red meat, organ meat, dark fowl, and fish are prime sources of "heme" iron, which is more easily absorbed by the body than the "nonheme" iron in leafy green vegetables, nuts, dry beans, apricots, prunes, and raisins. If you eat foods having nonheme iron with foods rich in vitamin C, such as tomatoes or bell peppers, however, the vitamin C will help your body take in the iron. This mineral is key to hemoglobin, a substance in red blood cells that carries oxygen throughout your body and keeps you alive. Girls need more iron than boys because monthly menstruation can deplete the iron supply. Eating iron-rich foods during these years is important, though, not only because you have begun menstruating, but because you are growing and you need a strong red blood supply for your maturing body.

Selenium. Seafood, organ meats, red meat, and poultry are the foods with the most selenium. Grains, seeds, fruits, and vegetables may offer some levels of selenium, depending on the amount of the mineral that was in the soil in which they grew. Selenium helps to keep your muscles, red blood cells, hair, and nails in good health. It also protects and strengthens your heart, and it works with vitamin E to fight free radicals and prevent cancerous tumors from forming.

Zinc. Oysters, liver, lean ground beef, lamb, pumpkin seeds, tuna, and the dark meat of turkey and chicken are all foods with zinc. This mineral helps build bones, cure certain skin problems, and keep your blood supply healthy.

Omega-3 Fatty Acids. Deep-sea, cold-water species of fish, such as salmon, tuna, mackerel, herring, and sardines, are rich in omega-3 fatty acids. New reports show that omega-3 may help suppress cancer. It has been found effective in fighting cancers of the breast, colon, and pancreas. So eat your seafood!

I recommend that you always eat a variety of the foods mentioned in this section for a good mix of the vitamins, minerals, and food components, such as carotenoids, that can contribute to your attractiveness and confidence.

IF YOU ARE THINKING OF BECOMING A VEGETARIAN

Nutritionists are encouraging all of us to eat less of the high-fat foods, such as meat and cheese, and more of the low-fat foods, such as vegetables and fruit. If the experts have their way, in the future we will be eating more food that grows from the ground, and we will be healthier.

Vegetarians have less chance of getting heart disease, diabetes, and certain kinds of cancer, and environmentally, vegetarianism is good for the planet. If Americans were to cut back on their meat eating by 10 percent, 60 million people could be fed on the grain used as animal feed. Cattle are vegetarians!

Does this mean that you should become a vegetarian? My advice is to learn about the different ways you can make changes in your diet without taking any sudden, radical steps. It's not a good idea to decide that the sliced steak on your dinner plate should be instantly converted into tofu and steamed vegetables. If you change your diet overnight, you will shock your system. You may become headachy and disoriented, and you may experience cramps and gas from a sudden increase in your consumption of

WHY EAT CERTAIN FOODS?

Food	Contains	Good for
carrots, squash, pumpkin, sweet potato, cantaloupe, spinach, watermelon, greens, and other yellow-orange and dark green leafy vegetables	Vitamin A and carotenoids	Preventing certain cancers (esp. lung), immunity, eyesight, healthy skin
romaine lettuce, beans, broccoli, spinach, beets, brussels sprouts, whole grains, wheat germ, liver	The B vitamin folic acid, also called folate	Growth, maintaining strong blood supply, healthy pregnancies, may fight precancer in the cervix
oranges, lemons, limes, berries, melons, cherries, tomatoes, green peppers, cabbage, broccoli, brussels sprouts, cauliflower	Vitamin C	Fighting effects of stress and pollution, healing wounds, fighting colds
wheat germ, seeds, nuts	Vitamin E	Attacking cells that can cause cancer, circulation of blood, eyes

Food	Contains	Good for
red meat, organ meat, dark fowl, fish, leafy green vegetables, nuts, dried beans, apricots, prunes, raisins	Iron (heme and nonheme)	A strong red blood supply, strength, growth
seafood, organ meats, red meat, poultry	Selenium	Healthy muscles, red blood cells, hair, nails
oysters, liver, beef, lamb, pumpkin seeds, tuna, dark turkey and chicken	Zinc	Strong bones, skin, blood
salmon, tuna, mackerel, herring, sardines	Omega-3 fatty acids	Fighting certain cancers (esp. breast, colon, and pancreas)

fiber-rich foods. If you want to eat less animal, and more plant foods, there are a number of approaches you might consider.

• **Lacto-icthyo vegetarians** do not eat meat of any kind, but they do eat fish, eggs, and dairy products.
• **Lacto-ovo vegetarians** do not eat meat or fish, but they eat everything else, including dairy products and eggs.
• **Lacto-vegetarians** do not eat meat, fish, or eggs, but

they still consume dairy products along with their fruits and vegetables.

• **Vegans** follow the most restrictive type of vegetarian diet. They stay away from meat, fish, eggs, dairy products, and any food that may have a remote connection to an animal or animal food. They do not eat a pie that has a crust made with butter, for instance.

Although you may have good reasons to cut back on meat and other foods from animal sources, you have to consider how you are going to get enough nutrients from a new diet. You especially want to think about getting enough calcium, iron, and protein. Normally you would be getting your calcium mostly from dairy, and iron and protein mostly from meat.

About Calcium. I always recommend that every teen stay on a diet that includes milk and other dairy foods. As I emphasized in the How to Quench Your Thirst section in this chapter, these are the years of rapid bone growth, when your bones are expanding in thickness as well as in length. If you do not take in high levels of calcium during your teens, you will not reach your peak bone mass and may more easily develop osteoporosis, the bone-thinning disease that can disfigure and cripple you when you are older.

About Iron. Iron can be a little tricky with a vegetarian diet. (See more about iron in the section Eating to Feel and Look Good.) Even if you continue to eat dairy foods and eggs, they offer little in the way of iron. You lose iron in your menstrual bleeding, and the easiest way to replace it is by eating meat, organ meat, dark fowl, and fish. The iron in leafy green vegetables, nuts, dry beans, and dried fruit, such as apricots, prunes, and raisins, is more difficult for your body to absorb. Yet the Chinese eat little meat and do not suffer from iron deficiency. They prepare iron-rich foods, such as legumes and nuts, in dishes that also contain foods high in vitamin C, such as broccoli and peppers, and it's well known that vitamin C helps the body absorb iron from food. Other foods that are high in vitamin C are citrus fruits, tomatoes, cabbage, cauliflower, and potatoes.

You can also increase your iron by cooking your food in cast-iron pots. The iron from the pot seeps into the food. On the other hand, tea and coffee can inhibit your body's intake of iron, so you would want to stay away from these drinks when you are eating for iron.

About Protein. Strung together in many ways, amino acids form protein, and we could not exist without them. Muscles, organs, blood vessels, skin, bone, hair, enzymes and hormones, even our genes, have protein. Our body can manufacture thirteen of the twenty-two different kinds of carbohydrate- and nitrogen-containing amino acids that create protein, but we must bring in the nine other essential amino acids from the protein we eat every day.

Most meat, fish, poultry, eggs, and dairy products contain considerable amounts of the nine essential amino acids. Vegetable protein sources also have the essential amino acids, but often only a small amount of one or another of them. You can get a good portion of the essential amino acids, however, by combining high-protein vegetables, such as dried beans, peas, and soy foods, with grains, such as corn, rice, and wheat. That's why it makes sense to mix rice and beans, for example. If you include fish in your nonmeat diet, you are already getting high-quality protein without combining vegetables. (Vegans, who do not eat dairy, eggs, meat, fish, or fowl, must also be aware of finding new sources of vitamin B_{12}, which is in these foods. I do not recommend a vegan diet, but those who are vegans ought to choose cereals fortified with vitamin B_{12}. Nutritional yeast also provides that vitamin.)

For more information on understanding vegetarianism, you can request the pamphlet "Vegetarian Nutrition for Teenagers" from The Vegetarian Resource Group, P.O. Box 1463, Baltimore, MD 21203 (enclose a stamped, self-addressed envelope). You can also gain excellent insights into vegetarian diets by reading *Diet for a Small Planet* by Frances Moore Lappé (Ballantine Books) and *The Gradual Vegetarian* by Lisa Tracy (Dell). Vegetarian cookbooks, such as *The Moosewood Cookbook* by Mollie Katzen (Ten Speed Press), can help you become your own cook.

A daily multivitamin with minerals is part of my philosophy of good nutrition, whether you are a strict vegetarian, a big meat eater, or simply a food lover.

ARE YOU TOO UNHAPPY TO EAT RIGHT? DO YOU HAVE AN EATING DISORDER?

Do you think of food as the enemy? While it is true that a large number of young people are gaining weight from lack of exercise and too much snacking in front of their television sets, many teenage girls are overexercising and undereating. They see "big" rather than "beautiful" bodies when they stand in front of their mirrors. They are unhappy, and when these unhappy girls become determined, they can decide to hardly eat at all, or to gorge themselves.

"If you are so focused on your weight that that's all you can think about, there is something else you are not looking at," says Natasha, a nineteen-year-old who starved

herself through high school while suffering from the eating disorder **anorexia nervosa**, then went through cycles
of stuffing herself and throwing up while suffering from
the eating disorder **bulimia**. Your feelings about food are
often linked to your feelings about yourself.

Anorexia Nervosa

Do people tell you that you should eat more because
you look too thin? Do you think they are completely
crazy? Do you see a fat girl in your mirror and believe
that you have to diet more? If you can answer yes to these
questions, you may be moving toward anorexia nervosa,
which is a life-threatening eating disorder that often has
underlying emotional causes. Try to judge your approach
to eating. You may be anorexic if you are

• Extremely thin and have lost 15 percent or more of
your body weight.
• Always counting calories and dieting.
• Sure you are fat even though everyone says you
have a terrific figure.
• Never hungry.
• Excessively exercising.
• Weighing yourself whenever you get the chance.
• Sick when you eat more than a few morsels of food.
• Chilly even when the temperature is not that cold.
• Not menstruating.

Bulimia

On the other hand, it is known that girls who are
afraid to gain weight but do not want to stop eating can
sometimes be driven to bulimia nervosa, another serious
eating disorder. Unlike anorexia, which is a form of self-
starvation, bulimia is characterized by cycles of out-of-
control eating (binging) of thousands of calories of food,
such as whole pizzas and half-gallon cartons of ice cream,

then getting rid of the food (purging) through vomiting, laxatives, diuretics, or overexercise. Sometimes after a binge/purge cycle, a bulimic girl will become anorexic for a while and not eat anything, but eventually she will binge/purge again. Like anorexia, bulimia is deeply rooted in emotional conflicts. Do you recognize any of the symptoms of bulimia in yourself? You may be bulimic if you are

• Gorging yourself with food during solitary eating orgies.
• Not getting your menstrual period regularly.
• Noticing that your weight goes up and down all the time.
• Always weighing yourself.
• Following your binges with strict diets.
• Ashamed of eating.
• Running to the bathroom right after you eat.
• Feeling depressed, and eating in response to your depression.

WHAT HAPPENS TO YOU WHEN YOU HAVE AN EATING DISORDER

While I do not want to scare you, you should know that both anorexia and bulimia are very serious health risks.

Anorexia virtually stops your sexual development. You do not menstruate. Your hair can fall out, and you can stop growing. Your brain can shrink, your heartbeat can slow, and your blood pressure can drop. You can have liver, kidney, and lung problems, a low white blood cell count, and anemia. You can dehydrate and eventually suffer congestive heart failure. In other words, anorexia can kill you!

Bulimia (which comes from a Greek word meaning

"ox hunger") can also make you sick to death. The vomiting can rot your teeth and gums, weaken all of your muscles, including your heart, and may lead to kidney failure. You can tear your esophagus and rupture your stomach by throwing up constantly. You could also set up a situation wherein your body becomes so dependent on laxatives that you cannot have a bowel movement without them. If you use drugs to get rid of the food through vomiting, urination, or bowel movements, you may cause the potassium level in your body to drop, and that can trigger a heart attack. You may die!

HOPE FROM GIRLS WHO ARE RECOVERING FROM EATING DISORDERS

You may see food as an enemy you have to overpower and control, but think about whether you are controlling the food or it is controlling you. Do you understand how your emotions may be affecting your eating?

I have met smart, attractive young women who have fought lifelong problems of self-esteem to conquer their eating disorders, and their insights are more valuable than anything I might say about eating a well-balanced diet.

I started restricting my food in seventh grade, and I didn't think anything about it. I wanted to lose weight and I didn't realize that I was hurting myself. I always had headaches—all the time—and I was not very clear. I thought that I had no energy because I was tired. I didn't think I had a problem. Now I have a better sense of how my emotions affect my eating and my body. Instead of facing my emotions when I couldn't make a decision, I would get concerned about my legs, my stomach, and my eating. Now I've learned that there's a lot of good in me and I'm more sure of the good part, my strength. Now I face things.

> Juliet, age 18, recovering anorexic

I've spent a lot of time [at a treatment center] dealing with issues of my sexuality and my sexual abuse as a child. I realize how much the abuse affected how I look at my body, how I carry myself, how I am in danger of not caring about my body, and how I don't care when I binge and purge. Yet when I was bulimic I felt very in control, but I really had no self-confidence. I'd feel lost so I'd want to eat everything.

> Debra, age 19, recovering bulimic

I started skipping meals when I was eleven. When I wouldn't eat I felt like I was floating, like I was walking on air. I could walk for miles because my feet weren't touching the ground. I felt like I could get my parents to do what I wanted them to do by not eating, but afterwards I learned about "bad" attention. I wanted my father's attention and I got it, but it was negative attention. Now I want to be noticed for my strength, but what really got me to start eating again was that I wanted to grow, to be tall. By not eating, I had stopped myself from growing. I want to be tall, with a really nice body, because your body is the shell of who you are, yourself.

> Alexis, age 16, recovering anorexic

"The most important thing is that girls who have eating disorders become decision makers," says Merrily Karpell, Ph.D., the associate clinical director of The Renfrew Center. "A lot of girls feel out of control, and they see life as something that happens to them. They tend to be people-pleasers, who are extremely concerned about others.

"So many young women with anorexia and bulimia

have to know that it's not selfish to have a self. Often these girls get confused and think that if they say they want something for themselves it means that they are selfish. I ask them to talk about themselves for three minutes, and instead it's the boyfriend, the mother, the father."

The Renfrew Center (475 Spring Lane, Philadelphia, PA 19128, 1-800-334-8415) is the country's first women's residential facility for the treatment of anorexia and bulimia. Forty women at a time can stay at Renfrew and take their first steps toward feeling good about themselves. A nine-week program, which is usually covered by health insurance, focuses on family therapy. Conquering an eating disorder is easier for a girl when she and her family discuss family dynamics, and everyone is open, aware, and supportive.

There are other centers for the treatment of anorexia and bulimia, and some of the organizations that can help you, and help you find ways to be treated, are listed on the next page. It is so important to talk to someone before you affect your health to the point of no return. Listen to Alexis:

My advice for a girl who might be like me, like I was, is to just go and talk to somebody, a friend, even call a hotline. I went to my doctor, who is a pediatrician. He talked to me, helped me figure out how I felt about my father. He made me feel like I could do anything, and that all this was really about getting control.

If you can see yourself in this section on anorexia and bulimia, do not try to keep your eating disorder all to yourself. If you feel uncomfortable telling your mother or father, share your secret with a trusted relative, friend, a doctor, a counselor at school or at your place of worship, or do what Alexis suggested and call a hotline. A number of organizations are available to help you.

National Association of Anorexia Nervosa and
     Associated Disorders (ANAD)
P.O. Box 7
Highland Park, IL 60035
708-831-3438

Anorexia Nervosa and Related Eating Disorders Inc.
P.O. Box 5102
Eugene, OR 97405
503-344-1144

Bulimia Anorexia Self-Help, Inc.
6125 Clayton Ave., Suite 215
St. Louis, MO 63139
800-227-4785

Center for the Study of Anorexia and Bulimia
1 W. 91st St.
New York, NY 10024
212-595-3449

Overeaters Anonymous Headquarters
World Services Office
383 Van Ness Ave., Suite 1601
Torrance, CA 90504
213-618-8835

NUTRITIOUS FOOD PLUS REGULAR EXERCISE EQUALS A FIT, GOOD-LOOKING BODY, EVEN IF YOU THINK YOU'RE TOO HEAVY

This chapter is devoted to giving you tips on how to eat
and drink for a healthy body, but food can only do so

much. Regular exercise is right up there with a well-balanced diet for good health. Whether you dance, run, swim, cycle, skate, or take an aerobics class, you owe it to your body to keep it moving for thirty minutes three or four times a week. (The exercises in Chapter 3 are a start.) Experts say you spend over twenty hours a week watching television. Here's your chance to prove them wrong.

Many young women are overweight (if your doctor says you are 20 percent above the healthy body weight for your age, sex, and height, you are too heavy), and they tell me that they want to lose. I recommend eating more of the low-fat foods I have described in this chapter, and less of the fatty fast foods and snacks, such as french fries, onion rings, and ice cream. In addition to cutting back on fatty foods, I strongly urge you to exercise. When you are a growing teenager, you need extra amounts of the essential nutrients, which means more good food than you used to eat. So do not concern yourself with dieting as much as with exercising.

Your bone structure and even your metabolism can be inherited. Are your parents small or big boned, high or low energy? You are born with your body type and your metabolism, the rate at which your body converts calories to energy. You may have inherited a slow metabolism, which would mean that you retain calories longer. Exercise will help you burn off calories; in fact, what exercise does is create a balance in your body—you take in calories from food and use up calories through exercise. Without exercise, many calories enter and don't exit. Also, exercise works with calcium to strengthen your bones. You may have gained a few pounds when you entered puberty. Now you can think about reshaping those pounds through exercise.

A FEW FREQUENTLY ASKED
QUESTIONS ABOUT NUTRITION

IS THERE ANY WAY I CAN BE TALLER AND HAVE A
FLATTER STOMACH?
When I check myself out in the mirror I think I have an OK
face, and I like my breasts, but I hate my stomach. It's too
round. If I could, I'd make myself over. Is there any way I can
be taller and have a flatter stomach?

Saskia, age 15

Each of us inherits genes from our parents, genes that
influence our body type, height, weight, and appearance
in general. Saskia's genes will set a pattern for her body
to follow, but within that pattern there's a lot she, and
every girl, can do.

She can eat a well-balanced diet so that her body produces growth hormones for her to become as tall as possible. She can be physically active by swimming, running,
cycling, dancing, or doing exercises to tone her muscles.
Active girls usually have trim bodies and as long as a girl
is healthy and fit, she is beautiful—no one will even notice
her height and weight.

DO DIET PILLS WORK? ARE THEY SAFE?
I am going to be the maid of honor at my sister's wedding,
and if I gain an ounce I won't fit into the dress I'm supposed
to wear. In fact, the dress is so clingy I'd like to lose at least
five pounds to look really great in it. I don't have a lot of will
power around food, so I bought some diet pills in the drugstore
to help me lose weight. Some of my friends say the pills don't

work, but how can they sell them if they're a fraud? Do diet
pills work? Are they safe?

Jane, age 17

First, I'd like to talk about the safety of diet pills. Over-the-counter diet pills, such as Dexatrim, Acutrim, StayTrim, and Control, contain a drug called phenylpropanolamine hydrochloride, or PPA. Although PPA is not addictive like amphetamines (stimulants that imitate your own brain chemicals), PPA is chemically similar to amphetamines. A controversy over the safety of PPA has been ongoing, and while the Food and Drug Administration decides whether PPA is safe, it continues to allow it to be used in over-the-counter diet pills. With all the testing, by the way, people under eighteen years old have not been studied for the effects of PPA. Pills with PPA carry a warning against taking them if you have high blood pressure, diabetes, heart, thyroid, kidney, or other disease. Yet you might not know if you have these conditions when you take the pills, and you could put yourself in the position of becoming seriously ill.

I believe in staying away from chemicals that can have an unknown or serious effect on your health. Since the safety of diet pills is still in dispute, my advice to Jane and any girl who wants to spend money on these "weight loss" products is *don't do it*. Even the over-the-counter pills that do not have PPA but offer weight loss through fiber have come under scrutiny. Pills that contain guar gum expand with moisture, so if you take a glass of water with them they can swell into a mass in your throat and cause a dangerous blockage.

Now, do over-the-counter diet pills work? First, I want to remind Jane that all diet pills are sold with instructions to go on a low-calorie diet and exercise. So often when girls diet with the pills they give the pills, instead of themselves, credit for their weight loss. If you eat fewer calories and exercise, you will lose weight. You do not need pills. (Usually, when researchers test weight reduction among people who take pills with PPA, they find that the pill takers lose about a half-pound a week or two pounds a month, which is hardly "fast" weight loss.)

I think that if Jane eats low-fat foods and gets involved in regular physical activity, her dress will look terrific on her. If she continues to feel that she would like help losing weight, however, she might ask her doctor about diet programs designed for teens.

ISN'T IT ALL RIGHT TO SKIP A COUPLE OF MEALS WHEN I KNOW I'M GOING TO BE EATING A LOT, LIKE AROUND THE HOLIDAYS?

Whenever I know I'm going to stuff myself, like at Thanksgiving or some other big family event, I try not to eat so much beforehand. Sometimes I skip meals to make room for more eating. I don't see anything wrong with this, but my mother always gets on my case. Isn't it all right to skip a couple of meals when I know I'm going to be eating a lot?

Dana, age 15

My experience with girls who skip meals is that they get hungry and snack on either fatty or sugary foods, a bag of potato chips, or a couple of cookies. If Dana wants to eat less before she feasts, she might try eating smaller meals of low-fat foods, in effect grazing throughout the day. Instead of three square meals, she might eat small meals four or five times a day, a tuna salad, or fresh fruit and yogurt, or a vegetable/pasta dish. That way she will still be eating a well-balanced diet without skipping meals or reaching for junk food.

SHOULD I TAKE VITAMINS?
My mother always gives me vitamins with my breakfast. When I told this to a friend of mine, she said that her mother says that she gets all of her vitamins from food and doesn't need to take vitamin pills. Who is right? Should I take vitamins?
Andrea, age 14

The debate over whether any of us should take vitamin supplements continues to rage among health experts. Some say that we can get all the vitamins and minerals we need by eating a balanced diet, while others say that there are added health benefits when a nutritious diet includes vitamin supplements.

I usually recommend that my teenage patients take a daily multivitamin/mineral supplement. Although a well-balanced diet may offer adequate vitamins and minerals, I am not convinced that all young women eat well-balanced diets. Also, studies have shown that women who took multivitamin supplements with extra folic acid before and during their pregnancies were less likely to give birth to babies with the serious birth defect known as spina bifida. Folic acid may actually help prevent birth defects! Although I would not recommend megadoses of vitamins to a young, healthy woman, I see no harm in taking a daily multivitamin/mineral.

HOW YOU EAT REVEALS HOW YOU FEEL ABOUT YOURSELF

Do you feel a different sense of self-confidence than you did when you were eleven? The work of Harvard's Dr. Carol Gilligan, who is in the vanguard of understanding how girls develop psychologically, shows that you have high self-esteem when you are eleven. You offer confident opinions and are unafraid to question authority. Yet as young girls move into adolescence, they become more caught up in meeting society's standards for femininity. They say "I don't know" more often because they're anxious to please others and don't want to be perceived as opinionated. Dr. Gilligan's study shows that teenage girls become less determined, less ambitious, less confident, and generally have lower self-esteem. They are also less interested in science and math.

Please remember that the title of this book is *You're In Charge*—of your mind, your body, and your life. You do not have to try to watch your weight, gain or lose to have the "perfect" body. Your eating and exercising habits can reveal your individual beauty and your self-confidence. Eat healthful, low-fat foods, lean meat, seafood, lots of fruits and vegetables, and especially remember to include low-fat dairy foods to strengthen your bones. Try to be physically active at least three times a week, by doing exercises, swimming, cycling, dancing, skating—whatever you like to do. You will allow your self-esteem to endure throughout your life if you eat and exercise, not to be skinny, but to be fit.

CHAPTER TWELVE

Why Making Healthy Choices (Even When You're Stressed Out) Makes Life Easier

This is the time in your life when your emotional highs and lows are most intense, and not just because of hormones. While hormonal levels can affect your mood (especially if you suffer from the hormonal shifts of PMS), they are only one influence on your mood swings. You are experiencing new pressures in your daily life as you move from being a girl whose decisions were made for her by her parents to a young woman who can make her own decisions. You enter your teens with one mind and body and leave with another.

You are a young woman discovering many things: different kinds of relationships, your sexual self, a sense of independence, a self-image, and all the while you are watching your figure change before your eyes. Then there are the pressures of new responsibilities to cope with, such as getting good grades, deciding what you want to do after high school, and earning your own money. No wonder you have good days and bad. If, as discussed in Chapter 11, you are not eating a nutritious diet, you may feel tired and edgy.

During those times when you are stressed out and in a bad mood, maybe you were disappointed by a guy or you had a hard time with a test, you can find yourself tempted to make unhealthy choices. You may pig out on junk food, or decide to party and drink a lot of beer, or light up a cigarette because it makes you feel more glamorous and you could use a lift. For a moment, you may feel better, but when you make an unhealthy choice, there is often a price to pay. As I have said before, *you're in charge*, but you ought to know what kinds of situations you may find yourself in as you make your decisions about how you want to live.

WHAT TO DO IF YOU'RE ANGRY OR DEPRESSED

Sometimes I meet girls whose parents punished them for being angry and they learned to hide their feelings. I encourage these girls to express themselves. We all need outlets for our feelings.

For some girls, one of the best releases is talk, to talk out problems with a close friend, to get an opinion from a respected source. Smoldering anger can often lead to resentment, which can be more difficult to conquer than the incident that upset you in the first place, and talking about what is bothering you helps. Sometimes you can talk to the person who made you mad and resolve your differences. Of course, the other person must be in an approachable mood at the time of your talk.

What do you do with your anger? How do you handle sadness? You probably know how to show your happiness, because happiness is an "acceptable" emotion, but do you know that other feelings are acceptable, too? It's human to be angry about some*thing* or angry at some*one* once in a while. It's also natural to feel sad or depressed on occasion, sometimes for no reason at all.

You may not have experience handling emotions that you consider negative, however, and you may turn your feelings inward. You may smoke because it makes you feel above it all, or you may turn to alcohol or other drugs to escape. These releases will ultimately bring you down even more.

There are other, more positive, ways to face your feelings and express yourself, and they do work. If you haven't already tried them you might find comfort and gain a sense of self-satisfaction if you do the following:

• **Write down your feelings in your own personal journal.** Be honest with the blank page in front of you and record what's on your mind. The process of writing helps you sort out your thoughts. You can express yourself free from embarrassment. No one is going to read what you wrote but you.

• **Create a short story or a poem.** Sometimes you can use your mood as the motivating force behind a short story or a poem. Perhaps you have been hurt by a girlfriend or a boyfriend, or a pet has died, or you lost a competition that was especially important to you. You can place a character in a short story in your shoes and work out an ending that makes you feel better, or you can write a poem that conveys your emotions.

• **Sketch or paint a picture.** Many girls are more visually than verbally oriented, and they transmit their feelings more accurately through drawing or painting. Just as with writing, the thought behind the creation helps you clarify your feelings.

• **Play an instrument or listen to music.** Music is a wonderful means of self-expression. Even if you don't play a musical instrument, listening to music, dancing to its beat, can be an emotional release.

• **Put yourself in a new environment.** Sometimes going to a funny movie or visiting a friend you haven't seen in a long time can help you make an emotional adjustment. By yourself, you might take a solitary bike ride or spend a day at a museum or a beautiful garden.

• **Get physical.** Exercise and sports help your brain release calming chemicals called endorphins, which are natural mood regulators. The more physically active you are, the more endorphins you have working for you.

• **Scream, cry, throw things.** Allow yourself a release in the best way you know. If you can let out a scream at a time and place that won't scare anyone, do it. Cry if it makes you feel better. Pound your mattress or throw rocks into streams. I once knew a woman who kept a cheap set of glasses in her house so she could hurl one or two against her large stone fireplace when she was angry. She always enjoyed a sense of relief afterward.

If you cannot seem to find a method that works for you, that lifts a depression, then it's time to ask yourself how long you have been living in despair. If your blue mood has lasted for weeks, and you don't know what's bothering you, and you are unable to do schoolwork or any of the things you used to do automatically, you may be seriously, clinically depressed.

Have you drastically changed your lifestyle?
Are you eating a lot more or a lot less food?
Do you have trouble sleeping?

When you wake up in the morning do you feel a sense of hopelessness?

Have you ever thought that death might be better than life?

If you answer yes to any of these questions, you must get help from a professional therapist. Talk to your parents if you can, or ask your favorite teacher, or the school nurse, or the gym teacher, or your clergyman, who you can call for help. You can also look in your local telephone directory for the phone number or hotline of the nearest chapter of the Mental Health Association. Clinical depression can be cured. Someone will always be there to help you if you ask for help, but the first step is the asking.

AN UNHEALTHY CHOICE CAN BECOME A HABIT

Almost all of you will experiment with unhealthy choices during your teens. You will see what it's like to smoke a cigarette or sip an alcoholic drink, sometimes because you are looking for a way to cope with stress, but more often because you are simply curious. If you go beyond your initial experiment and continue to use nicotine, alcohol, or other drugs to escape from your problems, or to help you fit in with the crowd, you risk a lifetime addiction. Once you are hooked on a substance, your popularity is more likely to fall than rise, and when those "friends" of yours disappear, you will be left in ill health. What you do to be cool can work against you.

SMOKING

Tobacco

Girls light up much more than boys. For some reason, a teenage girl is much more attracted to smoking than a guy is, and the American Cancer Society has the statistics to prove it. As the number of men dying from lung cancer drops each year, the number of lung cancer deaths among women rises. The younger you are when you start smoking, the harder it is to stop.

Right after you inhale nicotine, the addictive, poisonous substance in a cigarette, your heartbeat increases and your blood pressure rises. Carbon monoxide enters your bloodstream. Tar settles in your lungs. The cigarette smoke leaves a stale odor on your breath, skin, and clothes. Your teeth start to yellow. Your blood vessels constrict, which makes your skin start wrinkling at a young age.

Many guys don't like going out with girls who smoke. They consider smoking to be an annoying habit that creates an unpleasant odor. Also, they do not want to expose themselves to the smoke from your cigarette.

Disease may seem a long way off, but if you smoke you are more likely to get cancer of the lung, mouth, esophagus, pancreas, bladder, and uterus than a nonsmoker. Your chances of having a heart attack, stroke, and emphysema, a respiratory disease that blocks your breathing, are many times greater than they would be if you were a nonsmoker. Also, if you smoke when you are pregnant, you are more likely to have a miscarriage or a low-birth-weight or stillborn baby.

If you are smoking to cope with stress, you are making a mistake. Smoking will add health problems and stress *to* your life. A lit cigarette pollutes the air and puts people off. Also, since everyone knows the health risks

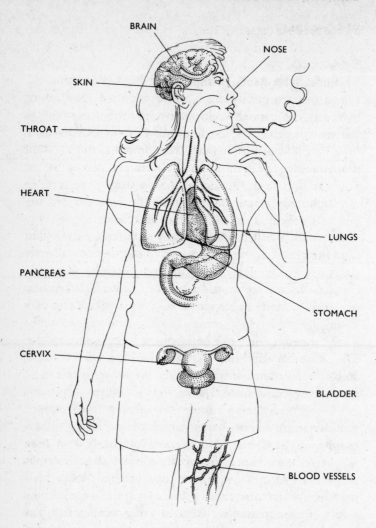

35. *Smoking Is Dangerous to Your Health. Notice all the organs affected by smoking: your brain, lungs, heart, stomach, reproductive organs, skin, and blood vessels. Please do everything you can to prevent yourself from picking up this terrible habit.*

of smoking, a cigarette resting between your lips makes you look like you don't know what you're doing.

Marijuana and Hashish

Marijuana is the most widely used illicit drug among teenagers, but surveys continue to show that overall, high school students are losing interest in marijuana as well as other illicit drugs (although cigarette smoking and alcoholic drinking are still quite popular). A recent survey by the American Medical Association found that 17 percent, or more than three and a half million, twelve- to seventeen-year-olds had tried smoking marijuana ("grass" or "pot" as it's commonly called), and 3 percent, or half a million, had sampled cocaine, but these figures are new lows.

The active ingredient in marijuana and hashish (the concentrated resin from marijuana flowers), tetrahydrocannabinol (THC), affects a receptor in your brain that alters your mood and the way you think. You can suddenly think that you are brilliant, that you are a person with great ideas. Marijuana can give you a sense of peaceful euphoria. Some people have a wonderful time when they're high on grass, but marijuana has its down side. People who smoke grass regularly can become tense and paranoid. They can lose their perspective and their ability to concentrate. Also, teens who are heavy users can upset their hormonal balance at a time when their hormones and bodies are restabilizing themselves. There is a possibility that this hormonal interference may affect fertility. Finally, as a marijuana smoker you face the same health risks as a cigarette smoker—you are more vulnerable to cancer, heart disease, emphysema, and other illnesses.

DRINKING

Although buying alcoholic beverages when you are under twenty-one years old is illegal in every state, alcohol is the drug of choice among teens. A national survey found that 10.6 million of the nation's 20.7 million students in grades seven through twelve drink alcoholic beverages. That's more than half the students in the United States! Sadly, that's not all. Eight million drink at least once a week, and almost half a million of them down five or more drinks in a row. The survey also estimates that more than three million students drink alone, and more than four million drink when they're upset. These last two are classic signs of problem drinking and alcoholism. This is not a drug to take casually, in spite of the good times people are having in beer commercials.

Every ounce of beer, the most popular beverage, has 4.5 percent alcohol; wine, 10 to 14 percent; and hard liquor, up to 50 percent. Translated, that means that twelve ounces of beer can have as much alcohol as one ounce of whiskey!

In addition, as a girl you are much more susceptible to alcohol's effects. As soon as you take a drink, even if it's only a wine cooler, the mucous membranes in your mouth begin to absorb the alcohol. Soon the alcohol reaches your stomach, and if you haven't recently eaten food, your stomach is going to absorb the alcohol quickly and you are going to get drunk fast. The alcohol depresses your central nervous system and slows your functioning. It affects your coordination, emotional control, and thought processes. You can't concentrate or react quickly.

Because you tend to weigh less than a guy, your body metabolizes alcohol faster. Also, alcohol becomes diluted in water, and women have less body water and more body fat than men. This means that the alcohol has more of a "kick" in your body. Your body and brain begin absorbing the drug, and soon it numbs your thought processes. The more you drink, the less you reason. You lose your sense of judgment as you lose your inhibitions, and for a girl, that can be especially dangerous:

• Many instances of date rape have involved episodes of drinking beforehand.

• If you consent to sexual intercourse, you may not have "safe sex," and you may expose yourself to a sexually transmitted disease, or you may become pregnant.

• Against your normally better judgment, you may get into a car with a driver who has been drinking, and drunk driving is the number one killer of teens.

• Under the influence of alcohol, thousands of teenagers have died, not only in cars, but by drowning, in fires, in accidental suicides and homicides, and in senseless accidents. If you are drunk, you cannot be trusted to walk home, much less, cycle, skate, or drive.

In our society, having a drink is still socially acceptable. Yet the research I have seen shows that most of you do not "have a drink." Teens seem to fall into one of two extreme camps: either you are a binge drinker or a person who completely abstains from alcohol. Where is the middle ground? Binge drinking signals drinking to get drunk and escape. This worries me.

When you drink a lot, you put your body in jeopardy in many ways. You assault your intellect, slow your reflexes, and over time can give yourself ulcers, completely destroy your liver, and contribute to the risk of certain kinds of cancer. You slowly kill your quality of life and, eventually, your life itself. If you consume a quantity of alcohol all at once, like the fifteen-year-old New Jersey girl who at a party had six Jell-O shots (chilled cubes of gelatin and vodka) and two wine coolers, you may die. First you may have trouble breathing, then you may pass out forever, as she did. If you mix alcohol with barbiturates, commonly known as "downers," you will be drinking a fatal cocktail that can send you into a coma, then into death. **Never mix pills and alcohol.**

Whatever your reason for drinking, if you're consuming alcohol to the point that you're no longer functioning normally, and your problem is obvious to others, try to get help. You are an alcoholic. You can call the National Council on Alcoholism and Drug Dependence Hope Line at 1-800-622-2255 from a touch-tone phone, or contact the local chapter of Alcoholics Anonymous.

As I mentioned earlier, at some point in your life you will probably take a drink to see why so many people seem to like alcoholic beverages so much. Alcohol is a drug that can make you physically and psychologically dependent, so treat it with respect.

OTHER DRUGS YOU MIGHT ENCOUNTER

Inner-city teens are more likely to encounter illicit drugs than teens who live outside urban areas, but these drugs are everywhere. There are hallucinogens like LSD and PCP (or "angel dust") that can bring on paranoia and hallucinations. They both distort your perceptions. LSD offers a high, but it can also trigger a future mental breakdown. PCP is quite dangerous in that it can cause your blood pressure and pulse rate to soar. It brings on a loss of memory, sometimes a brief paralysis, breathing difficulties, and kidney failure. Finally, it can leave you in a schizophrenic state.

Cocaine, a white powder that is sniffed or "snorted," affects your central nervous system, where it blocks the absorption of the brain chemicals dopamine and norepinephrine. Once blocked, these chemicals excite nerve impulses. Your pulse quickens, your blood pressure rises, and you feel a sense of energy, alertness, and self-confidence.

Crack is cocaine that has been mixed with baking soda and cooked in water, where it forms small pellets that are sold for $5 or $10 apiece. The pellets, or "rocks," are inserted in a cigarette or a small pipe and smoked. The high from crack is instantaneous, which makes a user want to do it again. It is highly addictive and highly dangerous. (A crystal methamphetamine, or "ice," is a relatively new hard drug that has many of the same effects as crack.)

Cocaine and crack constrict blood vessels, which endangers your heart. These drugs seem to fill you with charm and self-confidence at the start, but later they bring on depression and paranoia. They also cause heart attacks, strokes, convulsions, and death. Cocaine can kill you the first time you try it. If you survive its use, you can still ruin the lining of your nose by constantly snorting it. Crack can give you a skyrocketing high as the stimulating effect of the drug travels from your lungs to your brain. That zooming experience is what gets people hooked so fast. They want more and more and soon they can't think of anything else but where they can get more crack.

There are also amphetamines known as uppers, barbiturates known as downers, and the narcotic heroin. All of these substances assault your physical and emotional well-being, and most teens already stay away from them. And that's my advice:

Stay far away from every one of the drugs we have mentioned. If you are looking for ways to cope with difficulties, try to look within and marshal your inner strengths.

You're in Charge

As you travel through your teens and move toward greater personal independence, look for role models to give you direction. Who are the women you admire? Why are they worth your admiration? Do they have high self-esteem? Think about the choices the women you look up to have made and how their lives have unfolded as a result. You are in the process of directing your own life right now.

As I have mentioned before, studies have made the point that girls feel most self-confident at age eleven, and then they begin questioning and qualifying their opinions. Stay strong and be thoughtful. "Nobody can make you feel inferior without your consent," said the late American stateswoman Eleanor Roosevelt. Others sense how you feel about yourself, and if you believe in a healthful approach to life, and you respect your body, others will be respectful, too.